TINY BUBBLES
Biblical Teaching on Alcohol

DR. T. S. WISE

Tiny Bubbles: Biblical Teaching on Alcohol

Copyright © 2015 Terry S. Wise. All rights reserved. No part of this book may be reproduced, stored in a retrieval system, or transmitted in any form or by any means, electronic, mechanical, photocopying, recording, or otherwise, without the express written permission of Dr. Terry S. Wise.

Scripture quotations taken from the New American Standard Bible®,
Copyright © 1960, 1962, 1963, 1968, 1971, 1972, 1973,
1975, 1977, 1995 by The Lockman Foundation
Used by permission." (www.Lockman.org)

First Edition

ISBN: 978-0-9860613-0-1

Published by
Servant Communications, Inc.
Kirksville, Missouri 63501

Cover Picture © Jagcz | Dreamstime.com - Glasses Of Champagne Photo. Used with permission.

Cover & Interior Design: Lissa Auciello-Brogan

Printed in the United States of America.
14 13 12 11 10 / 10 9 8 7 6 5 4 3 2 1

*This book is dedicated to all who truly seek to
understand and live by the teaching of Scripture,
even when that teaching runs counter to contemporary
cultural values and conventional religious perspectives.*

CONTENTS

1. Another Book On Alcohol? 1
2. Approaching Scripture With Integrity 8
3. Drunkenology 101: The Abuse Of Alcohol 18
4. History 101: Alcohol Through The Ages 34
5. Biblical Teaching: An Overview 47
6. The Two-Wine Theory 61
7. Jesus And Alcohol 88
8. Perceived Problem Passages 115
9. Abstinence In The Bible 136
10. The Weaker Brother 148
11. Tying Up Loose Ends 169
12. What Now? A Practical Conclusion 182

ANOTHER BOOK ON ALCOHOL?

This chapter introduces the contentious issue of alcohol consumption by Christians. I share why I am writing on the topic and what I hope to accomplish by doing so. The three most common positions on the use of alcohol within the church are briefly introduced in setting the stage for the teaching to come.

Her name was Ida, a longtime lover of God with a strong German work ethic. A crusty personality occupied her stocky frame while her husband was thin and meek—a "yes-man" if there ever was one. It seems this contrast is not uncommon between married couples. One spouse wears the pants in the family and the other seems to know his or her place. Both were strong supporters of mine and earnestly sought to obey Scripture as best they could. I loved them dearly and was grateful for their presence in our local assembly of believers.

Freshly minted from seminary, this was my first full-time pastorate. Quite by accident, the issue of alcohol arose during a Wednesday evening service and caught me by surprise. I quickly scoured my mind for seminary training on the topic and realized I received none. To my knowledge, the issue never came up in any of my classes.

Ida piped up, "My God would never condone the use of alcohol." Clearly her mind was settled on the matter. It was not up for debate.

"Why is that, Ida?" I pressed.

"Alcohol is dangerous and hurts so many people that God couldn't possibly approve of it." Realizing she had painted herself into a corner, I stirred the pot a bit to liven up the discussion. "Would your God condone driving a car?" I sheepishly inquired. She responded in the affirmative.

"But cars can be dangerous, Ida, and many people are hurt in automobile accidents each year, losing loved ones, enduring emotional turmoil, living with lifelong physical infirmities, and struggling to rebuild their lives. If we say that God doesn't condone alcohol because of its potential dangers, wouldn't we also have to extend that reasoning to other areas of potential danger in our life?"

Would God condone investing in the stock market, walking across the street, flying in an airplane, serving as a police officer, or just living life? Each can be dangerous. The pot was indeed stirred; from that point on, a spirited conversation ensued. We didn't all agree or arrive at a definitive solution that evening, but the discussion prompted a mental reminder for me to study the issue. I wanted to arrive at a biblically reasoned conclusion in my own mind. After all of these years, I am finally getting around to it.

Books written from varying perspectives are readily available—some supporting the moderate use of alcohol, some prohibiting all use as sinful, and still others advocating abstention as the wisest of all paths. My contribution is by no means *the* definitive answer on the subject. Far be it from me to claim expertise in anything, especially when there are so many who are wiser and far more masterful in expressing their thoughts. I am thankful for the many gifted theologians and Bible teachers faithful to God's Word, but as a fellow sojourner in the faith, I seek my own answers to this firestorm. I want to know what Scripture teaches on the subject, not necessarily what others *claim* Scripture teaches. After all, God asks us to reason together (Is. 1:18), and I want to reason with Him. If Scripture is His inspired Word, it carries significance and authority beyond what any one individual could say, including me.

This book is the fruit of my own personal study on the subject, and I humbly share it with you. Many will disagree with where I land on the subject, of that I am certain. I learned a long time ago that trying to please everyone is an exercise in futility. Even Jesus couldn't do it. On non-essential issues such as this one, certainly we can live together without condemning each other to a fiery eternity. I encourage you to think critically, dig deep, and approach the topic with as much objectivity as you can muster. We dare not bend Scripture to fit our personal view of things, whether it be politics, doctrine, or alcohol. What we are most interested in is what Scripture says and means so we can align our thinking and behavior to its teachings, not the other way around. My personal investigation into this arena has been a wonderful and fulfilling journey. While I believe my conclusions are biblically sound and well-reasoned, I realize you may not agree with me, in which case I hope this book inspires you to clarify the matter in your own mind.

With such a sensitive cultural issue, some may accuse me of writing a book to promote my own personal agenda or to justify a desire to engage in something they believe the Bible condemns. In other words, "He is writing about alcohol because he loves to drink!" Writing on a subject like this is certainly a no-win situation. I will be a hero to some and a devil to others, depending on which side of the fence you're on. Whether a devil or a hero, I do not know, or care. What is important to me is that I am as faithful to Scripture as I can be, and to that end I have labored.

For the record, I am not an alcoholic, nor a recovering one. I find the taste and smell of beer to be utterly disgusting, and since I am diabetic, I stay away from wine because of the high sugar content. Alcoholic drinks are filled with many unnecessary calories, and the excess thermal insulation covering my bones constantly reminds me that extra calories are the last thing I need; although, I have been known to enjoy a good margarita once in a blue moon. I do not abstain from beer, wine, or hard liquor because of moral, religious, or theological reasons; I simply don't care for the taste, want to stay away from excess calories, and try to keep my blood sugars in check. But whether or not I moderately consume alcohol or like its taste is absolutely irrelevant to the heart of the issue. What matters is what Scripture teaches on the subject—end of story.

There are many reasons why biblical teaching regarding alcohol is of interest to me and why I am writing this book. First, many Christians are confused about the subject and I desire to bring clarity and simplicity to the many disparate and chaotic voices clamoring for attention.

Waiting for the congregation to clear the sanctuary, an elder cornered me after the morning service and whispered, "Pastor, is it sinful for me to serve wine to guests during a meal in my own home?" He was a bright individual who didn't want to undermine his leadership role or violate Scripture. The question surfaced out of confusion regarding what the Bible teaches. Is it sinful to serve wine at a meal? Do the specific circumstances determine whether it is right or wrong? Do we possess the right to serve wine at a meal, and yet, also be under obligation to curtail that right because of what others might think? Do we have full freedom to serve wine during a meal no matter what? I hope to share biblical teaching on the subject in a simple and clear manner that lifts the fog of confusion.

Second, this issue evokes passionate discourse among Christians, and I hope to talk us down from the ledge by bringing sanity to an insanely emotional issue. Sound reasoning is often clouded by personal experience—like a dog constantly kicked by its owner who now tucks its tail and hides every time someone raises a leg. Enduring great pain and trauma affects how we feel about the person, item, or situation causing such anguish.

Many know firsthand the destructive power of alcohol addiction. When you've gone to numerous support groups, hurt your family and friends, and allowed addiction to rule and ruin your life, the thought of this demon drug being sanctioned by God seems incredulous. You don't have to be a Harvard graduate to recognize the devastating influences alcohol abuse creates in our society.

As a young boy, I loved to go fishing. Dad and I rose early one day to fish a local pond with my step-grandfather. After a couple of hours, we turned to go home and took an unexpected detour to my step-grandfather's favorite watering hole. His addiction was screaming for attention while it was yet morning. We were the only ones in the place. Dad and I drank pop while the addictive fix temporarily satisfied my step-grandfather's craving.

Sound reasoning requires that we back away from the ledge, climb down from the emotional fervor, and approach Scripture with objectivity. When we are held hostage to strong and unchecked emotions and Scripture is filtered through personal preferences, biases, and perspectives, our ability to reason well is undermined. I hope to bring sanity to an insanely emotional subject.

Third, this topic brings unwarranted division among the people of God and I hope to reduce the caustic behavior and attitudes accompanying the issue. Factions on both sides of the fence can respond unlovingly to those who disagree with them, as though they are unworthy of being called sons and daughters of the Most High. Even the famous preacher to New York City street gangs and founder of Teen Challenge, David Wilkerson, writes, "I seriously doubt Christians who drink can be called saints."[1] He goes on, "Show me a man in the pulpit who drinks, even moderately, and I'll show you a coward when it comes to preaching the truth."[2] Stinging words like these builds walls instead of bridges, but we can empathize with his skewed perspective knowing that he witnessed the depths of human depravity out on the street. Division often brings with it harsh words, even by those who dearly love the Lord.

We should keep in mind that the use or non-use of alcohol by Christians is not a fundamental doctrine of the church. The doctrine of Christ's resurrection from the dead, for instance, is of the utmost importance because of its foundational nature to the Christian message. Paul notes in I Corinthians 15:3–4, "For I delivered to you as of first importance what I also received, that Christ died for our sins according to the Scriptures, and that He was buried, and that He was raised on the third day according to the Scriptures." He further states in I Corinthians 15:12–20:

> Now if Christ is preached, that He has been raised from the dead, how do some among you say that there is no resurrection of the dead? But if there is no resurrection of the dead, not even Christ has been raised; and if Christ has not been raised, then our preaching is vain, your faith also is vain. Moreover we are even found to be false witnesses of God, because we testified against God that He raised Christ, whom He did not raise, if in fact the dead are not raised. For if the dead are not raised, not even Christ has been raised; and if Christ has not been raised, your faith is worthless; you are still in your sins. Then those also who have fallen asleep in Christ have perished. If we have hoped in Christ in this life only, we are of all men most to be pitied. But now Christ has been raised from the dead, the first fruits of those who are asleep.

The resurrection is a pillar doctrine—a doctrine worth dying for since without it, everything we believe and hope in becomes nothing more than wishful thinking. Sorry, I am not going to die over whether or not Christians can moderately consume alcohol. A proper perspective about what we are fighting over is imperative, and since this is a non-pillar issue of faith, it doesn't warrant the kind of armor-bearing readiness that the resurrection doctrine requires. I hope that my work lowers the heated rhetoric and reduces troublesome divisions encompassing the issue.

The last reason for writing such a book is that truth demands it. In fact, the only thing worth believing is truth, even if it means swimming upstream. I certainly do not possess all truth, for the Lord knows how fallible and frail I really am. I do, however, think that scriptural truth is to be believed, proclaimed, and followed. Truth is not necessarily what any one denomination teaches or believes, and quite frankly, it is not determined by what you and I may believe about a topic, either. Whether it aligns with our beliefs or not, it is the truth of Scripture itself that is of paramount importance. Truth demands that we discover biblical teaching on the subject and believe, proclaim, and follow it without alteration. Peddling personal perspectives and biases as scriptural truth is not only unconscionable, it promotes bad theology, detracts from the truth, and enables false teaching to abound.

I weary of shallow thinking, shallow theology, and shallow living. A Ph.D. isn't necessary to understand God's Word, but we must invest time to study what it says. Unfortunately, we allow others to do our thinking for us, whether a popular megachurch pastor or some flamboyant televangelist prancing about the stage as if the louder he shouts the greater the truth. Popularity or decibel level has nothing to do with it; do your own thinking, make time to study and ponder Scripture, and come to your own reasoned conclusion.

When it comes to the drinking of alcohol, people typically hold one of three positions: some say you *can't* (prohibitionists), some say you *shouldn't* (abstentionists), and some say you *may* in moderation (moderationists).

Prohibition Position

This position holds that God absolutely forbids the consumption of alcohol. Alcohol is evil, and Proverbs 23:29–32 presents an absolute prohibition against its use. To explain that alcohol is sometimes spoken of positively in Scripture and sometimes negatively, prohibitionists believe there are two kinds of wine in the Bible. When wine is spoken of in positive terms it refers to nutritious grape juice while negative passages refer to fermented wine.

Abstention Position

This position holds that while wine was approved in Bible days, the times have changed. To avoid the social evils caused by alcohol and the negative stigma associated with its use, it is best not to even touch the stuff. While it may be permitted, it is unwise to engage in such activity given the negative perception surrounding alcohol. Abstaining becomes the proper pathway in today's world.

Moderation Position

This position holds that Scripture permits the moderate consumption of alcohol while drunkenness is condemned. In the Old Testament, wine is viewed as a blessing from God while its scarcity is seen as a curse. Jesus turns water into wine, institutes wine as the symbol of the New Covenant, and promises to partake of it again with His followers in the new kingdom. Church leaders are prohibited from being addicted to wine, not from ever drinking. Moderate use is approved while immoderate use is forbidden.

VIEWS ON ALCOHOL USE

View	Description	Basis	Result
Prohibition	God absolutely forbids alcohol use	Law	Can't Drink
Abstention	Prudent not to drink in light of the many social evils of alcohol	Love	Shouldn't Drink
Moderation	May drink in moderation while drunkenness is condemned	Truth	May Drink Moderately

While this is an oversimplification of each position, it allows us to see the options available. I suspect that you already have a preferred view on the issue. The prohibitionists' position, in my view, completely lacks credible biblical support and relies on circular reasoning akin to a dog chasing its own tail. I would be their biggest supporter if the Bible actually forbid alcohol consumption, but it doesn't. While it appears to be a righteous position, it is without biblical support and becomes just another ill-informed opinion confusing people and twisting Scripture. Abstentionists believe we should abstain from alcohol consumption due to its social stigma and the many evils it creates in society. Why play with fire when getting burned is a real possibility? The potential dangers far outweigh the risk of indulging. Why jeopardize our Christian testimony for the sake of something so unattractive? Yet, why must we refrain from what God permits? Isn't God's Word on the matter sufficient? Wouldn't it be far more prudent to actually abide by scriptural teaching than allow contemporary culture and its social agendas to define our actions?

I believe the view of moderation most accurately represents scriptural teaching. While permitted to consume alcohol in moderation, we are also free *not* to drink, not because we must or we should, but because we can if we desire. I have no personal agenda with regard to alcohol and am not trying to force or encourage anyone to consume fermented beverage. My goal is to be true to the biblical text, which doesn't command or require that we imbibe—only that moderate alcohol consumption is permitted while inebriation is forbidden. I simply asked myself, "What does the Bible teach regarding the consumption of alcohol?" What follows is my answer.

Summary: Though the use of alcohol by Christians is a nonessential issue of faith, the subject is shrouded by confusion, passion, and division, and sound biblical reasoning is needed so the truth of Scripture can be identified, believed, proclaimed, and followed.

APPROACHING SCRIPTURE WITH INTEGRITY

This chapter presents the need to approach Scripture objectively rather than sifting passages through our preferred and predetermined conclusions. Instead of reading modern biases into Scripture, the importance of drawing out the author's meaning by entering his world is essential. Why this is necessary and how we do it is described here.

When Christians argue over hotly contested issues, the first thing that often flies out the window is fidelity to the Word of God. Though both sides vehemently declare allegiance to Scripture and promote their views as correct interpretation, in reality, all sorts of interpretive gymnastics can be utilized to arrive at predetermined viewpoints.

One author believes Satan's most effective lie is that Jesus turns water into fermented wine at a wedding feast in Cana.[1] Really? I would have thought Satan's *most effective lie* was persuading Adam and Eve to sin in the Garden of Eden with such catastrophic results that turning water into wine pales in comparison.

That believers would drink wine, or that Jesus would turn water into wine, is nothing short of a "cleverly orchestrated Satanic hoax" according to the author, and "that at some point in history, the rules were completely changed when someone switched the drinks for all Christians and Christianity by changing the labels on the bottles."[2] He further claims,

> Noah was misled simply because Satan had contaminated, changed, and mislabeled the wine, and I was misled because some or all modern Bible translators erred in their false translations of the Holy Bible from Hebrew and

Greek into Latin, and later into all other languages, and because few modern theologians have discovered their errors.[3]

These off-the-wall statements are colored by his personal negative experience with alcohol. Sound biblical reasoning is cast aside while interpretive gymnastics fuel the journey to predetermined destinations. A non-essential issue is now elevated by a "cleverly orchestrated Satanic hoax" to be the devil's "most effective lie"—switching the drinks by sneakily mislabeling wine bottles and messing us up for thousands of years. This kind of nonsense occurs when personal bias interferes with the genuine discovery of scriptural teaching. It is reminiscent of a leader in one of my churches who said to me, "Pastor, the Bible says that God loves a cheerful giver and since I am not giving cheerfully, I have stopped giving altogether so I won't disobey Scripture." Yes, you read that correctly! Incredible, isn't it, how we deceive ourselves when we find it advantageous to do so. I later discovered that he was saving money to purchase a coveted piece of property and found it necessary to relieve his guilty conscience by creating a spiritual-sounding rationale for doing what he wanted to do. Personal biases can cloud objectivity and preclude the discovery of biblical truth.

The goal of studying the Bible is to correctly understand what it means so we can align our life to its teaching despite popular opinion, cultural bias, predetermined outcomes, or personal experiences. Forcing Scripture into modern cultural perspectives is like shooting at a moving target—the proverbial square peg in a round hole syndrome. As the winds of culture shift with every new generation or world crisis, the meaning of Scripture must also change to accommodate the constantly moving trajectory. Approaching Scripture with such lunacy means that there is no such thing as unchanging, timeless truth upon which to stand. The next time the wind shifts, so will the truth. With this approach, the Bible is meaningless. Besides, which modern culture becomes the standard by which we measure the shifting wind currents? Can a subculture of the main culture be utilized as the measuring rod? Can they both be used at the same time by different groups with differing interests and outcomes? Do we use African culture, Asian culture, Latin American culture? As you can see, there is no such thing as a modern day measuring stick. So pick up whatever cultural measuring device you desire—any will do, since it won't matter anyway.

A Backwards Approach

In many ways, our approach to Scripture is backwards. We examine the holy writings searching for support of our foregone conclusions, when we should be discovering what God says and means, *despite* our preconceived notions. This way we can align our lives according to the teaching of Scripture.

While having lunch with two faculty members, this tension rose to the surface regarding a Bible exploration course for nursing students. One adamantly believed nursing students should identify issues they were struggling with, such as fear, self-esteem, etc., and explore what the Bible says about the subject. This would show nurses that God cares about their problems and the Bible is relevant to their lives. This method didn't sit well with the other faculty member. It epitomized, in his mind, an incomplete approach to Scripture. We should discover what the Bible teaches and align our lives to its instruction rather than searching out verses that sooth our perceived needs.

God's Word does address many of our needs—some specifically and others through general principles. Rather than considering the Bible solely as a smorgasbord of self-help tips, wouldn't it be far more profitable to actually learn what the Bible says and means and shift our thinking, words, and behaviors into alignment? With the subject of alcohol, it is important that we go to the Bible itself, discover what it says and means, and align our perspective with its teaching, rather than expecting it to align with ours.

The Catch-All Verse

The Bible doesn't address every topic known to humankind. For instance, it doesn't address how to change a sparkplug, whether or not to chew gum or send humans into space. In those areas lacking clear biblical direction, legalists like to break out the "catch-all" verse of I Thessalonians 5:22: "abstain from every form of evil," or as some might say "avoid the very appearance of evil." Like a drug-sniffing police dog, this verse is used to sniff out all kinds of sin such as women wearing shorts, sunbathing in public, or wearing slacks to church, men with hair below their shirt collar or wearing beards, and Christians going to movies, playing card games, dancing, or embracing tattoos. Someone has labeled these items "the very appearance of evil" and now seemingly finds biblical support to back up the dubious pronouncement.

All we have to do is label something "the very appearance of evil" and throw in a good rendition of I Thessalonians 5:22, and we can guilt and coerce others into abstaining from all sorts of activities we find disagreeable. This is nothing more than an attempt to squelch others' freedom, prevent them from doing things we find offensive, and build fences where the Bible never does.

A rookie faculty member sought to include the following statement in her newly designed course: "This syllabus can be changed by the instructor at any time and for any reason." She clearly didn't understand the ramifications of such a statement. It gave her power to alter assignments, grades, textbooks and anything else she desired whenever she wanted, for whatever reason. If you received an A on a mid-term exam, the professor could arbitrarily change it to a D if it tickled her fancy. This is what the supposed biblical "catch-all" verse does. It allows for arbitrary definitions and abuse by those who feel it is their duty to identify and decry "the very appearance of evil." In modern lingo, "You are not allowed to do anything that I don't like." Anything can be a sin at any time, for whatever reason, as long as I label it "the very appearance of evil."

If we can never do anything that anyone finds objectionable, then we live in a prison defined by others, devoid of joy or freedom. If I happen to feel that dancing is sinful or could appear to be sinful (depending on how close you are to your partner and the rhythm), and you dance, I feel justified in throwing I Thessalonians 5:22 in your face for violating Scripture. How infantile. Do we really think that God engages in these kinds of romper room antics? Among the many problems with this approach to Scripture, two stand out.

First, Scripture can stand on its own without any attempt by us to prop it up. By adding our own rules and regulations to God's written Word, we actually detract from it. Let me be clear; Scripture doesn't need me or you propping it up as though it were weak in some spots and desperately in need of our assistance. When it comes to alcohol, what Scripture says is enough. This is the sufficiency of God's Word to speak for itself. When we go above and beyond what the Bible teaches, we go too far and misunderstand its powerful nature.

Second, using "the very appearance of evil" in preventing Christians from engaging in what others find questionable shows a total disregard for the proper interpretation of this verse in its contextual setting. Here is what I Thessalonians 5:19–22 says: "Do not quench the Spirit; do not despise prophetic utterances. But examine everything carefully; hold fast to that which is good; abstain from every form of evil."

In the context of prophetic utterances, Paul instructs the Thessalonians not to quench the Spirit, but test the declarations carefully so they can retain what is good and abstain from what is not. Some idle brothers were abusing this gift by making false statements regarding the Lord's return. It seems wherever the Lord is at work, Satan is right there seeking to bring confusion. When God plants a seed, Satan often plants a weed right next to it. Paul is not instructing us to refrain from actions others find objectionable; he is encouraging the careful testing of prophetic utterances for the purpose of discerning which ones to embrace and which ones to avoid.

Christians sure adore their faith formulas. Don't ask us to think deeply, reason soundly, or study methodically; instead, give us a formula of do's and dont's, and if we can't find one in Scripture, we'll make one up. But Scripture is powerful enough to stand on its own, and if God calls alcohol good, then it is good, and if He calls it bad, then it is bad. By adding to Scripture, we end up dumbing down God's Word; we dilute it while thinking we are making it stronger. This eventually leads to sloppy interpretation and inaccurate application. Scripture must speak for itself, stand by itself, and sound interpretation requires that we align our lives with its teaching. We desire an honest look at biblical teaching—nothing more and nothing less.

The Abuse Argument

No one disagrees that alcohol can be abused. Inebriation occurs when too much of it is consumed. This abuse can result in a loss of one's senses and a loss of self-control. People have done some pretty stupid things under the influence of alcohol, not to mention becoming a danger to others. My friend Ida was correct in believing that too much alcohol can cause pain to oneself and others, but she used the argument of abuse to justify her conclusion on alcohol itself. When we use the abuse argument, we are in danger of becoming judgmental and arriving at incorrect conclusions.

Never judge a religion or a doctrine by its abuses. If we did, we couldn't believe anything and would be nullifying our own faith. Individuals from every conviction sometimes act outside of their religion's principles, go to extremes, or extend a doctrine far beyond its intention. Do we judge Islam by the acts of Muslim extremists? No, Islam rises or falls on the tenants of its belief system, not on its abuse by some followers. Do we judge Christianity by the abuses that occurred during the Crusades of the Middle Ages? Of course not! Do we judge all Catholics by the perverted acts of some priests? Catholic theology rises or falls on its own merits, not on its abuses.

During my seminary days, several scandals broke out among highly visible televangelists that became national news. While out at a local restaurant, I overheard a couple discussing their contempt for such hypocrisy. They were judging the whole of Christianity by the abusive acts of a few. I wanted to butt in and say, "Hey, I am a Christian. I don't act that way. Please don't judge all of us because of what they did. They do not speak for me, represent me, or stand for what Christianity teaches."

Let's say I travel to several of the largest cities in the United States, climb the tallest building with hundreds of Bibles, and drop those Bibles on the people below. Can you imagine that? People are just minding their own business, talking on cell phones, listening to music, or lost in thought as they walk on the sidewalk below. From the towering skyscraper above, I suddenly drop a large Bible on their head and kill them. Individuals from other countries see this on national television and follow suit so that in major cities throughout the world, Bibles are being dropped on the heads of thousands.

The Bible, of course, teaches us to love fellow humans and treat them as we would like to be treated. It does not instruct us to drop Bibles from tall buildings on the heads of people below. Yet, Bibles are being dropped, good citizens are dying, chaos ensues, and an international Bible crisis erupts. With such misuse of Scripture, families begin throwing their Bibles in the trash. They don't want to be associated with something so dangerous and harmful to others. The owning of Bibles is frowned upon, believers are warned to avoid the very appearance of evil, the National Anti-Bible League is formed, and Scripture is interpreted to support its non-ownership.

Do you see the silliness of such an argument? We don't throw away all Bibles because some use them in an abusive and dangerous manner. The baby is not thrown out with the bathwater. We do not believe the Bible is evil simply because some have mistreated its true intention.

The same principle applies to alcohol. Without a doubt, its abuse can be dangerous, and the Bible speaks unequivocally against inebriation. But just because some abuse alcohol to the point of drunkenness doesn't mean that alcohol is intrinsically evil. Whether the moderate use of alcohol is sinful rises or falls on what the Bible teaches, not on its abuse. Employing the abuse argument to prohibit all use of alcohol means that we must also nullify the whole of Christianity. I am not prepared to do that. The use of alcohol is to be judged by what the Bible teaches about it rather than how some might abuse it.

Honest Biblical Study

Cultural pressure to arrive at certain predetermined outcomes is one reason we find such dissension over the Bible's teaching on alcohol, and it often leads to shoddy interpretation. When culture presses us to lean one way, we often do—even at the expense of sound biblical reasoning. In the legal profession, lawyers are expected to interpret evidence in the best light of their client. If you hire an attorney, you want them to do the same for you and actually engage the legal process toward your favor.

Many approach Scripture with this same mentality. Bible verses are interpreted in the best light of a specific viewpoint. If you are Catholic, you interpret the Bible through Catholic traditions. Anabaptists, such as Mennonites, interpret passages on baptism differently than do Lutherans, Quakers, or Church of Christ folks. This bias infects us all, even me, in more ways than we can imagine. It is a tendency we must strive to counteract. While we may never be totally free from such biases, we can be intentional in its recognition and strive toward honesty and integrity in our approach to Scripture.

Our role is not to interpret Scripture through the lens of modern culture, thereby forcing it to fit our viewpoint. That is what lawyers do; it is not what Christians do when studying the Bible. Lawyers try to convince and persuade a jury; Christians try to discern what the Bible means regardless of their own personal views. It is a tall order given the pressure for conformity to contemporary cultural biases, regardless of what the Bible really teaches.

The Bible was written over a period of sixteen hundred years by forty different authors in cultures and times different than our own. Because of this, we have to be careful. By reading Scripture solely through the lens of our own experience, our own culture, and our own theology, we wind up reading *into* Scripture issues, ideas, and interpretations the original authors never intended.

The changing vocabulary between generations reminds me of this principle with my own children. One day I put on my flip-flops and happened to call them "thongs," the term used when I was a young kid. My children were horrified since "thong" means something totally different in their world. In my father's generation, the word "gay" meant "happy" and is heard in songs and movies of that era. The word has a completely different meaning today. Is it appropriate to place the modern day definition upon those who used the word in song and movies of old? Of course not, because we would be projecting onto the songwriters and filmmakers our present understanding and use of the word rather than their own. This is exactly what happens when twisting Scripture to prove a predetermined viewpoint. We arrive at our intended destination but use an unsuitable method in doing so. We read *into* Scripture things that just aren't there.

We counteract this dangerous propensity by seeking to enter the world of the original author. Instead of reading our modern biases *into* Scripture, we should *draw out* the author's meaning by entering his world, and only then can we make application to our own culture. Before determining what the verse means for us, we must first determine what it means to its original audience. This path of discovery typically involves investigating the historical and cultural setting of the text as well as its grammatical structure of words, characters, and literary genre. In essence, we go back in time and place ourselves in the authors' world rather than first bringing them into ours.

It might be illustrated this way:

Incorrect

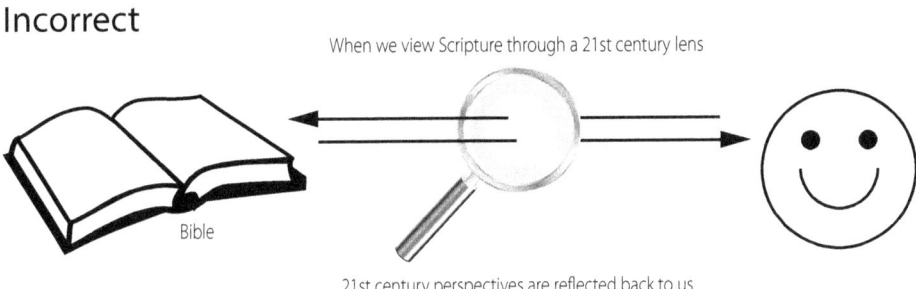

Correct

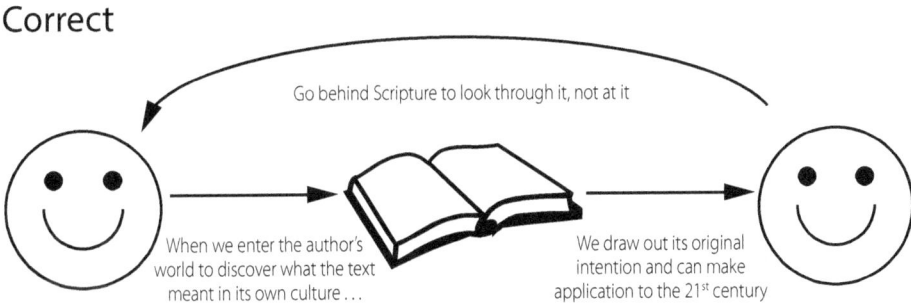

The interpretation of Matthew 7:1 is a prime example: "Do not judge so that you will not be judged." Insisting that Christians keep their nose out of everyone's business, this verse is offered as proof that even Jesus doesn't want us involved in the affairs of others. After all, who are we to judge anyone for anything? To judge another is to go against what Christ stood for and what He taught. How dare we! If I embezzle from my employer, who are you to judge? If I drink myself silly and get behind the wheel of a car, who are you to judge? If I want to behave in a manner denounced by Scripture, who are you to judge? To do so is to disobey the very words of Christ Himself. What escapes the attention of those who use this verse to denounce the judging of others is the fact that they actually declare judgment on the individual they think is being judgmental. In other words, they do the very thing they denounce and despise.

Tolerance is highly valued in our culture. It is okay to believe what we want and do what we want without interference from anyone. All religious beliefs are deemed equally valid, notwithstanding their contradictory teachings, and challenging another's belief or behavior is intolerable and uncouth. Swimming in a sea of relativity, we interpret Christ's words in light of our tolerant, everything-goes culture.

But this is reading *into* Scripture, the very thing we *shouldn't* be doing. We bypass the historical, cultural, and grammatical context of Jesus' words and arrive at faulty, but socially acceptable solutions.

Does Jesus really mean that we can never judge—ever, for anything? Is not Jesus Himself making a judgment by stating that those who judge will be judged? Jesus is doing the very thing He tells us not to do. How can that be? Jesus makes judgments in other scriptural passages, most notably in Matthew 23 where He judges the scribes and Pharisees as hypocrites, blind guides, sons of hell, whitewashed tombs, brood of vipers and the like. Harsh words of judgment from a kind and generous Savior.

According to John 7:24, we are not to "judge according to appearance, but judge with righteous judgment." Luke 12:57 asks, "why do you not even on your own initiative judge what is right?" Paul judges false teachers and even Leviticus 19:15 notes, "you are to judge your neighbor fairly." From a larger context, it seems the Bible doesn't prohibit all judging as our cultural warriors suggest.

By carefully examining the passage, we discern that Jesus' words are taken out of context to support a bias at odds with the Bible. Clouded by the lens of cultural relativity, it is easy to read *into* Scripture conclusions already deemed appropriate without regard for solid biblical reasoning. But what does the passage actually say in its context?

> Do not judge so that you will not be judged. For in the way you judge, you will be judged; and by your standard of measure, it will be measured to you. Why do you look at the speck that is in your brother's eye, but do not notice the log that is in your own eye? Or how can you say to your brother, "Let me take the speck out of your eye," and behold, the log is in your own eye? You hypocrite, first take the log out of your own eye, and then you will see clearly to take the speck out of your brother's eye. Do not give what is holy to dogs, and do not throw your pearls before swine, or they will trample them under their feet, and turn and tear you to pieces (Mt. 7:1–6).

We are invited to judge ourselves before we judge others—a principle worth living by and one the scribes and Pharisees neglect. In fact, they feel superior to everyone else, look down on others, and pride themselves on keeping the tiniest of commandments, even tithing mint, dill, and cumin while neglecting weightier matters (Mt. 23:23). Of all people, they are most deceived and blinded by their own self-righteousness. The kingdom is trampled underfoot by dogs and hogs with no regard for truth. Better to invest in those who are receptive to the moving of God.

Jesus is not prohibiting all judgments; after all, how can we determine who the hogs and dogs are without some form of discernment? Jesus is teaching that making judgments like the scribes and Pharisees do, without self-examination and in a manner that reflects hypocrisy and self-deception, is to be avoided. In order to judge correctly, these things must first be dealt with since we are obligated to take the log out of our own eye before examining the speck in another's.

Our task is not to read cultural or personal biases *into* Scripture, but to enter into the world of the author and original audience so we can discover how they understood the teaching in their day. Only then can we *draw out* meaning and application for our own culture. When we interpret Scripture solely through cultural biases, we easily get off on the wrong track. However, as we examine the historical, cultural, and grammatical context of the passage, we engage in sound biblical reasoning, even when it comes to alcohol.

Summary: *Alcohol isn't inherently evil simply because it can be abused, and since Scripture sufficiently speaks truth in its own right, we should first seek to understand what a passage means to the original audience in its own culture and time before making application to our own world.*

DRUNKENOLOGY 101: THE ABUSE OF ALCOHOL

This chapter contends that Scripture denounces drunkenness, something virtually all Christians agree with. It is a boundary God establishes that we are not to cross. By setting forth biblical support for the condemnation of drunkenness, we can find quick agreement on the matter before moving on to more controversial areas.

No thinking person denies the well-documented adverse effects of alcohol abuse. It is easy to quote statistics from the United States Department of Transportation, Centers for Disease Control and Prevention, various special interest groups, and other medical and law enforcement agencies, but doing so would only serve to support what we already know—the abuse of alcohol greatly costs our society.

Statistics can easily be manipulated to support just about anything. If I said three out of four pastors prefer the New International Version of the Bible, you might think that 75% of all pastors in the United States use this version over all others. In reality, I only asked four pastors of which I knew the NIV was preferred by three of them. I can now say that three out of four pastors prefer one version over all others. Tricky and misleading isn't it?

Current statistics reveal that alcohol-impaired traffic fatalities have been declining over the years despite an increase in drivers, vehicles, and miles driven. These statistics may go up or down over time and may be manipulated by the unscrupulous, but the truth of Scripture always remains intact. Even if there were ten billion people on this planet and only 2,500 abused alcohol (an astounding low percentage of 0.00000025%), would drunkenness be less of a sin? Would the small statistic void the clear teaching of God's Word? The answer is a resounding "no." While the statistical game can be played, I don't find it helpful in determining what the Bible actually teaches.

In no way am I trying to minimize the negative effects of alcohol abuse. Rather, I quite readily concede the point. In the legal system, only issues of disagreement are litigated. To deny what we already know is an act of desperation and a colossal waste of time. Quoting myriad statistics won't make what is true any truer. We know that the abuse of alcohol creates a host of medical problems such as cirrhosis of the liver, from which my step-grandfather died. Its abuse dangerously impairs judgment and reaction times for those behind the wheel, placing countless lives in danger. The misuse of alcohol can affect one's personality and cause serious harm to unborn children of pregnant women. Excessive consumption can even play a significant role in the commission of crimes.

While I find no need to display statistical support for what is blatantly obvious, this should not be construed that I am treading lightly on the potential dangers of excessive consumption. Quite the opposite is true. I readily comprehend its dark side, as should any breathing human being. In fact, we are merely agreeing with what the Bible already states: that alcohol abuse is dangerous and wrong. Disagreement arises not over its abuse, but over its casual use by Christians. Although abuse *can* occur, which we all agree is wrong, the question is whether that abuse precludes *all* use of alcohol, even use that doesn't amount to abuse.

Statistics are impersonal numbers lacking the attachment of emotion or experience. To say that forty thousand women in the United States die from breast cancer each year is one thing; it is quite another when one of those forty thousand happens to be your spouse, your sister, your mother, or your daughter. Statistics become real when someone we know, love, and miss is counted among them.

Personal experience becomes the face of statistical data. We all know someone who has been touched by the abuse of alcohol. A childhood friend who played organized baseball with me was recently arrested for driving under the influence of alcohol. A high school friend became an alcoholic as an adult and struggles daily with her addiction, is faithful to her AA meetings, and regularly meets with her sponsor for accountability. I will not soon forget my college experience of sharing the gospel with homeless alcoholics in the inner city, each carrying their own bottle of booze in brown paper bags. My grandmother, for a time, was a bartender and I remember visiting her in that dark and dirty small town joint.

During my first full-time pastorate, a rural teenager was in an alcohol-impaired automobile accident. The driver, who had been drinking, lost control of the truck and this young girl was thrown onto the pavement with a broken skull and fragments of glass lodged in her brain. She was airlifted to the big hospital in our city, and I was called to support the family. Medical personnel didn't think she would survive. I frequently visited the hospital, prayed with her, and watched her parents struggle to overcome the pain. She miraculously recovered. God had other plans for her. It was a close call, an expensive incident, and one that forever altered the lives of many people.

The abuse of alcohol can and does ruin lives—just ask the millions of people trounced in its wake. Their stories are heartbreaking, and the harmful effects are real. We must acknowledge this up front, openly, and unapologetically. In standing with the Bible, we dare not in any way glamorize or support the overindulgence or abuse of alcohol.

Whether Christians should abstain from using alcohol, freely enjoy it in moderation, or prohibit its use altogether is a debate that will probably continue until the Lord returns. But when it comes to drunkenness, Christians agree that God's Word unequivocally condemns such abuse. There is no dissension surrounding this point. But just to be sure, what does the Bible teach regarding the abuse of alcohol?

Scripture and Abuse

The perils of alcohol abuse are addressed quite clearly in Scripture. From its pages, much can be gleaned about overindulgence.[1] In Ephesians 5:18, for instance, we are explicitly told, "do not get drunk with wine, for that is dissipation, but be filled with the Spirit." Does it get any clearer than this? One might say, "It says not to be drunk *with wine*, but it doesn't prohibit being drunk on beer or hard liquor." Is the heart of Paul's prohibition against the *state of being drunk* or only *using wine* to get there? Some may argue over such nonsense, but when the context of Ephesians 5 is considered, along with other supporting biblical passages, we discover that Paul is prohibiting drunkenness itself.

Ephesians 5 may be captured this way:

5:1	Please the Heavenly Father by walking in love and imitating the Lord.
5:2	After all, Christ gave His life as a sacrificial offering for humankind. Living for Him is one way of showing gratitude.
5:3–5	A life pleasing to God involves the giving of thanks, not the pursuit of immorality or impurity which is contrary to His kingdom.

5:6–14   A life pleasing to the Lord entails vigilance against deception and eschewing unfruitful deeds.

5:15–21   When we walk with care in pursuit of the Lord's will, we escape being misled down the road of foolishness. Being filled with the Spirit of God enables choices and travels along paths of righteousness with a melody in our heart. Rather than give ourselves to the control of alcohol, Paul desires that we yield to the Spirit's oversight so we can lead a life pleasing to our Lord.

EPHESIANS 5:1–21

Pleasing to the Lord	Displeasing to the Lord
Imitating God, walking in love, giving thanks, goodness, righteousness, truth, learning to please God, exposing unfruitful deeds, careful in our walk, being wise, making the most of our time, refraining from foolishness, understanding the will of the Lord, being filled with the Spirit, speaking to one another in psalms, hymns, and spiritual songs, making melody in our heart, always giving thanks, being subject to one another	Immorality Impurity & Greed Filthiness Silly Talk Course Jesting Coveting Idolatry Being Deceived Unfruitful Deeds Drunkenness

A life pleasing to God is a life lived with intentionality. We *intentionally* pursue imitating our Lord. We *intentionally* rebuff immorality and impurity. We *intentionally* take time to give thanks. We *intentionally* remove ourselves from unfruitful deeds and foolishness. We *intentionally* seek to be led down paths of righteousness under the Spirit's control instead of voluntarily yielding ourselves to drunkenness. The issue is what controls us—alcohol or the Holy Spirit. A Spirit-controlled life is one that pleases God and receives His favor. An alcohol-controlled life displeases God and leads away from Him.

Plenty of Bible passages denounce the abuse of alcohol. Many describe the destructive consequences and noxious behavior associated with such abuse. A sampling of scriptural teaching on drunkenness reveals God's displeasure with overindulgence.

Drunkenness Condemned

The Bible explicitly prohibits drunkenness in Ephesians 5:18, and Paul indicates that drunkards will not inherit the kingdom of God. The Old Testament clearly confirms the many ruinous outcomes inebriation brings upon its victim.

> Ephesians 5:18
> And do not get drunk with wine, for that is dissipation, but be filled with the Spirit.
>
> Romans 13:13
> Let us behave properly as in the day, not in carousing and drunkenness, not in sexual promiscuity and sensuality, not in strife and jealousy.
>
> Galatians 5:19–21
> Now the deeds of the flesh are evident, which are: immorality, impurity, sensuality, idolatry, sorcery, enmities, strife, jealousy, outbursts of anger, disputes, dissensions, factions, envying, drunkenness, carousing, and things like these, of which I forewarn you, just as I have forewarned you, that those who practice such things will not inherit the kingdom of God.
>
> 1 Corinthians 6:9–10
> Or do you not know that the unrighteous will not inherit the kingdom of God? Do not be deceived; neither fornicators, nor idolaters, nor adulterers, nor effeminate, nor homosexuals, nor thieves, nor the covetous, nor drunkards, nor revilers, nor swindlers, will inherit the kingdom of God.
>
> Isaiah 28:1
> Woe to the proud crown of the drunkards of Ephraim, and to the fading flower of its glorious beauty, which is at the head of the fertile valley of those who are overcome with wine!

Drunken Fellowship Avoided

Associating with so-called brothers who abuse alcohol undermines the faith. In other words, pleasing God involves willingly placing ourselves under the control of the Holy Spirit who leads us down paths of righteousness, not the undisciplined and problematic trail of drunkards. Being under the influence of alcohol and being under the influence of the Holy Spirit are diametrically opposed to one another and leads to opposite outcomes.

> Proverbs 23:20
> Do not be with heavy drinkers of wine, or with gluttonous eaters of meat.
>
> 1 Corinthians 5:11
> But actually, I wrote to you not to associate with any so-called brother if he is an immoral person, or covetous, or an idolater, or a reviler, or a drunkard, or a swindler—not even to eat with such a one.

Drunkenness a Metaphor for the Imprecation of God

Drunkenness can depict the curse of God upon a land. Through the prophet Jeremiah, the Lord declares He will fill all the inhabitants of Jerusalem with drunkenness. He declares through Ezekiel that He will fill the land with drunkenness and sorrow. Used as a metaphor for the displeasure and curse of God, drunkenness is never a positive attribute; rather, it is the very opposite of our Lord's blessing and favor.

> Jeremiah 13:13–14
> Then say to them, "Thus says the Lord, 'Behold I am about to fill all the inhabitants of this land—the kings that sit for David on his throne, the priests, the prophets and all the inhabitants of Jerusalem—with drunkenness! I will dash them against each other, both the fathers and the sons together,' declares the Lord. 'I will not show pity nor be sorry nor have compassion so as not to destroy them.'"

> Ezekiel 23:28–33
> For thus says the Lord God, "Behold, I will give you into the hand of those whom you hate, into the hand of those from whom you were alienated. They will deal with you in hatred, take all your property, and leave you naked and bare. And the nakedness of your harlotries will be uncovered, both your lewdness and your harlotries. These things will be done to you because you have played the harlot with the nations, because you have defiled yourself with their idols. You have walked in the way of your sister; therefore I will give her cup into your hand." Thus says the Lord God,
>
> "You will drink your sister's cup,
> Which is deep and wide.
> You will be laughed at and held in derision;
> It contains much.
> You will be filled with drunkenness and sorrow,
> The cup of horror and desolation,
> The cup of your sister Samaria."

Drunkenness Leads to Ruin

Nothing good comes from the abuse of alcohol. Instead of arousing a solid work ethic, its victims become lazy and irresponsible. It was when Elah, the king of Israel, was drunk that his servant Zimri knew he had the advantage and assassinated him. In Deuteronomy, a stubborn and rebellious son is called a drunkard and stoned to death. In order to avenge Amnon's violation of his sister Tamar, Absalom waits for Amnon to become inebriated prior to killing him. Drunkenness creates a state of vulnerability for its abusers who then become easy prey for calamity. Only ruin comes from the abuse of alcohol.

> Proverbs 23:21
> For the heavy drinker and the glutton will come to poverty, and drowsiness will clothe one with rags.

Nahum 1:9–10
Whatever you devise against the Lord, He will make a complete end of it. Distress will not rise up twice. Like tangled thorns, and like those who are drunken with their drink, they are consumed as stubble completely withered.

Habakkuk 2:15–16
Woe to you who make your neighbors drink,
Who mix in your venom even to make them drunk
So as to look on their nakedness!
You will be filled with disgrace rather than honor.
Now you yourself drink and expose your own nakedness.
The cup in the Lord's right hand will come around to you,
And utter disgrace will come upon your glory.

Lamentations 4:21–22
Rejoice and be glad, O daughter of Edom,
Who dwells in the land of Uz;
But the cup will come around to you as well,
You will become drunk and make yourself naked.
The punishment of your iniquity has been completed, O daughter of Zion;
He will exile you no longer.
But He will punish your iniquity, O daughter of Edom;
He will expose your sins!

Deuteronomy 21:18–21
If any man has a stubborn and rebellious son who will not obey his father or his mother, and when they chastise him, he will not even listen to them, then his father and mother shall seize him, and bring him out to the elders of his city at the gateway of his hometown. They shall say to the elders of his city, "This son of ours is stubborn and rebellious, he will not obey us, he is a glutton and a drunkard." Then all the men of his city shall stone him to death; so you shall remove the evil from your midst, and all Israel will hear of it and fear.

1 Kings 16:8–10
In the twenty-sixth year of Asa king of Judah, Elah the son of Baasha became king over Israel at Tirzah, and reigned two years. His servant Zimri, commander of half his chariots, conspired against him. Now he was at Tirzah drinking himself drunk in the house of Arza, who was over the household at Tirzah. Then Zimri went in and struck him and put him to death in the twenty-seventh year of Asa king of Judah, and became king in his place.

2 Samuel 13: 28–29
Absalom commanded his servants, saying, "See now, when Amnon's heart is merry with wine, and when I say to you, 'Strike Amnon,' then put him to death. Do not fear; have not I myself commanded you? Be courageous and be valiant."

The servants of Absalom did to Amnon just as Absalom had commanded. Then all the king's sons arose and each mounted his mule and fled.

Drunkenness Skews Perspective

The consumption of too much alcohol affects accurate perception—skewing perspective. Confusion sets in and the ability to render sound judgment is hampered. When reeling from strong drink, the presence of understanding flees. Inebriation doesn't enhance our ability to view things from God's perspective; instead, understanding vanishes and sound decision-making deteriorates to the point of nonexistence.

> Proverbs 23:29–30, 33
> Who has woe? Who has sorrow?
> Who has contentions? Who has complaining?
> Who has wounds without cause?
> Who has redness of eyes?
> Those who linger long over wine,
> Those who go to taste mixed wine.
>
> Your eyes will see strange things
> And your mind will utter perverse things.
>
> Jeremiah 25:16
> They will drink and stagger and go mad because of the sword that I will send among them.
>
> Isaiah 28:7
> And these also reel with wine and stagger from strong drink:
> The priest and the prophet reel with strong drink,
> They are confused by wine, they stagger from strong drink;
> They reel while having visions,
> They totter when rendering judgment.
>
> Hosea 4:11
> Harlotry, wine and new wine take away the understanding.

Drunkenness Impacts Calling

God not only calls us to serve and worship Him, but He leads us vocationally as well. He is the potter and we are the clay. Our lives are designed by Him and for Him, no matter what our occupation. Even the prophets and priests of the Old Testament, who should know better, discover that the ability to fulfill their God-ordained vocation is impacted by alcohol abuse. When inebriation adversely affects our ability to perform or respond to the Lord's call upon our lives, we dishonor Him.

Isaiah 28:7
And these also reel with wine and stagger from strong drink:
The priest and the prophet reel with strong drink,
They are confused by wine, they stagger from strong drink;
They reel while having visions,
They totter when rendering judgment.

Jeremiah 13:13
Thus says the Lord, "Behold I am about to fill all the inhabitants of this land—the kings that sit for David on his throne, the priests, the prophets and all the inhabitants of Jerusalem—with drunkenness!"

Leviticus 10:1–3
Now Nadab and Abihu, the sons of Aaron, took their respective firepans, and after putting fire in them, placed incense on it and offered strange fire before the Lord, which He had not commanded them. And fire came out from the presence of the Lord and consumed them, and they died before the Lord. Then Moses said to Aaron, "It is what the Lord spoke, saying, 'By those who come near Me I will be treated as holy, and before all the people I will be honored.'" So Aaron, therefore, kept silent.

Drunkenness Degrades Behavior

Living life for the glory of God under the guidance of the Holy Spirit is the desire of every Christian. The Bible duly notes the outrageous and revolting behavior to which drunkenness leads. Drunkards can be obnoxious, violent, and contentious—something we witness even in our own culture.

Jeremiah 25:27
Thus says the Lord of hosts, the God of Israel, "Drink, be drunk, vomit, fall and rise no more because of the sword which I will send among you."

Psalm 107:27
They reeled and staggered like a drunken man, and were at their wits' end.

Job 12:25
They grope in darkness with no light, and He makes them stagger like a drunken man.

Proverbs 23:29–30, 33
Who has woe? Who has sorrow?
Who has contentions? Who has complaining?
Who has wounds without cause?
Who has redness of eyes?

Those who linger long over wine,
Those who go to taste mixed wine.

Your eyes will see strange things
And your mind will utter perverse things.

Habakkuk 2:16
You will be filled with disgrace rather than honor.
Now you yourself drink and expose your own nakedness.
The cup in the Lord's right hand will come around to you,
And utter disgrace will come upon your glory.

Proverbs 4:17
For they eat the bread of wickedness and drink the wine of violence.

Proverbs 20:1
Wine is a mocker, strong drink a brawler,
And whoever is intoxicated by it is not wise.

Drunkenness Erodes Morals

Christians are salt and light (Mt. 5:13–16)—a positive influence upon this world. Our presence restrains sin and thwarts the collapse of morality. Under the control of alcohol, proper judgment vanishes, perspective is skewed, senses are dulled, and inhibition is stripped away. Without proper senses, drunkards engage in corrupt behavior they would not normally pursue. Noah is a prime example of this as he lay naked in his tent after becoming inebriated. Lot becomes drunk and sleeps with his daughters. Even David, the apple of God's eye, tempts Uriah to abuse alcohol in an effort to cover his own sin with Bathsheba (2 Sam. 11:13ff).

Isaiah 56:12
"Come," they say, "let us get wine, and let us drink heavily of strong drink;
And tomorrow will be like today, only more so."

Genesis 9:1
He drank of the wine and became drunk, and uncovered himself inside his tent.

Genesis 19:32
Come, let us make our father drink wine, and let us lie with him that we may preserve our family through our father.

Lamentations 4:21
Rejoice and be glad, O daughter of Edom,
Who dwells in the land of Uz;

But the cup will come around to you as well,
You will become drunk and make yourself naked.

Joel 3:3
They have also cast lots for My people,
Traded a boy for a harlot
And sold a girl for wine that they may drink.

Drunkenness Leads to Spiritual Indifference

Alcohol abuse is an evil master who moves us toward fulfilling addiction as the primary focus in life. God takes a back seat and our heart's ambition is no longer the pursuit of spiritual realities, but the satisfying of physical pleasures. Drunkenness is never equated with spirituality. In fact, it is an obstacle—a stumbling block to knowing and serving God. The incompatibility of alcohol abuse with Christianity is so strongly felt by Paul that he declares drunkards unfit for an inheritance in the kingdom. When abusing alcohol, our sensitivity toward spiritual things is diminished, even to the point of indifference.

Isaiah 5:11–12
Woe to those who rise early in the morning that they may pursue strong drink,
Who stay up late in the evening that wine may inflame them!
Their banquets are accompanied by lyre and harp, by tambourine and flute, and by wine; but they do not pay attention to the deeds of the Lord, nor do they consider the work of His hands.

Galatians 5:19–21
Now the deeds of the flesh are evident, which are: immorality, impurity, sensuality, idolatry, sorcery, enmities, strife, jealousy, outbursts of anger, disputes, dissensions, factions, envying, drunkenness, carousing, and things like these, of which I forewarn you, just as I have forewarned you, that those who practice such things will not inherit the kingdom of God.

1 Corinthians 6:9–10
Or do you not know that the unrighteous will not inherit the kingdom of God? Do not be deceived; neither fornicators, nor idolaters, nor adulterers, nor effeminate, nor homosexuals, nor thieves, nor the covetous, nor drunkards, nor revilers, nor swindlers, will inherit the kingdom of God.

Drunkenness Undermines Judgment

That too much alcohol affects one's judgment really needs no explanation. God desires that we maintain sober judgment and sound minds (Rom. 12:3; 2 Tim. 1:7; 1 Pt. 5:8). In an inebriated state, proper judgment falls by the wayside. Jesus tells the story of a faithless and irresponsible servant overseeing his master's possessions. Instead of working hard, his drunkenness impedes a proper response toward his master and his responsibilities (Lk. 12:41–48). Nabal misjudges his response to David's request for food, and if it wasn't for the intervention of his wise wife Abigail, the drunkard would be dead (I Sam. 25:32–38).

> Proverbs 20:1
> Wine is a mocker, strong drink a brawler,
> And whoever is intoxicated by it is not wise.
>
> Habakkuk 2:5
> Furthermore, wine betrays the haughty man,
> So that he does not stay at home.
> He enlarges his appetite like Sheol,
> And he is like death, never satisfied.
> He also gathers to himself all nations
> And collects to himself all peoples.
>
> Isaiah 22:13
> Instead, there is gaiety and gladness,
> Killing of cattle and slaughtering of sheep,
> Eating of meat and drinking of wine:
> "Let us eat and drink, for tomorrow we may die."
>
> Hosea 4:1
> Harlotry, wine and new wine take away the understanding.

Drunkenness a Leadership Disqualifier

Qualifications for leadership within the church are found in Titus 1:5–9 and I Timothy 3:2–7. These verses list required leadership attributes such as sound judgment, moral behavior, good reputation, as well as negative traits leaders are not to possess, like a hot temper, addiction to wine, and greediness. Alcohol abuse is a barrier to church leadership for all the reasons listed in this chapter. Proverbs even notes that overindulgence is unfit for kings and rulers while Titus says it isn't even fit for older women.

> Titus 1:7–9
> For the overseer must be above reproach as God's steward, not self-willed, not quick-tempered, not addicted to wine, not pugnacious, not fond of sordid gain, but hospitable, loving what is good, sensible, just, devout, self-controlled, holding fast the faithful word which is in accordance with the teaching, so that he will be able both to exhort in sound doctrine and to refute those who contradict.

I Timothy 3:2–3
An overseer, then, must be above reproach, the husband of one wife, temperate, prudent, respectable, hospitable, able to teach, not addicted to wine or pugnacious, but gentle, peaceable, free from the love of money.

I Timothy 3:8
Deacons likewise must be men of dignity, not double-tongued, or addicted to much wine or fond of sordid gain.

Prov. 31:4–5
It is not for kings, O Lemuel,
It is not for kings to drink wine,
Or for rulers to desire strong drink,
For they will drink and forget what is decreed,
And pervert the rights of all the afflicted.

Titus 2:3
Older women likewise are to be reverent in their behavior, not malicious gossips nor enslaved to much wine, teaching what is good.

G. I. Williamson sums it up pretty well in his book titled *Wine in the Bible & the Church:*[2]

> The problem of the abuse of wine and strong drink is not new. It was well known to the inspired writers of the Old Testament. They tell us that in their day too there were those who drank until they were "merry" (2 Sam. 13:28; Est. 1:10), then "boisterous" (Zech. 9:15), and finally violent (Pr. 4:17). They vividly describe the drunken man "overcome with wine" (Ps. 78:65). He reels, staggers, is confused, totters, and finally vomits (Isa. 28:7). He sees "strange things" and utters "perverse things" (Pr. 23:33). He becomes "like one who lies down in the middle of the sea, or like one who lies down on the top of a mast" (Pr. 23:34). In his drunken condition a man may strike him and he will not even feel it (Pr. 23:35), and then, as soon as he is sober he will seek another drink (23:35). The "skid-row" derelict is evidently nothing new under the sun. The inspired writers also knew about the "woe ... sorrow ... contentions ... wounds ... (and) redness of eyes" (Pr. 23:39) suffered by the man "sick with the heat of wine" (Hos. 7:5). They knew what it could do to human behavior, when a man drank too much—how he would sell a girl for wine (Joel 3:3)—lose all sense of modesty (Gen. 9:21)—or even commit incest (Gen. 19:32–35). They didn't hesitate to compare the powerful effects of wine and strong drink to the "venom of serpents and the deadly poison of cobras" (Deut. 32:32). The Scripture confirms the testimony that the drunkard himself makes in his sober moments: "it bites like a serpent and stings like a viper" (Pr. 23:32).

The biblical portrayal of someone under the control of alcohol resonates with what we find in life. We shake our head in agreement, mumbling, "Yep, that is exactly what the abuse of alcohol does to a person." It is Drunkenology 101 and easy to understand.

Crossing the Line

Our Creator knows what is best for us and often establishes boundaries we are not to cross. He knows that when we cross those lines, we harm ourselves and our relationship with Him. In the Garden of Eden, Adam and Eve are given the task of tending the garden while enjoying both its blessings and its Creator. They are free to enjoy the bounty of the Lord with one exception: they cannot cross the line of eating fruit from a particular tree. Everything was theirs, except one tree. It is not the only tree in the garden bearing fruit; there are many other trees to enjoy. The prohibition is not a difficult one to abide by, for it is but one tree out of many. The Creator establishes a line over which Adam and Eve are not to cross. The loving Heavenly Father knows the devastation and ruin a trespass will bring. It isn't the tree that is important, but the test of faithfulness and obedience. Will our human parents obey the Lord, or will they cross the line into sin?

There are lines in life we are not to cross; some are restrictions established by God and others are logical and natural limits. When God says, "Have no other gods before Me," "Do not commit adultery," or "Do not eat from tree of the knowledge of good and evil," the restriction comes directly from our Creator. Logical or natural limits, on the other hand, are restricted by design. For instance, humans can create vehicles for flight, but the ability to fly ourselves is limited. We are unable to sprout wings. Monsanto, a large agricultural company, may be able to genetically modify soy beans to withstand pesticide, but the bean cannot be modified to withstand the destruction of a backhoe.

In other words,

> Alcohol involves both types of boundaries. There is only so much alcohol an individual can consume before enjoyment cedes to inebriation, and then sickness. One can die from alcohol poisoning. On top of this natural limit, God has decreed an ethical limit. Indulging oneself to the point of such inebriation—we commonly call it "drunkenness"—is an infraction of God's right way of living. Thus, drunkenness trespasses both kinds of boundaries—it defies God in both His created order and His revealed Word.[3]

Scripture is crystal clear in its condemnation of alcohol abuse. Drunkenness steps over a line God instructs us not to cross. When we step over the line, we disobey and displease our Heavenly Father, allow alcohol to control us instead of the Holy Spirit, and exhibit egregious behavior. Drunkenness is such a serious trespass that it prevents one from serving in church leadership or inheriting the kingdom of God. However, here is where we need to be careful.

Just because God strongly denounces drunkenness doesn't mean that He denounces all use of alcohol. In other words, being drunk, which is a sin, is not to be confused with drinking alcohol, which is not a sin. The Bible clearly condemns the *abuse* of alcohol, not the *use* of alcohol. There is a difference between being drunk and drinking. Some folks are unable to separate the two, maybe because they don't want to, but sound thinking demands it.

In his book titled *What Would Jesus Drink?*, Brad Whittington notes, "In the Old and New Testament there are 228 references to wine and 19 references to strong drink" which he organizes into positive, neutral, and negative categories.[4] He discovers forty negative references to alcohol in the Bible, which amounts to 16% of the verses.[5] He goes on to say,

> All but one of the forty negative references to alcohol in the Bible concern the abuse of alcohol. There are seventeen warnings against abusing alcohol, nineteen examples of people abusing alcohol, and three guidelines for selecting leaders. The three references to selecting leaders caution that those who abuse alcohol should not be selected as leaders.[6]

After studying the 247 positive, neutral, and negative references to wine and strong drink in the Bible, Whittington concludes, "As these are warnings against abuse, they seemed to indicate that total abstinence is not required or expected of leaders."[7] He further notes,

> By the time I had come to this point in my research, I sensed a fairly clear picture of the larger sort. Based on the content and number of positive references to alcohol . . . . it seemed to me that the scriptural position is an emphasis on moderate use of alcohol with a caution against drunkenness.[8]

The following chart reveals the flawed reasoning that exists when we extend Scripture's prohibition against alcohol abuse to all uses of alcohol.[9]

FLAWED REASONING

Alcohol	Food	Sex
Scripture condemns drunkenness	Scripture condemns gluttony	Scripture condemns infidelity
Drinking alcohol can lead to drunkenness	Enjoying food can lead to gluttony	Enjoying sex can lead to sexual infidelity
Therefore, Scripture condemns all alcohol drinking	Therefore, Scripture condemns all food consumption	Therefore, Scripture condemns all sexual activity

A study in the use of alcohol by Christians would be far easier if we could just conclude, "Can't touch it, can't look at it, can't drink it, can't own it, can't do anything with it, and we must be totally against it at all times and in every circumstance." Unfortunately, it is not quite that black and white. We must engage our mind, study the issue, and reason well.

It is good to be a generous person, but generosity extended too far becomes irresponsibility and poor stewardship. It is good to deeply care for others, but to do so in a manner that neglects our own self-care crosses the line of God's intention. Work is a positive activity, but taken to the extreme, it becomes a greedy love of money or a workaholic addiction. Sex is an enjoyable activity, but becomes a trespass when extended beyond God's boundaries. Food wonderfully sustains us, but becomes gluttony when taken too far. Moderate consumption of alcohol is permitted, but inebriation crosses a line which the Lord forbids. Christians agree that drunkenness is prohibited by the Lord, but is all use forbidden as well? This is where the road parts and Christians from all branches of the faith take divergent paths.

Summary: Recognizing the destructive nature of overindulgence, Scripture clearly condemns the abuse of alcohol whereas a life pleasing to the Heavenly Father is one under the control of the Holy Spirit.

HISTORY 101: ALCOHOL THROUGH THE AGES

This chapter traces views of alcohol throughout the centuries—before Jesus to the Temperance Movement in the United States. How do those who have gone before us understand biblical teaching on alcohol? We discover that views of total abstinence were uncommon until the Temperance Movement's social agenda altered the way alcohol is perceived by the modern church.

History is an exciting subject, though I didn't always feel this way. I used to be a quitter. I quit just about everything I tried—football, basketball, wrestling, stamp collecting, drums—you name it, I quit. Then came a point in my life when I decided to quit quitting and force myself to stick with something. So I intentionally pursued a college major that I knew absolutely nothing about and couldn't tolerate at the time, just to prove to myself that I could stick with something. It wasn't long before I began loving the subject, appreciating its value, and allowing it to broaden my perspective on life. I graduated with an undergraduate degree in history.

Though our focus is on scriptural teaching, a brief survey of alcohol within Christendom is beneficial. Sometimes we fall into the trap of thinking that all that ever was, is, or will be is our own generational perspective. It reminds me of growing up amid Iowa cornfields, sheltered from the world at large by a hard-working, blue-collar hometown. I didn't realize there was such a thing as Chinese food until I went off to college. Mistakenly, I believed Iowa was pretty much the only world that existed, or mattered. It didn't occur to me the world was bigger than Iowa, let alone my hometown. Later in life I would travel far beyond familiar cornfields to various countries, eat numerous ethnic cuisines, experience diverse cultures and perspectives, and gain a larger picture of life and what God was up to around the globe. Don't get me wrong, I revere the cornfields of Iowa and deeply appreciate growing up in such a wonderful environment, but I am also grateful for the many eye-opening experiences that have enlarged my world.

Exploring past practices and attitudes from distant panoramic vistas helps broaden our sphere of understanding. Seeing things only from the cornfields is merely one piece of the puzzle; stepping back to look through wide-angle lenses is also profitable. Though history is merely one piece of data for us to consider, it is certainly an important piece. While not prescriptive in nature, history is always a helpful teacher. We learn lessons from the experiences of others throughout the ages.

Some may sarcastically quip, "Well, if everyone in history jumped off a bridge, would you jump too?" Others might counter, "Well, if the Christian church throughout the ages believed that Jesus is the Christ, would you believe that too?" Like anything else, even history can be skewed to one's perspective. Though the historical record is not on par with the authority of Scripture, its importance and influence must not be denied. I do not hold myself out to be an historian by any stretch of the imagination, and my brief excursions into the past merely provide big-picture, broad-stroke snippets of how others before us felt about an issue so divisive to Christians today.

Winemaking

Before conducting a 35,000-foot historical flyover of alcohol throughout the centuries, it might be wise to warm up the engine by first understanding a bit about winemaking itself.

Wine is basically fermented juice from crushed grapes:

> Just as the egg must be fertilized, the grape juice or must requires for its transformation the attack of bacteria. For some reason, so long as the grapes remain on the vine this cannot occur. From the very moment when a bunch of grapes is picked, however, or sometimes even a little bruised, the bacteria begin their work of metamorphosis and the birth of the wine has begun. The winemaker does not really make the wine, therefore, he merely helps nature accomplish her work perfectly. He is thus a kind of obstetrician: he must be professionally competent but also a little inspired and very patient, for the process can last a number of weeks. He adds yeasts to insure victory over the bad ferments which would turn the developing wine into vinegar."[1]

Like farming in America during the early 1900s, harvesting grapes became a family affair—everyone participated. If the vineyard was large, additional workers were hired and "some grapes were eaten immediately, while others were turned into raisins. Most of them, however, were put into the wine press where the men and boys trampled them, often to music."[2] Crushed to release their juices,

> The fermentation process started within six to twelve hours after pressing, and the must was usually left in the collection vat for a few days to allow the initial 'tumultuous' stage of fermentation to pass. The wine makers soon transferred it either into large earthenware jars, which were then sealed, or, if the wine were to be transported elsewhere, into wineskins (that is, partially tanned goat-skins, sewn up where the legs and tail had protruded but leaving the opening at the neck). After six weeks, fermentation was complete, and the wine was filtered into larger containers and either sold for consumption or stored in a cellar or cistern, lasting for three to four years. Even after a year of aging, the vintage was still called 'new wine' and more aged wines were preferred.[3]

Vineyards today can be small operations or large commercial ventures. While modern equipment and preservation methods make the work much easier, the basic process remains the same—bacteria cause the liquid to ferment.

Palestine was filled with vineyards. The Hebrew spies returned from their Promised Land expedition with a cluster of grapes so large it had to be carried on a pole between two men (Num. 13:23). Winemaking was so common in Jesus' day that laboring in the vineyard sets the stage for one of His many parables (Mt. 20:1–16). He even views Himself as the vine and His Heavenly Father as the vinedresser (Jn. 15:1–11). A Christian winemaker in the early 1900s writes,

> First, we find vineyards—many of them, and from all of them wine is being made; and as fast as the juice runs from the press it is put into skins or amphoras. These are the only bottles they have. The skins will hold from two to four gallons, and the amphoras from six to nine gallons each. No precaution is taken to exclude the air from the juice; and as the laws of fermentation were as fixed in Palestine nineteen hundred years ago as they are in the United States to-day, when the juice flows from the press just at that instant does fermentation begin. As soon as the skin of the grape is broken the yeast spores enter.[4]

The Promised Land is a fertile environment for growing and harvesting grapes. Wine is so prevalent in the Mediterranean that it becomes a prized commodity.

Among other things, Solomon gave twenty thousand baths of wine (approximately 118 thousand gallons) to Huram, king of Tyre, in exchange for cedar to build the house of the Lord (2 Chr. 2:3, 10). Highly valued, vineyards are protected by hedges, walls, and watchtowers to keep out thieves and plundering animals according to Psalm 80:12–13 and Isaiah 5:1–5. Even Jesus begins a parable with the following phrase: "A man planted a vineyard and put a wall around it, and dug a vat under the wine press and built a tower" (Mk. 12:1). Wine is being produced in a land made for just such cultivation and its product becomes a central part of everyday, religious, and commercial life.

Before Jesus

Looked upon favorably in Old Testament times, wine is embraced with joy and thanksgiving as a reflection of His blessing, though inebriation is clearly condemned. We delve more deeply into Old and New Testament teaching about wine in the next chapter, but suffice it to say at this point that wine is a blessing from God that gladdens the heart and becomes a normal part of Jewish life with use in festive celebrations and sacrificial offerings:

> As the Jews returned from the Babylonian exile (starting in 537 BC) and the events of the Old Testament drew to a close, wine was "a common beverage for all classes and ages, including the very young; an important source of nourishment; a prominent part in the festivities of the people; a widely appreciated medicine; an essential provision for any fortress; and an important commodity." And it served as "a necessary element in the life of the Hebrews." Wine was also used ritualistically to close the Sabbath and to celebrate weddings, and circumcisions, and Passover.[5]

Vineyards already existed in the Promised Land long before the Hebrews entered it (Num.13:23; Dt. 6:11) and "An exiled Egyptian official who observed life in Syria-Palestine near the beginning of the second millennium B.C. remarked that there was 'more wine than water.' Probably the scarcity of water and its frequent contamination were practical incentives to produce wine."[6]

The Early Church Fathers

Even the early Church Fathers do not stray from the longstanding Old Testament perspective that moderate use of wine is to be enjoyed, while abuse is prohibited. They do not insist on abstinence, view wine as inherently evil, or prohibit its use altogether.[7]

Jerome (AD 347–420)

The son of Eusebius, Jerome is a Latin priest, theologian, and historian who translates the Bible into Latin (called the Vulgate). He is a prolific writer who approves the use of wine in moderation:

> I do not say we are to condemn what is a creature of God. The Lord, Himself, was called a 'wine-bibber,' and wine in moderation was allowed to Timothy because of his weak stomach. I only require that drinkers should observe that limit which their age, their health, or their constitution requires.[8]

Clement of Alexandria (AD 150–215)

Educated in philosophy and literature, Clement of Alexandria winds up teaching at a theological school in Alexandria after his conversion. He is keenly aware of alcohol's dark side and warns of its dangers for young people unable to control their impulses, believing that we are at our best when we are sober. Wine, he believes, is an appropriate symbol of the shed blood of Christ. Using wine medicinally or for purposes of relaxation and enjoyment is acceptable, but only by those who are mature enough by time and reason to drink without becoming intoxicated. He even recommends watering down wine to reduce the risk of overindulgence. Fully aware of the dangers of alcohol abuse, he does not suggest or promote absolute prohibition or abstinence as the solution to drunkenness.

Augustine (AD 354–430)

Augustine is a contemporary of Jerome and serves as a bishop in Africa. As one of the most beloved and influential Church Fathers, he writes *City of God* and *Confessions* which are still revered today. Though Augustine writes that the saints practiced "perpetual abstinence from meat and wine, he also states that wine is "licit [lawful or permissible] as a bodily refreshment."[9] A one-time adherent of Manichaeism before becoming a Christian, Augustine goes to great lengths in distancing himself from the Manichaean heresy. Countering their view that everything in this life is inherently evil, he defends wine as a perfectly good gift from God. Augustine isn't promoting total abstinence as a way of becoming pure from something inherently evil; rather, he promotes the moderate use of wine, knowing that it is a perfectly good gift from our Maker. Neither Jerome or Augustine negate this conclusion: "The Patristic tradition of the Church in regard to intoxicating liquor holds that drunkenness is wrong, total abstinence is praiseworthy, and that it is licit to partake in moderation of inebriating beverages."[10]

Methodius (AD 270–312)
Methodius is the Bishop of Olympos and clearly understands the two uses of wine: (1) moderate use that produces joy for sober individuals, and (2) overindulgence that becomes the poison of dragons.

Basil the Great (AD 329–379)
Basil is born into a wealthy family and pursues a career in law and teaching, but soon recognizes the vanity of his labors and is transformed by the gospel. He later becomes the Greek Bishop of Caesarea Mazaca (in modern day Turkey) and refutes those who condemn marriage and prohibit wine—those who believe wine is inherently evil.

John Chrysostom (AD 347–407)
Chrysostom is known for his outstanding preaching and public-speaking abilities. He emphasizes moderation and states,

> Let there be no drunkenness; for wine is the work of God, but drunkenness is the work of the devil. Wine makes not drunkenness; but intemperance produces it. Do not accuse that which is the workmanship of God, but accuse the madness of a fellow mortal.[11]

Also agreeing with the moderate use of alcohol and the prohibition against drunkenness is Justin Martyr and Bernard of Clairvaux. In fact, of the four cardinal virtues described by Ambrose and Augustine (prudence, justice, temperance, fortitude), the concept of temperance readily applies to the use of alcohol. Drunkenness, on the other hand, is considered a manifestation of gluttony, one of the seven deadly sins as compiled by Gregory the Great in the sixth century.[12] Even the *Didache*, a teaching manual for Christians near the end of the first century, instructs believers to give a portion of their wine to prophets and to the poor.

The Middle Ages (5th–15th century)
The monks of medieval days were known for making excellent wine and beer. In the middle ages, monks "were allotted about five liters of beer per day, and were allowed to drink beer (but not wine) during fasts."[13] Though there are exceptions to this, such as the Olivetan Order that uprooted their vineyards, destroyed their wine-presses, and became fanatical total abstainers for a short time,[14] "The Church of the Middle Ages, if anything, became even softer in its attitude toward the consumption of intoxicating drinks."[15] During this time there was only one organized church, until the Great Schism of 1054 when the Eastern Orthodox Church

split from the Catholic Church. Since both groups believe that proper communion (Eucharist) must use fermented wine, they plant vineyards everywhere they spread their faith.

The Reformation (AD 1517–1648)

While the Reformation initially sought transformation within the Catholic Church, it brought no fundamental changes to the longstanding perspective of alcohol and its use—moderation is a blessing to be enjoyed from God, while drunkenness is wrong. In fact, most of the Reformers were avid drinkers, delighting in the fruit of the vine without apology, while at the same time condemning intoxication.[16]

Martin Luther (AD 1483–1546)

Born in Germany, Luther is a central figure in the Reformation. He is a monk, theologian, and a former Catholic priest who disputes the practice of selling indulgences—paying money to priests for the forgiveness of sins. He believes salvation is the free gift of God, not something to be earned or obtained by good deeds. In his desire to make the Word of God accessible to common folks, he translates the Bible into German instead of using Latin. He becomes a threat to Papal power and is excommunicated from the church and categorized as a troublemaker.

Martin Luther loves his beer and wine as seen in his wedding invitation to a friend: "I am to be married on Thursday. My lord Katie [his wife] and I invite you to send a barrel of the best Torgau beer, and if it is not good, you will have to drink it all yourself."[17] In a letter to his wife during a time of travel, he writes, "You must wonder how long I am likely to stay, or rather, how long you will be rid of me. I keep thinking what good wine and beer I have at home, as well as a beautiful wife, or shall I say 'lord'?"[18] His wife was a trained, licensed, and competent brewer of beer.

Luther said that drunkenness was "when the tongue walks on stilts and reason goes forward under a half sail."[19] Intoxication extends beyond the boundaries established by God, yet Luther feels no compulsion to prohibit its moderate use altogether: "Do not suppose that abuses are eliminated by destroying the object which is abused. Men can go wrong with wine and women. Shall we then prohibit and abolish women?"[20]

John Calvin (AD 1509–1564)

Originally trained in France as a lawyer, Calvin flees to Switzerland after breaking away from the Catholic Church around 1530. Six years later he writes *Institutes of the Christian Religion*. His teachings become the foundation for what is today known as Calvinism. One criterion for distinguishing the elect, according to Calvin, is an upright life that manifests itself in abstention from dancing, card playing, gambling, obscenity, and drunkenness.[21] Alcohol is not to be avoided, only intoxication is prohibited. He writes, "If a man knows that he has a weak head and that he cannot carry three glasses of wine without being overcome, and then drinks indiscreetly, is he not a hog?[22]

Realizing the large number of visitors Calvin entertains, the Geneva town council provides barrels of wine as part of his salary. In his famous *Institutes of the Christian Religion*, Calvin writes of his gratitude for wine: "We are nowhere forbidden to laugh, or to be satisfied with food . . . or to be delighted with music, or to drink wine," and "It is permissible to use wine not only for necessity, but also to make us merry."[23] In his commentary on Psalm 104:15, he warns against using inebriation as "a pretext for a new cult based upon abstinence."[24] Calvin puts forth two conditions for consuming alcohol: (1) drinking must be done in moderation, and (2) in drinking, one must "feel a livelier gratitude to God."[25]

John Knox (AD 1514–1572)

John Knox, the Scottish Reformer and friend of Calvin, is credited with founding Presbyterianism in Scotland. Knox encourages daily Bible reading and finds that some are becoming weary of such a regiment, so he quips, "why weary they not also every day to eat bread? Every day to drink wine? Every day to behold the brightness of the sun?"[26] Drinking was an everyday occurrence for godly people in his day. Eating his last dinner before death, Knox sits with friends and orders a hogshead of wine (about sixty-three gallons), knowing he will never live long enough to drink it all.[27]

Huldrych Zwingli (AD 1484–1531)

Even Zwingli, a Swiss pastor and theologian leading the Reformation movement in Switzerland, believes wine comes from God, but drunkenness crosses boundaries. For Zwingli, the issue is not about the wine itself. In his comparison of wine to God's Word, he states the following:

> To the healthy it warms the blood. But if there is someone who is sick of a disease or fever, he cannot even taste it, let alone drink it, and he marvels that the healthy is able to do so. This is not due to any defect in the wine, but to that of the sickness. So too it is with the Word of God. It is right in itself and its proclamation is always for good. If there are those who cannot bear or understand or receive it, it is because they are sick.[28]

Early Puritans (16th–17th century)

Unable to change the Anglican Church from within, the Puritans in England believe the Reformation doesn't go far enough. For many, the church is so steeped in corruption that separating from it altogether is the only viable alternative. As the name suggests, Puritans believe in moral purity for both the organized church and one's personal life.

Samuel Rutherford declares, "I drink the Lord's choicest wines in the cellar of affliction," and Thomas Watson uses wine in his numerous analogies of Christ and His kingdom, while Hugh Latimer drinks a goblet of spiced ale with his meal just before being burned at the stake.[29] Before coming to Christ, William Perkins was a well-known alcoholic. He sobers up and becomes known as "The Calvin of England;" yet, despite his own adverse experience with alcohol, he does not advocate for abstention or prohibition, but now drinks in moderation to the glory of God.[30] The Reformers, from Luther to the early Puritans, view the moderate use of alcohol as God's blessing from which we need not abstain or prohibit. Drunkenness, on the other hand, clearly crosses a boundary set by God.

The Confessions

We should keep in mind that "Three Reformation confessions of faith note that wine is obligatory in the Lord's Supper: the *Second Helvetic Confession*, the *Westminster Confession*, and the *Heidelberg Catechism*," and the latter actually "glorifies wine drinking not only in the Lord's Supper, but in common repasts, when it speaks of 'wine that sustains this temporal life.'"[31] Additionally,

> The Lutheran Formula of Concord (1576) and the Reformed Christian confessions of faith also make explicit mention of and assume the use of wine, as does the 1689 Baptist Confession of Faith and the Methodist Articles of Religion (1784). In the Dordrecht Confession of Faith (1632), even the radical Anabaptists, who sought to expunge every trace of Roman Catholicism and to rely only on the Bible, also assumed wine was to be used, and despite their reputation as killjoys, the English Puritans were temperate partakers of 'God's good gifts,' including wine and ale.[32]

Colonial America (AD 1607–1783)

As Pilgrims set sail from Europe toward American soil, they bring with them a hearty amount of beer and wine, along with an Old World frame of mind. Wine and beer are the national beverages of the motherland. In the hull of one ship, the *Arabella*, which sailed for America in 1630, was recorded forty-two tuns of beer, ten thousand gallons of wine, fourteen tuns of fresh water, and 120 hogshead of malt for brewing.[33] Of all the things a group of immigrants could bring across a vast ocean to begin a new life, they bring alcohol. For them, life just wouldn't be the same without it.

Once the sea voyagers hit American shores, they begin preparations for a brewery—the first permanent building in Plymouth. Shipments of beer and wine from England couldn't keep up with the expansion and need of the new colonies.[34] The first Thanksgiving by the Pilgrims contained homemade sweet wine from wild grapes.[35] At one point liquor sales to Native Indians is forbidden, but the decision is soon reversed, noting that prohibition is "not fit to deprive the Indians of any lawful comfort which God allows to all men by the use of wine."[36] Even the esteemed Quaker and statesman William Penn, who opens the first brewery in Pennsylvania in 1683, opposes drunkenness but not alcohol itself.[37]

In 1660, drunkenness is codified by the new colony at Plymouth: "By drunkenness is understood a person that either lisps or falters in speech by reason of overdrink or that staggers in his going or that vomits by reason of excessive drinking, or cannot follow his calling."[38] Clergyman and Harvard president Increase Mather got it right when he said, "Drink is in itself a good creature of God, and to be received with thankfulness, but the abuse of drink is from Satan; the wine is from God, but the drunkard is from the Devil."[39] Drunkenness was always seen as wrong, but "the colonists had assimilated alcohol use, based on Old World patterns, into their community lifestyles. As long as mores remained intact, communities held drinking excesses largely in bounds."[40] In reality, "The Anglicans of Virginia and Vermont brought their flasks as well as their Bibles. The same combination was enjoyed by the Puritans of New England and was no stranger to the Scotch-Irish on the western frontier."[41] One author sums up the period from 1750–1825 this way: "Nearly everyone drank intoxicating liquor. It was the family beverage. It was the prevailing mark of hospitality. It was regarded as a discourtesy, even an insult, to refuse it. At all functions, public and private, social and commercial, sacred and solemn, intoxicating beverages were used."[42]

The Awakening (mid–18th century—late 19th century)

Many early Methodist preachers were paid in rum, and Charles Wesley "drank ale and toward the latter end of his life listed certain expenditures for drinks for the guests attending his son's musical concerts. Sherry, port, and Madeira were the favorite wines of hospitality at that time."[43] It was not uncommon for colleges and churches to brew beer for special occasions and the list of special religious ale is legion.[44] George Whitfield, one of the great evangelists of this time, writes at the end of one of his letters, "Give my thanks to that friendly brewer for the keg of rum he sent us."[45] The great Charles Spurgeon, prince of preachers, was known to drink and smoke. Allegedly speaking of Spurgeon, a newspaper article writes that he "freely drank beer, brandy, and sherry" and after leading his family in devotions "before rising from his knees he struck a match and lighted his cigar."[46]

Hints of attitude changes toward alcohol begin to creep in during this period. Throughout church history, drunkenness is condemned while moderate use of alcohol is permitted. But now the wind begins shifting as social concern increases and emerging attitudes toward temperance sprout in the United States. Succumbing to the cultural pressure of his day, even Spurgeon eventually goes without wine and beer in an effort not to offend fellow Christians.[47] The Temperance Movement would not have progressed very far had it not been for the pioneering work of John Wesley and the Methodists. Wesley called on Methodist societies to boycott the use and sale of spirituous liquors not used for medicinal purposes.[48] It was John Wesley who said, "You see the wine when it sparkles in the cup, and are going to drink of it. I tell you there is poison in it! and, therefore, beg you to throw it away."[49]

In 1780 at the "Methodist Conference in Baltimore, the churchmen opposed distilled liquors and determined to 'disown those who would not renounce the practice' of producing it."[50] Francis Asbury, one of the first bishops of the Methodist Episcopal Church states, "I have had one thought about our citizens in general. I wish they would lay aside the use of wine and strong drink in general. God would suddenly and certainly work. I am determined not to go out of my way on that matter for five hundred presidents and all the bishops in the world."[51] The winds of change are gathering and will soon sweep across the country:

> This heightened concern paved the way for movements in the direction of organizations with which to implement this new attitude. Several outstanding preachers, led by Lyman Beecher with his famous Six Sermons on Intemperance, kindled the drive to fever pitch. The activities of Jeremiah Evarts and Jedidiah Morse figured prominently in the movement for organization of important temperance societies on the state level, the logical climax to which came in 1826 with the organization of the American Temperance Union.[52]

The Temperance Movement (19th–20th century)

With newfound freedom from England, increased national growth, and the "social upheaval accompanying the American Revolution and urbanization induced by the Industrial Revolution, drunkenness was on the rise and was blamed as a major contributor to the increasing poverty, unemployment, and crime."[53] It should be noted that "By 1830, the average American over 15 years old consumed nearly seven gallons of pure alcohol a year—three times as much as we drink today—and alcohol abuse (primarily by men) was wreaking havoc on the lives of many."[54]

While the Methodists emphasized personal holiness and rambled against the use of distilled drink, it was Benjamin Rush's 1875 tract titled "A Medical Inquiry into the Effects of Ardent Spirits upon the Body and Mind" that perked the ears of a larger audience. As a well-respected Quaker, physician, patriot, and original signer of the Declaration of Independence, Rush denounced "the use of distilled liquors as ravaging, useless, pernicious and universally destructive."[55] In 1826 the American Temperance Union was organized and at the National Temperance Convention in 1836 a resolution passed to "circulate the pledge for 'total abstinence from all that intoxicates.'" Methodists, Quakers, Presbyterians, and Congregationalists almost immediately gave official sanction to this plea."[56] "The Temperance Movement, rooted in America's Protestant churches, first urged moderation, then encouraged drinkers to help each other to resist temptation, and ultimately demanded that local, state, and national governments prohibit alcohol outright."[57]

The momentum behind this blossoming movement loses influence during the Civil War as the nation's energies are focused elsewhere, but once hostilities are settled, renewed momentum ensues with the creation of the National Woman's Christian Temperance Union in 1874. This hard-working new movement sees thirty-nine states adopt prohibitions so that "By 1920 . . . the vast majority of both the land and people of this country were in dry territory."[58] The Eighteenth Amendment is passed in 1919 prohibiting the production, transportation, and sale of alcohol in the United States; in 1933, it becomes the only amendment ever to be repealed.

G.I. Williamson briefly traces the rise of total abstinence within the Presbyterian Church and asks if the Temperance Movement arose from careful study of Scripture or from some other source.[59] Williamson declares, "It would be a mistake, however, to think of the Temperance Movement as a product of Scripture. The Washingtonian Temperance Movement which began in Baltimore, for example, professed no religious foundation at all. Even more important is the fact that the Scripture was not the 'proof' that was used to support the movement."[60] According to Williamson, the Presbyterian Church gets caught up in the euphoria of the day and in the General Assembly's pronouncements is seen "the utter lack of scriptural proof for what it declares."[61] He further states, "is it not perfectly evident that the Church simply assumed that the 'evil' was too notorious to require proof?" and "What then was the basis of the Church's assumption? The record will show that it was the influence of the temperance movement then sweeping over the American society."[62]

As the new world endures growth, two wars, and an Industrial Revolution, drunkenness is perceived to be a national problem in need of a national solution. The nation is experiencing the undesirable effects of alcohol abuse, and the Protestant Church's solution is to prohibit its use altogether. Total abstinence may curb alcohol abuse, but is it a biblical solution or one that impedes the clear authority of God's Word? Recognizing the problem of abuse, America declares all drinking evil, not just excessive consumption. The Eighteenth Amendment is seen as the national answer when in reality it is a colossal failure that clogs up the court system, enhances organized crime, and becomes exceedingly difficult to enforce. It reminds me of a rabbit that hops onto the road directly in your path, and in a moment of driver panic, overcorrection occurs and the car winds up in the ditch. The American Temperance Movement, in my opinion, is an overcorrection that throws the baby out with the bathwater and equates the moderate use of alcohol with inebriation itself. This is guilt by association whereby the intended blessing of God is turned into something inherently evil. The movement finally lands where Chrysostom, Luther, Calvin, Knox and virtually all of the Church Fathers and Reformers were unwilling to go in their fidelity to Scripture.

Throughout the centuries, Christendom views alcohol as a kind gift from the Heavenly Father to be enjoyed in moderation. Excessive consumption leading to drunkenness has never been sanctioned, while abstinence and prohibition has never been a biblical requirement. It isn't until the Awakening in America that rumblings of abstinence sprout up, take root, and find full voice in the birth of the Temperance Movement and the passing of the Eighteenth Amendment in 1919.

While America engages in total abstinence social reform, "there seems to be neither historical nor theological basis for the total abstinence movement, since . . . the Jews, Christ, and the founders of the major Protestant denominations all drank. Although drunkenness is condemned in both the Old and New Testaments, there is no condemnation of drinking in either."[63]

Summary: *A consistent view of scriptural teaching on alcohol can be seen throughout Christian history (abuse prohibited—moderation permitted) up until the Temperance Movement of the nineteenth and twentieth centuries when social pressure is brought to bear in the national crusade for total abstinence.*

BIBLICAL TEACHING: AN OVERVIEW

This chapter provides an overview of Old and New Testament perspectives on alcohol, particularly wine. Many are surprised at the overwhelming positive references to alcohol. In both testaments, wine is viewed as a good gift from a good God for the enjoyment of His people, while drunkenness is condemned.

The path of least resistance in approaching Scripture is to read modern-day cultural biases and perspectives *into* the text when the biblical author had no inkling of twenty-first century realities. Cultural influence is a substantial factor in how we interpret the Bible. In fact, it can be a doubled-edged sword. On the one hand, Scripture tells us to reject worldly perspectives in favor of biblical standards, and on the other hand, we often elevate cultural biases to scriptural standards without recognizing them as nothing more than another worldly bias, albeit, one that we prefer.

Christians are called to righteousness, service, and a lifestyle contrary to many modern-day perspectives. We are to be strikingly different in our values, beliefs, and practices—often swimming upstream in hostile waters. According to Romans 12:2, we are to think differently from prevailing viewpoints: "And do not be conformed to this world, but be transformed by the renewing of your mind." Similarly, we read in 1 John 2:15–17,

> Do not love the world nor the things in the world. If anyone loves the world, the love of the Father is not in him. For all that is in the world, the lust of the flesh and the lust of the eyes and the boastful pride of life, is not from the Father, but is from the world. The world is passing away, and also its lusts; but the one who does the will of God lives forever.

Jesus' kingdom is not of this world (Jn. 18:36) and rather than receiving the spirit of the world, we have received God's Spirit (1 Cor. 2:12). Jesus says that we are not of this world because He has chosen us out of this world (Jn. 15:19). We are aliens and strangers in this life (1 Pt. 2:11–12) with a true citizenship in heaven (Phil. 3:20).

In many ways, being a disciple of Christ necessitates a mindset different from what is commonly around us. We exemplify all that God is and desires by pursuing a holy life pleasing to Him, like keeping our minds pure, thinking on good things (Phil. 4:8), and doing "nothing from selfishness or empty conceit, but with humility of mind regard one another as more important than yourselves; do not merely look out for your own personal interests, but also for the interests of others" (Phil. 2:3–4). Love is the hallmark of our identification with Christ: "A new commandment I give to you, that you love one another, even as I have loved you, that you also love one another. By this all men will know that you are My disciples, if you have love for one another" (Jn. 13:34–35). Distinguishing characteristics of those transformed by the gospel are readily seen in the Bible.

We can easily highlight blatant cultural practices and beliefs at odds with the Bible such as self-promotion, fornication, and lying, but we are not quite as skilled at identifying our own petty cultural biases we love to pawn off as biblical standards. In other words, we can be inconsistent in scrutinizing our own worldly standards, attitudes, and practices that may be at odds with the Bible. For instance, we may condemn dancing as inherently evil and claim scriptural grounds for our position, but is this a cultural preference or a biblical mandate? In essence, we often fail to detect our own cultural biases while trying to pawn them off as scriptural standards. This form of self-deception is dangerous and wholly unbiblical.

It really does matter what the Bible teaches, and this chapter provides an overview of its instruction while later chapters examine specific passages in greater depth. Since we have already examined biblical teaching on drunkenness, there is no need to retrace ground already established. The Bible clearly condemns the abuse and overindulgence of alcohol.

Old Testament
Sacrificial and Festive Use

The use of wine in sacrificial offerings, feasts, and celebrations is seen throughout the Old Testament. In Numbers 15:4–5 we read,

> The one who presents his offering shall present to the Lord a grain offering of one-tenth of an ephah of fine flour mixed with one-fourth of a hin of oil, and you shall prepare wine for the drink offering, one-fourth of a hin, with the burnt offering or for the sacrifice, for each lamb.

First fruits of harvest were given to the priests as a sacrifice unto the Lord that helped sustain both the priests and the temple facilities (Dt. 18:3–5).

> Now this shall be the priests' due from the people, from those who offer a sacrifice, either an ox or a sheep, of which they shall give to the priest the shoulder and the two cheeks and the stomach. You shall give him the first fruits of your grain, your new wine, and your oil, and the first shearing of your sheep. For the Lord your God has chosen him and his sons from all your tribes, to stand and serve in the name of the Lord forever.

Upon returning to their homeland and rebuilding the city walls, thankful Jews make promises to obey the Lord of which one promise is giving wine to the priests. "We will also bring the first of our dough, our contributions, the fruit of every tree, the new wine and the oil to the priests at the chambers of the house of our God, and the tithe of our ground to the Levites, for the Levites are they who receive the tithes in all the rural towns" (Neh. 10:37).

We discover the following:

> Wine was kept in the Temple in Jerusalem, and the king had his own private stores. The banquet hall was called a "house of wine," and wine was used as the usual drink at most secular and religious feasts, including feasts of celebration and hospitality, tithe celebrations, Jewish holidays such as Passover, and at burials. Jesus instituted the Eucharist at the Last Supper, which took place at a Passover celebration, and set apart the bread and wine that were present there as symbols of the New Covenant.[1]

Wine "was used in sacrifice among not only the Hebrews but also the Canaanites and the Babylonians. In Israelite practice wine normally was not used independently but along with other sacrificial gifts:"[2]

Exodus 29:38–40
Now this is what you shall offer on the altar: two one year old lambs each day, continuously. The one lamb you shall offer in the morning and the other lamb you shall offer at twilight; and there shall be one-tenth of an ephah of fine flour mixed with one-fourth of a hin of beaten oil, and one-fourth of a hin of wine for a drink offering with one lamb.

Leviticus 23:12–23
Now on the day when you wave the sheaf, you shall offer a male lamb one year old without defect for a burnt offering to the Lord. Its grain offering shall then be two-tenths of an ephah of fine flour mixed with oil, an offering by fire to the Lord for a soothing aroma, with its drink offering, a fourth of a hin of wine.

The Blessing and Joy of God[3]

Revealing God's joyous care over all the earth, Psalm 104:14–15 makes plain His gracious provision for humankind:

> He causes the grass to grow for the cattle,
> And vegetation for the labor of man,
> So that he may bring forth food from the earth,
> And wine which makes man's heart glad,
> So that he may make his face glisten with oil,
> And food which sustains man's heart.

Wine is a gift from the goodness of our Heavenly Father as seen in Jeremiah 31:12–14:

> They will come and shout for joy on the height of Zion,
> And they will be radiant over the bounty of the LORD—
> Over the grain and the new wine and the oil,
> And over the young of the flock and the herd;
> And their life will be like a watered garden,
> And they will never languish again.
> Then the virgin will rejoice in the dance,
> And the young men and the old, together,
> For I will turn their mourning into joy
> And will comfort them and give them joy for their sorrow.
> I will fill the soul of the priests with abundance,
> And My people will be satisfied with My goodness, declares the LORD.

Wine reflects the blessing of God:

Joel 2:24–26
> The threshing floors will be full of grain,
> And the vats will overflow with the new wine and oil.
> "Then I will make up to you for the years
> That the swarming locust has eaten,
> The creeping locust, the stripping locust and the gnawing locust,
> My great army which I sent among you.
> "You will have plenty to eat and be satisfied
> And praise the name of the LORD your God,
> Who has dealt wondrously with you;
> Then My people will never be put to shame.

Joel 3:18
> And in that day
> The mountains will drip with sweet wine,

And the hills will flow with milk,
And all the brooks of Judah will flow with water;
And a spring will go out from the house of the Lord
To water the valley of Shittim.

Wine brings joy and gladness to the heart:

Judges 9:13
But the vine said to them, 'Shall I leave my new wine, which cheers God and men, and go to wave over the trees?'

Ecclesiastes 9:7
Go then, eat your bread in happiness and drink your wine with a cheerful heart; for God has already approved your works.

Ecclesiastes 10:19
Men prepare a meal for enjoyment, and wine makes life merry, and money is the answer to everything.

Zechariah 10:7
Ephraim will be like a mighty man,
And their heart will be glad as if from wine;
Indeed, their children will see it and be glad,
Their heart will rejoice in the Lord.

Drink before the Lord with rejoicing:

Deuteronomy 12:17–19
You are not allowed to eat within your gates the tithe of your grain or new wine or oil, or the firstborn of your herd or flock, or any of your votive offerings which you vow, or your freewill offerings, or the contribution of your hand. But you shall eat them before the Lord your God in the place which the Lord your God will choose, you and your son and daughter, and your male and female servants, and the Levite who is within your gates; and you shall rejoice before the Lord your God in all your undertakings. Be careful that you do not forsake the Levite as long as you live in your land.

Deuteronomy 14:22–26
You shall surely tithe all the produce from what you sow, which comes out of the field every year. You shall eat in the presence of the Lord your God, at the place where He chooses to establish His name, the tithe of your grain, your new wine, your oil, and the firstborn of your herd and your flock, so that you may learn to fear the Lord your God always. If the distance is so great for you that you are not able to bring the tithe, since the place where the Lord your God chooses to set His name is too far away from you when the Lord

your God blesses you, then you shall exchange it for money, and bind the money in your hand and go to the place which the Lord your God chooses. You may spend the money for whatever your heart desires: for oxen, or sheep, or wine, or strong drink, or whatever your heart desires; and there you shall eat in the presence of the Lord your God and rejoice, you and your household.

Isaiah 62:8–9

The Lord has sworn by His right hand and by His strong arm,
"I will never again give your grain as food for your enemies;
Nor will foreigners drink your new wine for which you have labored."
But those who garner it will eat it and praise the Lord;
And those who gather it will drink it in the courts of My sanctuary.

With no wine comes no joy:

Isaiah 24:7–11

The new wine mourns,
The vine decays,
All the merry-hearted sigh.
The gaiety of tambourines ceases,
The noise of revelers stops,
The gaiety of the harp ceases.
They do not drink wine with song;
Strong drink is bitter to those who drink it.
The city of chaos is broken down;
Every house is shut up so that none may enter.
There is an outcry in the streets concerning the wine;
All joy turns to gloom.
The gaiety of the earth is banished.

Jeremiah 48:33

So gladness and joy are taken away
From the fruitful field, even from the land of Moab.
And I have made the wine to cease from the wine presses;
No one will tread them with shouting,
The shouting will not be shouts of joy.

Wine as a hardship and judgment from God:

Amos 5:11

Therefore because you impose heavy rent on the poor
And exact a tribute of grain from them,
Though you have built houses of well-hewn stone,

Yet you will not live in them;
You have planted pleasant vineyards, yet you will not drink their wine.

Deuteronomy 29:2–6
And Moses summoned all Israel and said to them, "You have seen all that the Lord did before your eyes in the land of Egypt to Pharaoh and all his servants and all his land; the great trials which your eyes have seen, those great signs and wonders. Yet to this day the Lord has not given you a heart to know, nor eyes to see, nor ears to hear. I have led you forty years in the wilderness; your clothes have not worn out on you, and your sandal has not worn out on your foot. You have not eaten bread, nor have you drunk wine or strong drink, in order that you might know that I am the Lord your God.

Wine in the future kingdom:

Isaiah 25:6–9
The Lord of hosts will prepare a lavish banquet for all peoples on
this mountain;
A banquet of aged wine, choice pieces with marrow,
And refined, aged wine.
And on this mountain He will swallow up the covering which is over
all peoples,
Even the veil which is stretched over all nations.
He will swallow up death for all time,
And the Lord God will wipe tears away from all faces,
And He will remove the reproach of His people from all the earth;
For the Lord has spoken.
And it will be said in that day,
"Behold, this is our God for whom we have waited that He might save us.
This is the Lord for whom we have waited;
Let us rejoice and be glad in His salvation."

Jeremiah 31:12–14
They will come and shout for joy on the height of Zion,
And they will be radiant over the bounty of the Lord—
Over the grain and the new wine and the oil,
And over the young of the flock and the herd;
And their life will be like a watered garden,
And they will never languish again.
"Then the virgin will rejoice in the dance,
And the young men and the old, together,
For I will turn their mourning into joy
And will comfort them and give them joy for their sorrow.
"I will fill the soul of the priests with abundance,
And My people will be satisfied with My goodness," declares the Lord.

Matthew 26:29
But I say to you, I will not drink of this fruit of the vine from now on until that day when I drink it new with you in My Father's kingdom."

Wine as Symbol and Metaphor

Common and plentiful in Bible times, wine is often symbolized and used metaphorically, both positively and negatively. It is a symbol of God's grace, and the Song of Solomon compares it to romantic love. Plentiful wine represents the blessing of God while the absence of wine often represents His judgment. In Luke 5:36–39, wine represents the truth of God as seen in Jesus' opposition to the old, stale, legalistic traditions of the religious establishment. At the Last Supper, wine becomes a symbol of the New Covenant in Mark 14:22–25:

> While they were eating, He took some bread, and after a blessing He broke it, and gave it to them, and said, "Take it; this is My body." And when He had taken a cup and given thanks, He gave it to them, and they all drank from it. And He said to them, "This is My blood of the covenant, which is poured out for many. Truly I say to you, I will never again drink of the fruit of the vine until that day when I drink it new in the kingdom of God."

Israel is depicted as a God-owned vine and vineyard which the Lord brings out of Egypt: "You removed a vine from Egypt; You drove out the nations and planted it" (Ps. 80:8). As Jacob blesses his sons, the prosperity of wine symbolizes Judah's good fortune and blessing.

On the negative side, Proverbs 20:1 personifies wine as a mocker: "Wine is a mocker, strong drink a brawler, and whoever is intoxicated by it is not wise." In Zephaniah 1:12, the Lord searches Jerusalem for complacent individuals who are like stagnant wine:

> It will come about at that time
> That I will search Jerusalem with lamps,
> And I will punish the men
> Who are stagnant in spirit,
> Who say in their hearts,
> 'The Lord will not do good or evil!'

Wine is sometimes associated with God's wrath, as seen in Jeremiah 25:15: "For thus the Lord, the God of Israel, says to me, 'Take this cup of the wine of wrath from My hand and cause all the nations to whom I send you to drink it,'" and Revelation 14:18, "Then another angel, the one who has power over fire, came out from the altar; and he called with a loud voice to him who had the sharp sickle, saying, 'Put in your sharp sickle and gather the clusters from the vine of the earth, because her grapes are ripe.'" Even Jesus alludes to the cup of wrath which He must drink (Mk. 10:38–39; Mt. 20:20–22) and in the Garden of Gethsemane asks if it might pass from Him (Mt. 26:39; Lk. 22:42).

Medicinal Use

Wine is also used for medicinal purposes. The wine offered to Jesus during His crucifixion may have been an effort to dull His pain. In the parable of the Good Samaritan (Lk. 10:30–37), oil and wine are poured on wounds as the Good Samaritan "bandaged up his wounds, pouring oil and wine on them; and he put him on his own beast, and brought him to an inn and took care of him." The apostle Paul instructs Timothy: "No longer drink water exclusively, but use a little wine for the sake of your stomach and your frequent ailments" (I Tim. 5:23).

Vows and Priestly Duties

There are certain restrictions in the Bible on the use of alcohol. Though God orders the tithing of wine be given to the priests, they are not to drink while on duty (Lev. 10:9). Realizing the effect drunkenness has upon one's judgment and behavior, it is no wonder the Lord requires abstinence in the fulfillment of temple obligations. In fact, some priests may have disobeyed this requirement and served with drunken swagger, prompting the anger of the Lord (Lev. 10).

Nazarites who take a vow before the Lord abstain from wine, vinegar, grapes, and raisins during the term of their vow. When the vow is fulfilled, they present wine as a sacrificial offering unto the Lord. Many believe John the Baptist was a Nazarite who followed this practice. Jesus, however, does not take a Nazarite vow and does not abstain.

The Rechabites are another group of abstainers:

> The Rechabites, a sub-tribe of the Kenites, vowed never to drink wine, live in houses, or plant fields of vineyards, not because of any "threat to wise living" from these practices, but because of their commitment to a nomadic life-style by not being bound to any particular piece of land. The Rechabites's strict obedience to the command of their father (rather than nomadism and abstentionism) is commended and is contrasted with the failure of Jerusalem and the Kingdom of Judah to listen to their God [4]

During the Babylonian captivity, Daniel did not eat meat and wine provided by the king. He views it as defilement, maybe because it comes from an arrogant king who has defiled Jerusalem and God's people. Later, the book of Daniel implies that he drinks wine on occasion, presumably wine that wasn't furnished by the king.

The Practice of Judaism

Despite the Bible's clear stance on drunkenness, Scripture doesn't condemn wine or strong drink itself, only its abuse.

> He promises His people that, if they will obey Him, He will bless them with an abundance of wine (Deut 7:13, 11:14, Prov. 3:10, etc.). He threatens to withdraw this blessing from them if they disobey His law (Deut. 28:39, 51; Isa. 62:8). The Scriptures clearly teach that God permits His people to enjoy wine and strong drink as a gift from Him. "You may spend the money for whatever your heart desires, for oxen, or sheep, or wine, or strong drink, or whatever your heart desires; and there you shall eat in the presence of the Lord your God and rejoice, you and your household" (Deut. 14:26). Under certain circumstances it is even commanded of God that wine and strong drink be given (Pr. 31:6,7). And since wine was used in the worship of God (Ex. 29:40, Lev. 23:13; Nu. 15:5,7,10; 28:14), the Bible says wine is something that cheers God as well as man (Jud. 9:13).[5]

"When we turn from the Old Testament to the noncanonical literature of Judaism, the same general positive appraisal of wine is continued."[6]

> Ben-Sirach:
> What is life to a man who is without wine? It has been created to make men glad (Sir. 31:27b).

Noting the danger of overindulgence he also writes:

> Do not aim to be valiant over wine, for wine has destroyed many . . .
> Wine is like life to men, if you drink it in moderation . . .
> Wine drunk in season and temperately is rejoicing of heart and gladness of soul.
> Wine drunk to excess is bitterness of soul, with provocation and stumbling (Sir. 31:25–29)

> The Story of Ahikar:
> Son, God hath ordained wine for the sake of gladness (Arm. Ver. 2:95).

> Testament of Judah:
> Much discretion needeth the man who drinketh wine . . . and herein is discretion in drinking wine, a man may drink so long as he preserveth modesty (14:7).

> III Baruch
> The men who now drink insatiably the wine which is begotten of it, transgress worse than Adam . . . For those who drink it to surfeit do these things: neither

does a brother pity his brother, nor a father his son, nor children their parents, but from drinking of wine comes all evils such as murders, adulteries, fornication, perjuries, thefts, and such like and nothing good is established by it (III Baruch 4:16f.).

Philo thought wine had a proper use and condemned its misuse. The rabbis viewed wine as a gift from God to be enjoyed with a grateful heart while at the same time teaching moderation. "Like the prophets, however, they condemned drunkenness. A decision issued by a judge when drunk was not valid. A drunken man's prayers were of no value. A priest was not permitted to drink wine before entering the temple to serve. Indeed, the efficacy of any religious act was nullified when the performer was intoxicated."[7]

The attitude toward alcohol in the Old Testament and in Judaism can be summarized this way:[8]

1. Wine, as a part of God's creation, is an inherently good gift from the Creator and may be consumed with thanksgiving.
2. Wine, like all other good gifts from God, can be abused. Drunkenness is abuse and is vehemently condemned.
3. The condemnation of drunkenness is not merely from a pragmatic or social viewpoint, but it is seen in light of our relationship and obligation to God and others. This relationship and obligation cannot possibly be adequately fulfilled while inebriated.

New Testament

Though references to wine in the Old Testament are numerous, they aren't nearly as plentiful in the New Testament. We have already mentioned the medicinal purposes of wine for Timothy's stomach, wine to dull Jesus' pain during the crucifixion, and wine for cleaning wounds in the parable of the Good Samaritan. Jesus mentions wine and wineskins to illustrate truth about His kingdom. He speaks parables about a vineyard, building a wine press, and a drunken servant not expecting his master's return. At the wedding in Cana He turns water into wine and, "even though we may wish it otherwise, honest exegesis compels the candid admission that on this occasion Jesus deliberately added to the stock of wine available for consumption at the wedding feast."[9] Jesus warns against drunkenness in Luke 21:34: "Be on guard, so that your hearts will not be weighted down with dissipation and drunkenness and the worries of life, and that day will not come on you suddenly like a trap."

While John the Baptist maintains a vow not to drink, Jesus makes no such abstention vow. In fact, He is accused of being a drunkard who drinks with sinners: "The Son of Man came eating and drinking, and they say, 'Behold, a gluttonous man and a drunkard, a friend of tax collectors and sinners!'" (Mt. 11:19; Lk. 7:34). Though the statement is intended as a slur, it reveals that Jesus did not abstain from wine like John the Baptist. Jesus also uses wine during the Last Supper, though it is called "the fruit of the vine" (Mk. 14:25).

Wine in the New Testament is not forbidden; rather, its use is a normal and assumed aspect of life. The qualifications for church leadership require that one not be addicted to wine or be a drunkard (I Tim. 3:3,8; Titus 1:7), but it does not prohibit its use altogether, only its abuse. Paul instructs Timothy to use wine for the sake of his stomach and frequent ailments (I Tim. 5:23).

Paul assumes a strong stance on drunkenness, viewing it as a work of the flesh that prevents kingdom entrance (Gal. 5:21; I Cor. 6:10). When some are using the Lord's Supper as an opportunity for inebriation, Paul lays into them as they mock the significance of the event (I Cor. 11:17–22). Drunkenness is so opposite, so antithetical to the things of God, that Paul counsels against fellowshipping with those who claim to know Christ but live under the influence of alcohol: "But actually, I wrote to you not to associate with any so-called brother if he is an immoral person, or covetous, or an idolater, or a reviler, or a drunkard, or a swindler—not even to eat with such a one" (I Cor. 5:11). Paul inspires us to be filled with the Holy Spirit rather than under the problematic influence of alcohol (Eph. 5:18).

Paul encourages setting aside drunkenness and putting on the Lord Jesus Christ in Romans 13:12–14:

> The night is almost gone, and the day is near. Therefore let us lay aside the deeds of darkness and put on the armor of light. Let us behave properly as in the day, not in carousing and drunkenness, not in sexual promiscuity and sensuality, not in strife and jealousy. But put on the Lord Jesus Christ, and make no provision for the flesh in regard to its lusts.

Even the future kingdom will include wine, for Jesus said at the Last Supper, "Truly I say to you, I will never again drink of the fruit of the vine until that day when I drink it new in the kingdom of God" (Mk. 14:25).

The New Testament teaching on wine can be summed up this way: "Thus far we have surveyed the explicit references in the New Testament to the use of wine. They point to its casual acceptance as a common beverage of the day while condemning its excessive use which leads to drunkenness. This position might be summed up as one of moderation. It is essentially the same attitude as found in the Old Testament and in Judaism."[10]

Within the larger context of Greco-Roman culture, a similar stance is embraced. "The Stoic philosophers stressed temperance and self-control in the matter of drinking as in other activities. Seneca has a long tirade against the vice of drunkenness. Galen, one of the most famous physicians of the Graeco-Roman world, while recognizing the medicinal value of wine, condemns its immoderate use."[11]

Positive, Neutral, and Negative

Listed below is an analysis of scriptural references to alcohol organized according to their frequency:[12]

SCRIPTURE FREQUENCY TABLE

Use Category	Wine	Strong Drink
Use accepted as normal part of culture	58	1
Symbolic (the wine of His wrath, etc.)	32	1
Wine called a blessing from God	27	0
Use in offerings and sacrifices	24	1
Loss of wine an example of a curse from God	19	1
Examples of alcohol abuse	16	3
Vows of abstinence	15	6
Warnings against abuse	13	4
Gifts between people	9	0
Comparisons (x is better than wine)	5	0
False accusations of drunkenness	3	1
Rules for selecting church leaders	3	0
Miscellaneous	3	1
Abstinence in deference to a weak conscience	1	0
247 total references	**228**	**19**

When these references are divided into negative, positive, and neutral categories, we discover that 16% of the references (40 out of 247) are negative in nature. The positive category equates to 59% of the references (145 out of 247), while 25% fall into the neutral category (62 out of 247).[13] It comes as quite a surprise to those who believe alcohol is inherently evil that 84% of the scriptural references to wine and strong drink are either positive or neutral, while only 16% of the references are negative, mostly warning against its abuse or providing examples of such misuse.

The Old Testament, ancient culture, noncanonical writings of Judaism, New Testament, and the Greco-Roman world outside of the church all concur that alcohol is not intrinsically evil but can be enjoyed in moderation. It is the abuse of alcohol that is condemned.

Summary: The Bible teaches, in both testaments, that alcohol is not inherently evil but a gift from God to be enjoyed with thanksgiving, while the abuse of alcohol (drunkenness) is condemned.

THE TWO-WINE THEORY

This chapter examines a clever theory promoting two different kinds of wine in the Bible—positive references refer to grape juice while negative references refer to fermented beverage. Arising with the Temperance Movement, this theory lacks biblical support. Upon closer scrutiny, this modern perspective is debunked and close attention is paid to the Hebrew and Greek words for wine.

Realizing Scripture condemns the abuse of alcohol and not its moderate use, some seek to alter the biblical record through clever interpretive tricks. In other words, they don't like what the Bible *actually* teaches so they find ways to make it fit what they *want* it to teach—a ploy for arriving at predetermined outcomes. It is like the judge in a court of law deciding a ruling in her mind before the case is tried, and when it finally comes before her court, she selectively seeks evidence justifying her foreordained decision.

If you don't like what the Bible says, your only option is to find a way around it by redefining terms, defying common authorities, engaging in questionable interpretive tactics, or crucifying the messenger in an attempt to sully the message itself. One clever method of undermining biblical teaching is to posit a two-wine theory—whenever wine is spoken of in positive terms it refers to grape juice, while negative references speak of fermented wine. While I am not a trained linguist, this view, in my opinion, is nothing more than a delicate house of cards. If the thread is pulled too hard, the whole argument quickly unravels. Proponents of the two-wine theory are certainly not inane; most are smart, well-intentioned, and many hold sterling credentials. But when the truth of Scripture is rejected, any other approach is flawed and wholly inadequate. Put another way, "It is an old saying that bad arguments injure even a good cause, and there is some reason to fear that this saying will be proved true" with the two-wine theory.[1]

Scripture was originally written in Hebrew, Aramaic, and Greek, with multiple words for wine. In light of this, determining how these words are used and what they mean requires due diligence. However, this is where confusion enters the picture and proponents of the two-wine theory walk on shaky ground. Since the average person in the pew lacks training in biblical languages and lives a fast-paced and beleaguered lifestyle, he or she is dependent upon others to sort this out. Unfortunately, final conclusions differ depending on who the "sorter-outer" is. Prohibitionists, abstentionists, and moderationists all sort a little differently.

This puts the average churchgoer at a disadvantage in reaching an informed decision about the matter. It's like trying to eat healthy or deciding on which washing machine to purchase. One medical doctor says eggs are beneficial, while another totally disagrees. Which one do we believe? In search of a reliable washing machine at a local big box retail giant, we encounter so many models that cognitive dissonance sets in. Some washing machines carry brand names, others do not. A few are on sale or on clearance. Some tout metal tubs, others plastic. There are top loaders and front loaders. Some are high-efficiency models, others not so much. One salesman pushes a particular model while another promotes a different brand. Which model is best and which salesman are we to trust? When it comes to Christians using alcohol, each side struts its credentialed experts, indisputable data, iron-clad arguments, and advances its cause in the best light of its position. Just like buying a washing machine or deciphering nutritional labels, the average churchgoer runs into a wall of confusion without background or knowledge in the subject at hand.

Contrasting two different authors with two different views ought to drive home the problem of sifting through confusing and conflicting information. One author believes the Bible teaches total abstinence, not as a matter of prudence or Christian liberty, but as a matter of scriptural law:

> . . . how we manage to possibly assume wine in Scripture necessarily and always refers to intoxicating beverages remains inexplicable. Indeed this may be the grandest hermeneutical hoax of the ages. We believe the simple observation that when the Bible speaks of wine, the fact that this does not necessarily refer to intoxicating wine fundamentally corrects the bias almost universally imbedded in the evangelical world. As the evidence demonstrates, the ancients employed painful, meticulous means to keep some

wines from fermenting to the point of being toxic. They desired pure, unfermented grape juice. The evidence seems overwhelming.[2]

Since Scripture speaks of wine in negative terms (being a mocker, don't be drunk, etc.) and also in positive terms (blessing from God, enjoy with gladness, etc.), some handle the seemingly contradiction by positing a two-wine theory. Wine spoken of in negative terms refers to fermented wine while wine in positive contexts refers to grape juice. But why invent the grape juice distinction at all? Why not just believe what the Bible teaches—that the abuse of wine is always negative, but moderate use is a gift from God to be enjoyed? We know why—to do so jeopardizes preconceived notions and predetermined outcomes.

Another author presents quite a different viewpoint:

> The Old Testament makes no distinction between the fermented and unfermented juice of grapes or other fruits. Neither does it use one set of terms for intoxicating and another for nonintoxicating beverages, but it does have special words for potent drinks.
>
> One scholar goes so far as to say, after carefully studying the scriptural references to wine, that the use of unfermented wines by the Hebrews is a myth. He questions the existence of any ground for the pretense that the unfermented juice of the grape was ordinarily used.[3]

There is no need to invent or promote a two-wine theory because there is scant biblical basis for doing so. A Christian winemaker in 1902 writes, "It is the absurd plausibility of the name 'unfermented wine' that appeals to the casual person, and also their often repeated use of the term that has given it a sort of standing with the unthinking," and " ... not one unbiased, thinking man has ever been convinced on the two-wine theory."[4] Contrast this with David Wilkerson's statement, "As far as I am concerned, Scripture and historical facts prove there were two kinds of wine. One was intoxicating, the other was not."[5]

Which view are we to believe? Which washing machine model are we to purchase? Which credentialed expert is more "expert" than the other? For some, moderation feels like a compromised position in light of the fury surrounding the subject. When ministers, firmly planted behind the pulpit, preach passionate sermons and share a few horror stories on demon alcohol, we are shamed for believing otherwise. How could we? Swimming upstream not only means swimming against the tide of a nonbelieving culture, it may also entail swimming against the tide of prejudicial theology and sloppy biblical teaching.

I was in your shoes, searching for answers that made sense. I explored many works on the subject from various authors and viewpoints. I consulted numerous "experts" who all seemed to have an opinion on the matter—all of which were deemed "biblical." Having arrived at my own conclusions on the matter, I optimistically share the fruit of my labor hoping it might unclutter any confusion in your own mind. While we may not arrive at similar end points, I pray that my own search for answers will inform your own.

Two-Wine Origins

Where and when did this two-wine theory arise? It certainly isn't found in the theology or practice of the early church, the early Church Fathers, the Reformers, or American colonists, for they seemed quite clear on scriptural teaching regarding alcohol. Could this view coincide with the rise of the Temperance Movement in the United States during the nineteenth and twentieth centuries? Indeed it does.

Do the temperance folks of the nineteenth and twentieth centuries *finally* understand what no one else could discern—that there are two kinds of wine, fermented and grape juice? Is it only after God's people in the Old Testament cultivate grapes, produce wine, drink in moderation with joy and thanksgiving, view the bounty of wine as God's blessing and its scarcity as His curse, offer wine in required sacrifice to the Lord, and entwine wine with festive, ceremonial, and everyday life that we *just now* become enlightened? Even though Jesus turns water into wine at a wedding festival, institutes wine as the symbol of His blood and the New Covenant during the Last Supper, states that He will drink it again with His followers in the future kingdom, are we now finally realizing that the Bible has all along been referring to grape juice? If so, I have some ocean front property in Kansas I would like to sell you!

The Temperance Movement of the nineteenth and twentieth centuries tied their social concern for drunkenness with unemployment, crime, and numerous social issues. Methodists lead the charge as other denominations jump on the bandwagon and call for total abstinence. Under intense social pressure, reason and biblical thinking go down the drain, while the *abuse* of alcohol is equated with the *use* of alcohol, even moderate use. Realizing this, in 1887 Dunlop Moore writes in *A Religious Encyclopedia of Biblical, Historical, Doctrinal and Practical Theology*,

> In fact, the theory of two kinds of wine—the one fermented and intoxicating and unlawful, and the other unfermented, unintoxicating, and lawful—is a modern hypothesis, devised during the present century, and has no foundation in the Bible, or in Hebrew or classical antiquity.[6]

The Temperance Movement plowed the ground for several key writers to plant the seed of alleged biblical support.

Circular Reasoning

Do you sense something wrong with the following statement—whenever the Bible speaks of wine in negative terms it refers to fermented wine, and whenever the Bible speaks of wine in positive terms it refers to grape juice? This just doesn't sound right, does it? That's because it isn't right; it is circular reasoning.

Circular reasoning occurs when you begin with what you are trying to prove, or the conclusion becomes one of the premises. In other words, it is impossible to prove the conclusion because you are circling back to one of the premises instead of arriving at a proper conclusion. Here is an example of circular reasoning as it pertains to the Bible:

- The Bible is God's Word (how do we know this?)
- Because the Bible tells us it is God's Word (why do we believe this?)
- Because the Bible is infallible (how do we know it is infallible?)
- Because the Bible is God's Word (how do we know this?)
- Because the Bible tells us it is God's Word (why do we believe this?)
- Because the Bible is infallible (how do we know it is infallible?)

The reasoning continues in a circle, using one of the premises in the conclusion. It happens in the scientific realm as well:

> Joel Feinberg and Russ Shafer-Landau note that "using the scientific method to judge the scientific method is circular reasoning." Scientists attempt to discover the laws of nature and to predict what will happen in the future, based on those laws. However, per David Hume's problem of induction, science cannot be proven inductively by empirical evidence, and thus science cannot be proven scientifically. But as Bertrand Russell observed, "The method of 'postulating' what we want has many advantages; they are the same as the advantages of theft over honest toil."[7]

The circular reasoning of two-wine theorists might look like this:

- There are two types of wine in the Bible: fermented and grape juice (how do we know this?)
- Because negative references refer to fermented wine (how do we know this?)
- Because positive references refer to grape juice (how do we know this?)
- Because there are two types of wine in the Bible: fermented and grape juice (how do we know this?)

- Because negative references refer to fermented wine (how do we know this?)
- Because positive references refer to grape juice (how do we know this?)
- Because there are two types of wine in the Bible: fermented and grape juice (how do we know this?)

The reasoning continues in a circle, using one of the premises in the conclusion. Sound familiar? When standing on the precarious foundation of circular reasoning, arguments are sure to crumble at first light of logic. It will take more than circular reasoning to prove the two-wine theory.

Biblical Harmonization

The two-wine theory is an attempt to harmonize *apparent* conflicting passages on alcohol—the contrast between positive and negative verses. Trying to figure out some Bible passages is indeed difficult, largely because of our distance from the culture and time of the Bible. How do we harmonize the two natures of Christ—fully human and fully God at the same time? How do we harmonize the Trinitarian nature of God when the Bible never mentions the word "Trinity?" Our understanding of how He can be both one and three at the same time falls short. We are told that God is spirit, yet Scripture speaks of Him as having hands, eyes, ears, fingers, nostrils, etc. How do we explain the apparent contradiction? How can a baby be born of a virgin? How can we be born anew when we have already been born and are living? Even Proverbs 26:4–5 appears contradictory:

> Do not answer a fool according to his folly,
> Or you will also be like him.
>
> Answer a fool as his folly deserves,
> That he not be wise in his own eyes.

Which one is it? Are we to answer a fool or aren't we? How do we harmonize the use of the Old Testament in the New Testament? How much continuity is there between the two distinct emphases and teaching of each testament?

One author puts it this way:

> Finally we note our unwavering commitment to biblical inerrancy as the fundamental backdrop to biblical hermeneutics. Given our view of the God-breathed text of Scripture, we employ the *principle of interpretative harmonization*—that is, we do not believe Scripture contradicts itself.[8]

So far, so good. I don't believe Scripture contradicts itself either, but he goes on,

> Similarly what we find in Scripture is two apparent contradictory views of wine. On the one hand we see wine [*yayin*] being both praised and commended (Ps. 104:14-15). On the other we observe wine [*yayin*] being both treacherous and condemned (Prov. 20:1).[9]

Believing the Bible contains apparent contradictions in its teaching on wine, the above author concludes the following:

> My final conclusion is this; viz, that wherever the scriptures speak of wine as a comfort, a blessing, or libation to God, and rank it with such articles as corn and oil, they mean—they can mean—only such wine as contained no alcohol that could have a mischievous tendency; that wherever they denounce it, prohibit it, and connect it with drunkenness and reveling, they can mean only alcoholic or intoxicating wine . . . I cannot refuse to take this position without virtually impeaching the Scriptures of contradiction or inconsistency. I cannot admit, that God has given liberty to persons in health to drink alcoholic wine, without admitting that his word and his works are at variance."[10]

In the mind of prohibitionists, fermented wine is not good or bad depending on its use; it is always bad because it is inherently evil. Any reference to its goodness *must* refer to grape juice, since an inherently evil substance cannot be good. Dr. Charles Wesley Ewing who was on the lecturing staff of the Temperance League of Illinois, formerly known as the Anti-Saloon League, advances the same rhetoric:

> Whenever disapproval, condemnation, warning, prohibition accompanies the word wine, it must be understood that fermented wine is indicated. When God's approval, blessings, sanctions are given to wine, it must be understood that the unfermented is intended. There is no other way of harmonizing the Scriptures dealing with the subject.[11]

There are certainly difficult concepts in the pages of Scripture where harmonization is helpful, but biblical teaching on alcohol isn't one of them. Harmonization reconciles apparent contradictions within Scripture and since there is no contradiction in its instruction regarding alcohol, harmonization is unnecessary. This "contradiction" viewpoint is relatively new, advancing with the rising ranks of the Temperance Movement. It is not a perspective seen throughout church history. The Hebrews in the Old Testament, Jesus in the New Testament, the early Church Fathers, the Reformers, and the American colonists see no need to harmonize apparent contradictions. Overindulgence leading to drunkenness is iniquitous, while moderate drinking to the glory of God can be enjoyed. What needs to be harmonized? What don't we understand? The substance hasn't magically changed from fermented wine to grape juice. What *has* changed is its use, one moderate and the other excessive. There is no contradiction, unless of course one is created to prop up a perspective contrary to biblical teaching.

If I said to you, "Food is a gift from God so give thanks for His goodness as you eat of it. Oh, and don't overeat, for that becomes gluttony and you could get sick." Where is the contradiction? What don't we understand? We don't say, "How do I interpret this statement? How can food be both a good gift from God and spoken of in negative gluttonous terms as well?" If I said to you, "Sex is a wonderful gift from God so be sure to enjoy it with your spouse. Oh, and don't engage in sexual relations outside of marriage because that goes against the will of God." Where is the contradiction? What don't we understand? We don't say, "How do I interpret this statement? How can sex be both good and at the same time be said to go against the will of God?"

Since there is no contradiction regarding biblical instruction on alcohol, there is no need for a harmonizing process. The Bible's teaching as understood for thousands of years prior to the Temperance Movement is that alcohol is a gift from God to be enjoyed in moderation. Oh, and don't overindulge and become drunk because that goes against the will of God. Okay, got it. It is a simple message and simple to understand without contradiction.

If harmonization must occur, it happens in the mind of prohibitionists, not within Scripture. In their mind, alcohol is an inherently evil substance. A holy God couldn't possibly condone that which can potentially cause so much pain and devastation as noted in Charles Wesley Ewing's statement, "To this writer, it is inconceivable that an all-wise God, with the best interests of His creatures in mind, would give His sanction to the use of any drink that contains poison, or that is an addiction-producing drug."[12] Their need for harmonization is not with apparent biblical contradictions, but between their predetermined conclusions and the Bible. In essence, they wrestle with the Word of God and invent superficial scriptural contradictions as a platform for advancing their alternative and preferred interpretation.

Let's suppose for the sake of argument that an apparent contradiction does indeed exist and we need to reconcile both the negative and positive references to wine. Though an unnecessary step, and one that doesn't change the outcome one iota, must we arrive at Ewing's conclusion that the only way to harmonize the apparent contradiction is to say that negative references speak of intoxicating wine while positive references refer to grape juice? This argument would never be utilized in regard to food or sex. Would we say that food, when spoken of in positive terms refers to food, but in negative references refers to "non-food?" When sex is spoken of in positive terms it is sex, but referred to in negative terms (outside of marriage) becomes "non-sex?" This is absolutely ludicrous. We would be inventing two kinds of food and two kinds of sex, when in reality it is not the *substance* of food or sex that is prohibited, only *certain uses* of food and *certain expressions* of sex. Is this a difficult concept to grasp? I think not!

The problem of harmonization completely disappears when we simply and humbly accept biblical teaching that moderate use can be enjoyed as a gift from God while overindulgence leading to drunkenness is condemned. We don't have to advance a change of substance theory (fermented wine vs. grape juice) when simply understanding a proper and improper use is all that is needed. One perspective reflects biblical teaching while the other reflects modifications that align with a preferred view.

Biblical Words

Several words in Scripture refer to alcoholic beverages, and some have overlapping meaning. The Bible was originally written in Hebrew, Aramaic, and Greek, and the early church read the Septuagint, a Greek translation of the Hebrew Old Testament. Some words are more significant than others because of their frequency and use in various contexts. For instance, the Hebrew Old Testament word *yayin* (141 occurrences) and the Greek New Testament word *oinos* (33 occurrences) are used more than other words and require our attention.

The various words for alcoholic beverages in the Bible include the following:[13]

OLD TESTAMENT WORDS

OT Words	Meaning
yayin	The common word translated as wine.
tirosh	Properly must; sometimes rendered as wine, new wine, or sweet wine. It can represent juice at any stage in the fermentation process, and in some places it represents wine made from the first drippings of the juice before the winepress was trodden. As such it would be particularly potent. It can certainly be alcoholic, as in Hos. 4:11.
shekar	Strong drink; denotes any inebriating drink with about 7–10% alcoholic content, not hard liquor, because there is no evidence of distilled liquor in ancient times. It was made from either fruit and/or barley beer; the term can include wine, but generally it is used in combination with wine and strong drink to encompass all varieties of intoxicants.

continues

OLD TESTAMENT WORDS *(continued)*

OT Words	Meaning
chemer	Wine; the word conveys the idea of foaming, as in the process of fermentation, or when poured out. It is derived from the root *hamar*, meaning to boil up.
'asis	Sweet wine or new wine, the vintage of the current year with intoxicating power.
chomets	Vinegar, which was made from wine or other fermented beverage and is used as a condiment or, when mixed with water, a slightly intoxicating drink.
shemar shemarim	Lees or dregs of wine; wine that has been kept on the lees, and therefore old wine; if the wine was intended to be kept for some time a certain amount of lees was added to give it body.
sobhe	Drink, liquor, wine.
mamsak mesekh	Mixed drink, mixed wine, drink offering; the word is properly a mixture of wine and water with spices that increase its stimulating properties.
mezeg	Mixture, mixed wine.

NEW TESTAMENT WORDS

NT Words	Meaning
oinos	The common word translated wine in the New Testament and Septuagint.
gleukos	Sweet wine (sometimes rendered new wine), only one use in NT and may be intoxicating while some feel it refers to grape juice.
sikera	A Hebrew loanword from *shekar* meaning strong drink.
oxos	Vinegar, sour wine; could be made from grape wine or other fermented beverages; when mixed with water, it was a common, cheap drink of the poor and of the Roman army.
methusma	An intoxicating drink.

Old Testament

Yayin

In most Bible translations of the Old Testament, wine generally comes from the word *yayin* and in nearly every case it refers to alcoholic drink. A search of various dictionaries, encyclopedias, and Hebrew lexicons reveals the same thing. *Brown-Driver-Briggs Lexicon, Theological Wordbook of the Old Testament, Strong's Concordance, Analytical Hebrew and Chaldee Lexicon, Nelson's Expository Dictionary of the Old Testament, Vine's*

Complete Expository Dictionary, The New Unger's Bible Dictionary, etc., all depict *yayin* as possessing alcoholic properties.

Of course, there are those who dispute this fact and defy common authorities on the meaning of the term. One vigorous proponent of the two-wine theory is Dr. Stephen Reynolds, an ancient Semitic language scholar, who helped translate the Old Testament for the New International Version of the Bible.[14] He staunchly believes it is wrong for Christians to drink alcohol under any circumstance, in any quantity, at any time. Well-intentioned perhaps, but evading the plain meaning of *yayin* reveals a bias that interferes with common sense.

Yet, even Reynolds admits that "the Talmud gives support to the idea that it was regarded as an intoxicant in post-biblical (but nevertheless ancient) Hebrew. Thus, in Yoma 76 b (p.372 of the Sonica edition) we read: 'Why is it (wine) called *yayin* and *tirosh*? It is called *yayin* because it brings lamentation into the world, and *tirosh* because he who indulges in it becomes poor.'"[15] "Thus, ancient Hebrews speaking in their *own language* affirm *yayin's* fermented quality—as even one of the most vigorous opponents of this view admits."[16]

The root word of *yayin*,

> means "to effervesce"—that is, to create lots of bubbles. This pretty clearly references the fermentation process where yeast converts sugars into ethyl alcohol and carbon dioxide. While this process occurs in a vat of mashed grapes and their juice, over time, teams of tiny bubbles escape (the carbon dioxide). Thus it seems obvious that the very Hebrew word for wine is descriptive of grape juice that has undergone this bubbly process.[17]

Another strong proponent of the two-wine theory is Dr. Samuele Bacchiocchi who believes that *yayin* refers to a variety of wines including newly pressed wine, prior to fermentation.[18] He suggests that prior to fermentation wine is called *yayin mi-gat*, older wine is referred to as *yayin yashan*, and very old wine is called *yayin meyushshan* or *yashan noshan*, concluding that *yayin* often refers to grape juice.[19]

There are several holes in Bacchiocchi's argument:[20]

1. No such distinctions can be found in the Old Testament. It is 500–1900 years after the Old Testament references that distinctions of various stages of *yayin* are found in rabbinic literature. Unless the distinctions are found within the Old Testament long before they were written in rabbinical literature, Bacchiocchi's argument holds no weight.
2. With no distinctive stages or classes of *yayin* in the Old Testament, circular reasoning must occur in order to uphold Bacchiocchi's argument—where *yayin* is condemned it refers to fermented wine, but where it is favorably

presented it refers to grape juice. We have previously exposed the logical fallacy of circular reasoning.

3. The rabbinic sources Bacchiocchi draws upon note that *yayin mi-gat* was in its unfermented stage for only three days. With such a short period of time, it is uncertain if *yayin* could even refer to non-alcoholic grape juice in the Old Testament.

Some folks go to great lengths in justifying their predetermined conclusions. Street preacher David "Wilkerson laments, 'I have searched out the old Bible commentaries and almost all of them suggest wine referred to in the Old and New Testaments was fermented.' Teachout does the same: 'Unfortunately Bible scholars have been equally misled by public opinion.' But when you search out all the scholars and find them unanimously differing with your opinion, who is really mistaken?"[21]

Translated as Wine

Bible translations agree that *yayin* is fermented wine. The translation committees comprise numerous scholars who translate *yayin* as wine, not grape juice or some other non-intoxicating drink. Having served on the Old Testament translation committee for the New International Version, Reynolds states, "'There is a word *must* which could be used . . . This definition would be a good word to substitute for wine when the sense of Scripture demand it.' Yet, no reputable translation does so."[22]

Speaking of the Nazarite vow in Numbers 6:2–4, the Lord states the following:

> Speak to the sons of Israel and say to them, 'When a man or woman makes a special vow, the vow of a Nazirite, to dedicate himself to the Lord, he shall abstain from wine and strong drink; he shall drink no vinegar, whether made from wine or strong drink, nor shall he drink any grape juice nor eat fresh or dried grapes. All the days of his separation he shall not eat anything that is produced by the grape vine, from the seeds even to the skin.'

Notice the words "grape juice"? That is the phrase *mishrath-enabiem* in the Hebrew language, and most Bible versions (NASB, KJV, NKJV, NRSV, HCSB, NAB, NRSVA, etc.) translate it "grape juice" as opposed to wine. This phrase could have easily been used in the Old Testament to differentiate fermented wine from non-intoxicating grape juice. In support of this point, the *New Bible Dictionary* says, "While there are examples of the grapes being pressed into a cup and presumably used at once (Gen. 40:11), it is significant that the term 'wine' is never applied to the resultant grape juice."[23]

First Mention & First Meaning

After the historic flood and Noah's ark lands safely on dry ground, a covenant sign (a rainbow) is given that the earth will never again experience such devastation by water. Now back on dry land, Noah begins farming, plants a vineyard, and becomes drunk, as noted in Genesis 9:21: "Then Noah began farming and planted a vineyard. He drank of the wine and became drunk, and uncovered himself inside his tent." This is the first time *yayin* (wine) is mentioned in the Bible.

The very first time we run across this word in Scripture we know it is not referring to grape juice, for Noah is drunk and you simply can't get drunk on grape juice. It is extremely difficult to argue that non-intoxicating wine is intended here, when the context assures us otherwise. With the "first mention/first meaning" argument, if the first mention of *yayin* results in Noah's drunkenness, there must later be some sort of correction or indication that the word has changed to mean grape juice, but alas, there is none. If *yayin* meant fermented wine with its first use in the Bible, surely it means the same in other uses, apart from some correcting event.

The Principle of Context

It has been said that a text without a context is nothing more than a pretext. In other words, correct interpretation always considers the context of a verse or passage. Otherwise, the text merely becomes a stand-alone pretext for propping up one's pet perspective.

Take the Noah incident in Genesis 9 where *yayin* is first mentioned in the Bible. No matter how desperately we want *yayin* to be grape juice and not fermented wine, the context alone becomes a huge mountain to climb. I can argue until the cows come home that *yayin* means grape juice, but context pulls the curtain back and we see the Wizard of Oz for what he truly is. For goodness sake, Noah gets drunk—so drunk that he lay naked in his tent. That's not the result of consuming too much grape juice.

Additionally, we find others who get drunk on *yayin*:

- Lot   Gen. 19:32–35
- Nabal   1 Sam. 25:36–37
- Uriah   2 Sam. 11:13
- Elah   1 Kgs. 16:9
- Ben-hadad   1 Kgs. 20:16
- Ahasuerus   Esth. 1:10–11
- Belshazzar   Dan. 5:1–6
- The proud drunkards of Ephraim   Is. 28:1
- Numerous negative consequences of drunkenness see Chapter 3

Believing *yayin* means grape juice when the context clearly shows otherwise is irresponsible. We must concur with the fundamentalist Old Testament scholar Merrill F. Unger who observes that "in most of the passages in the Bible where *yayin* is used . . . it certainly means fermented grape juice, and in the remainder it may be fairly presumed to do so. In no passage can it be positively shown to have any other meaning. The intoxicating character of *yayin* in general is plain from Scripture."[24]

Intentional Fermentation

In Isaiah 25:6 we see the Israelites purposefully preparing wine in a manner that strengthens its robust nature: "The LORD of hosts will prepare a lavish banquet for all peoples on this mountain; a banquet of aged wine, choice pieces with marrow, and refined, aged wine."

While the New American Standard Version utilizes "aged wine" to show the intentional aging process, the King James Version of the Bible translates it "wines on the lees."

> By means of gradation, Isaiah now characterizes the banquet as one of wine that is matured by resting undisturbed on the lees. A play upon words as well as gradation appears between *shemanim* (fat things) and *shemarim* (lees). This latter word originally signified holders or preservers and then came to designate the wines that had rested a long time on sediment or dregs, and so had become more valuable. The wine lay on the lees to increase its strength and color."[25]

The Israelites deliberately allow wine to age so that "its strength and color are preserved."[26] Isaiah 48:11 speaks of aging wine in metaphorical terms:

> Isaiah 48:11
> Moab has been at ease since his youth;
> He has also been undisturbed, like wine on its dregs,
> And he has not been emptied from vessel to vessel,
> Nor has he gone into exile.
> Therefore he retains his flavor,
> And his aroma has not changed.

The fact that Israel purposefully aged wines to increase its strength is devastating to grape juice advocates. Even the Hebrew scholar Reynolds finds this difficult to swallow: "The improbable must be the correct answer. That is, the hypothesis that *shemarim* in Isaiah 26:5 does not mean *lees* at all. It is true that the lexicographers do not recognize any other meaning for *shemar* than dregs, lees, or sediment, but we must face the improbable answer that they are incorrect in this particular verse."[27] With other references to lees or dregs as in Psalm 75:8, Reynolds admits, "I know of no previous writer who has suggested it," and "It is true that this translation may appear somewhat innovative."[28]

Others suggest the ancients actually worked to impede the process of fermentation and often quote Columella and Pliny the Elder for support. Unfortunately, they misrepresent what is actually said. Both Columella and Pliny are touted as "describing how to store wine by trying to keep it from the air, and thus from fermentation, by sinking wine casks under water."[29] However, we see that this initial euphoria of support for preventing fermentation is short lived:[30]

> Both of these ancient writers do spend a good deal of time describing how to keep and store wine, but not to keep it from fermenting. Columella devotes Book 12 of *On Agriculture* to the preservation of various food items against spoilage: vines, vineyards and wine production are covered in several chapters. It is important to understand why these writers spend so much time explaining the processes used for drying fruits, storing grain, and how to store wine – the goal was to make sure there was food and drink until the next harvest. Columella writes extensively about the storage of wine, but nothing is said to indicate that the purpose is to keep the wine from fermenting. A close reading reveals that Columella's real concern, reflecting a common concern in the ancient world, was to keep the wine from **too much** fermentation—becoming vinegar. This is borne out by his comments in 12.20.1, "Furthermore, boiled-down must, though carefully made, is, like wine, apt to go sour." Again, 12.20.8, "This, though it does not make the flavour of the wine last forever, yet at any rate generally preserves it until another vintage."

> There are numerous places where both Columella and Pliny indicate that their discussion concerns fermented wine . . . All of these texts indicate the presence of alcohol and fermentation, but the two from Pliny are particularly interesting: he describes the warming sensation one feels when alcohol is consumed and then describes the cooling, evaporative nature of using wine on the skin as a rub—both point to alcohol. Then the lower freezing point of alcohol which causes Pliny to marvel at how wine could ever freeze. Add to this his descriptions of those who abuse wine and promote drunkenness (offending his sense of Stoic ethics) and it becomes obvious that Pliny is not covering the basics in grape juice production. He is not concerned about trying to keep grape juice from becoming alcoholic. His concern was to keep wine from spoiling into vinegar and becoming useless as a beverage.

Additional places where we find Pliny and Columella speaking of fermented wine include the following:[31]

On Agriculture:
The following is the way to make sweet wine . . . when it has ceased to ferment . . . [add crushed spices and strain it]. This wine will be pleasant to the taste and will keep in good state and is wholesome for the body. 12.27.1

The best after-wine is made as follows . . . [add water to grapeskins which have been pressed and let it soak overnight] when it has fermented . . . 12.40 (See also, 12.28.3; 32; 37; 38.2,3)

Natural History:
Wine has the property of heating the parts of the body inside when it is drunk and of cooling them when poured on them outside. 14.7.58

In the neighbourhood of the Alps they put it in wooden casks and close these round with tiles and in a cold winter also light fires to protect it from the effect of the cold. It is seldom recorded, but it has been seen occasionally, that the vessels have burst in a frost, leaving the wine standing in frozen blocks—almost a miracle, since it is not the nature of wine to freeze: usually it is only numbed by cold. 14.27.132

While grape juice certainly exists in the Old Testament, Columella and Pliny are actually discussing purposeful actions to help wine ferment properly. We see intentionality with wine production of the Old Testament.

Specific Limitations

While wine is a gift from God to be enjoyed in moderation, specific limitations are instituted because of its intoxicating qualities. Drunkenness, for instance, is condemned and crosses a line from moderation to excess, a definite limitation on its use. In Proverbs 31:4–5, kings are prohibited from *yayin* consumption "while engaging in the affairs of the state, lest he diminish his perception."[32]

It is not for kings, O Lemuel,
It is not for kings to drink wine,
Or for rulers to desire strong drink,
For they will drink and forget what is decreed,
And pervert the rights of all the afflicted.

In Leviticus 10:8–10, Old Testament priests are prohibited from drinking *yayin* while performing their priestly functions:

> Immediately after God destroys Nadab and Abihu for offering "strange fire" which he had not commanded, he warns Aaron, "The Lord then spoke to Aaron, saying, 'Do not drink wine or strong drink, neither you nor your sons with you, when you come into the tent of meeting, so that you will not die—it is a perpetual statute throughout your generations—and so as to make a distinction between the holy and the profane, and between the unclean and the clean, and so as to teach the sons of Israel all the statutes which the Lord has spoken to them through Moses.'"[33]

The same sentiment is found in Ezekiel 44:21: "Nor shall any of the priests drink wine when they enter the inner court." An historian born in the first century, "Josephus mentions this as continuing for this reason in his day: 'The priests abide therein both nights and days, performing certain purifications, and drinking not the least drop of wine *while they are in the temple.*' (*Apion* 1:22)."[34]

Wine (*yayin*) is not totally, absolutely forbidden in any quantity, at any time, and for any reason as prohibitionists suggest. In reality, the moderation view is further supported by limited restrictions on wine. These restrictions show that we are talking about alcohol, not grape juice, and that moderation is not prohibited, only excess consumption. Restrictions on priests and kings were not from drinking *yayin*, only from drinking it while fulfilling priestly duties or engaging in the affairs of state. These are reasonable restrictions given the importance of state action and the need to avoid inebriation (like Nadab and Abihu) in priestly service. These limitations affirm *yayin* as an alcoholic beverage with limited restrictions, not the total abstinence demanded by prohibitionists.

Limited Interpretive Options

This isn't a case of choosing between three or four solid interpretive options. In fact, the only option advanced by prohibitionists is that *yayin* means wine in negative contexts and grape juice in positive references. Isaiah 16:10 is used to support the two-wine theory:

> Gladness and joy are taken away from the fruitful field;
> In the vineyards also there will be no cries of joy or jubilant shouting,
> No treader treads out wine in the presses,
> For I have made the shouting to cease.

Prohibitionists interpret the "no treading out *yayin*" statement this way: "This obviously means that no treader shall tread out grape juice in the presses, because fermentation is a time consuming process. Therefore alcohol is excluded from the word *yayin* in this passage."[35] Prohibitionist Reynolds states, "This is enough to establish the fact that *yayin* in the Bible need not be alcoholic" and "it would be absurd to translate *yayin* as *fermented grape juice*."[36]

This view of Isaiah 16:10 as a reference to grape juice is untenable for several reasons:

1. Authorities are vehemently against this interpretation.
2. Isaiah 16:10 is poetic in nature and uses a common literary devise known as prolepsis where "the anachronistic representing of something as existing *before* its proper or historical time. Prolepsis looks to the end result anticipated in the proleptic observation."[37] In other words, fresh grape juice being tread in the press can poetically be spoken of as alcoholic because that is what it becomes and why it is being pressed in the first place, just like speaking of wine as a brawler, when wine isn't a brawler, the person drinking it to excess is. Other examples of prolepsis can be found in Scripture:

   Judges 9:10–13: liquid wine (*tirosh*) is spoken of as on the vine, like figs exist on a tree, but it is actually gapes that appear on the vine, not the liquid.

   Is. 65:8: new wine (*tirosh*) is spoken of as "in the cluster."

   Jer. 40:10: speaks of new wine (*tirosh*) like it was still on the vine needing to be harvested.

   Gen. 40:10–11, Lev. 25:5, Num. 6:3–4: figuratively using *tirosh* instead of *enab*, the literal grape on the vine.[38]

3. Prohibitionists argue prolepsis elsewhere. Isaiah 65:8, for instance, is understood to be poetic when referring to wine being found in the cluster during a time of drought. Elsewhere they believe that the "end results are sometimes attributed to the substance which causes the result."[39]

There just aren't a great many options for understanding *yayin* to be anything other than an alcoholic drink. Common authorities agree that *yayin* refers to fermented juice and the use of prolepsis, a literary device of anticipation, can be used in Scripture to speak of end results (fermented wine) as being attributed to the grape itself. In reality, the two-wine option is not really an option, but a perversion of Scripture supported by circular reasoning and defiance of common lexical authorities.

Positive and Negative Together

Prohibitionists struggle when the *same* substance (wine) is used in the *same* context both positively and negatively. The substance hasn't all of the sudden switched from fermented wine to grape juice, for it is the same substance in the same context. If I said, "I ate my first foot-long hot dog at the ballgame and it was awesome. But the second hot dog made me sick and I had to leave the game," we have one context (hot dogs at a ballgame) and the same use of the word hot dog.

Should I conclude that the first hot dog is a non-hot dog since I didn't get sick while the second one is a real hot dog because it made me sick? Within the same ballpark context I eat two of the same hot dogs. Could it be that both hot dogs are the same, but in my game-time exuberance, I overate? Could it be that they were the same hot dogs but one I ate in moderation while the second one was excessive? I got sick not from the hot dog itself, but from the abuse of the hot dog. My hot dog story contains the same wieners within the same context with different results. We don't conclude that the hot dogs were different, only that I overate.

Joel 1:5, 10
Awake, drunkards, and weep;
And wail, all you wine drinkers,
On account of the sweet wine
That is cut off from your mouth.
The field is ruined,
The land mourns;
For the grain is ruined,
The new wine dries up,
Fresh oil fails.

1 Samuel 1:14, 24
Then Eli said to her, "How long will you make yourself drunk? Put away your wine from you."

Now when she had weaned him, she took him up with her, with a three-year-old bull and one ephah of flour and a jug of wine, and brought him to the house of the Lord in Shiloh, although the child was young.

1 Samuel 25:18, 37
Then Abigail hurried and took two hundred loaves of bread and two jugs of wine and five sheep already prepared and five measures of roasted grain and a hundred clusters of raisins and two hundred cakes of figs, and loaded them on donkeys.

> But in the morning, when the wine had gone out of Nabal, his wife told him these things, and his heart died within him so that he became as a stone.

Silence can be Golden

Arguments from silence must be approached with caution. To stand on silence alone is problematic, but combined with other information we know about *yayin*, it is interesting that the Bible itself never makes the distinction between "'safe' and 'unsafe' *yayin*—as if the 'problem' is in a certain kind of wine, rather than in the volume consumed or the person recklessly partaking."[40]

The Bible doesn't make a distinction between safe and unsafe *yayin*. If there was such a thing, why isn't this differentiation drawn out for us so we can avoid bad wine? There is no prohibition or denunciation of drinking or making fermented wine. Realizing this, prohibitionists simply speak of this as an enigma, an ambiguity that God has not revealed to us. This scarcity and obscurity is viewed as a test to see which believer can interpret the ambiguity faithfully. However, instead of walking in the dark trying to find the door, "maybe God meant what he said."[41] Why can't folks just use good ol' common sense and believe biblical teaching for what it is: abuse of alcohol is sinful while moderate use may be enjoyed as a gift from God.

Fermented Wine Offering

Some argue that first fruit offerings are grape juice and not fermented wine. But "this involves a misunderstanding of the notion of a 'first fruit.' It does not necessarily mean the *youngest* fruit appearing first, but may mean the first of a finished product."[42] Alfred Edersheim, a convert to Christianity from Judaism and an eminent scholar in the 1800s penned *The Life and Times of Jesus the Messiah* and *The Temple: Its Ministry and Services*. He writes, "Authorities distinguish between the *Biccurim* (*primitiva*) or first fruits offered in their natural state, and the *Terumoth* (*primitae*), brought not as raw products, but in a prepared state,—as flour, oil, wine, etc."[43] In other words, a first fruit can be a finished product like wine and not necessarily a raw product like a grape.

The Talmud addresses this as well:[44]

> Terumoth 1:4:
> Heave—offering may not be given from olives instead of from oil, or from grapes instead of from wine.

Maaseroth 1:7
Wine [is liable to the tithe] after it has been skimmed.

Skimming refers to removing the scum that appears on the surface of bubbling, fermenting wine.

Concluding that *yayin* means anything but fermented wine is nothing more than unsubstantiated opinion. It is this fermented *yayin* that God speaks so positively of when used in moderation. It is His gift to His people for celebration, worship, and joy. It reflects the blessing of God whereas the absence of *yayin* reflects the curse of God upon a land and people.

Tirosh

While *yayin* is the most popular word for wine in the Old Testament (141 occurences), *tirosh* is the second most common (used 38 times). The word is translated as wine, and even the King James Bible translates *tirosh* as wine. Some believe it refers to grape juice, but "technically, *tirosh* is a form of immature *yayin*, an early stage in the fermentation process."[45] The *International Standard Bible Encyclopedia* notes the following:[46]

> Unfermented grape juice is a very difficult thing to keep without the aid of modern antiseptic precautions, and its preservation in the warm and not over cleanly conditions of ancient Palestine was impossible. Consequently *tirosh* came to mean wine that was not fully aged (although with full intoxicating properties, Judg. 9:13; Hos. 4:11; Acts 2:13) or wine when considered specifically as the product of grapes (Deut. 12:17; 18:4).

Just because *tirosh* may be wine in an immature stage doesn't mean it is without intoxicating properties. Hosea 4:11 indicates that "wine and new wine take away the understanding." It is hard to see how grape juice can take away understanding if it is so healthy for us, but if it has intoxicating qualities, even in an immature stage, its abuse could lead to inebriation. *Tirosh*, like *yayin*, can be used in a right way and a wrong way. And like *yayin*, its abundance is a blessing from God while its absence is a curse.

Tirosh comes from a word meaning "take possession of, inherit, dispossess" and can be either "enlivening" or "injurious," and even prohibitionist Stephen Reynolds admits that "the case for assuming that *tirosh* was primarily an intoxicant is greatly strengthened."[47]

Shekar

Occurring twenty-two times in the Old Testament, *shekar* means "intoxicating drink" and is translated in the King James Bible as "strong drink." It is probably as close as we come to hard liquor. "The root of this word comes from a word meaning to be tipsy and is associated with strong alcoholic drink."[48] It is related to the word *shikkar* (drunkard) and *shikkaron* (drunkenness).[49] The word covers various types of fermented drinks made from apples, dates, barley, etc., but is separate and distinct from wine.

Eli wrongly assumed that Hannah was drunk from this strong intoxicating substance. Wine is said to be a mocker, but strong drink (*shekar*) is a brawler (Prov. 20:1). Like wine, priests may not drink of it while performing their temple duties (Lev. 10:9) and Nazarites may not partake during the time of their vows (Num. 6:3). "Yet, God never universally prohibits or discourages it. Rather, he commands *shekar* as a drink-offering," as seen in Numbers 28:7: "Then the drink offering with it shall be a fourth of a hin for each lamb, in the holy place you shall pour out a drink offering of strong drink [*shekar*] to the LORD."[50]

Even Moses permits the drinking of *shekar* and encourages its enjoyment in Deuteronomy 14:22–26:[51]

> You shall surely tithe all the produce from what you sow, which comes out of the field every year. You shall eat in the presence of the LORD your God, at the place where He chooses to establish His name, the tithe of your grain, your new wine, your oil, and the firstborn of your herd and your flock, so that you may learn to fear the LORD your God always. If the distance is so great for you that you are not able to bring the tithe, since the place where the LORD your God chooses to set His name is too far away from you when the LORD your God blesses you, then you shall exchange it for money, and bind the money in your hand and go to the place which the LORD your God chooses. You may spend the money for whatever your heart desires: for oxen, or sheep, or wine, or strong drink [shekar], or whatever your heart desires; and there you shall eat in the presence of the LORD your God and rejoice, you and your household.

With *shekar*, we may rightly conclude that "the attempt made to prove that it was simply the unfermented juice of certain fruits is quite without foundation."[52]

'Asis

'*Asis*, a word meaning "pressed out," occurs only five times in the Old Testament and is translated "sweet wine," "new wine," or "juice." '*Asis* "is properly the newly expressed juice of the grape. Yet again, despite the seeming innocence of this word lexically, '*asis* can and does have the power to intoxicate."[53]

Joel 1:5
Awake, drunkards, and weep;
And wail, all you wine drinkers,
On account of the sweet wine *['asis]*
That is cut off from your mouth.

Isaiah 49:26 (used metaphorically)
I will feed your oppressors with their own flesh,
And they will become drunk with their own blood as with sweet wine; *['asis]*
And all flesh will know that I, the Lord, am your Savior
And your Redeemer, the Mighty One of Jacob.

Used in a Messianic sense as "emblems of God's gracious blessings," we read the following:[54]

Joel 3:18
And in that day
The mountains will drip with sweet wine,
And the hills will flow with milk,
And all the brooks of Judah will flow with water;
And a spring will go out from the house of the Lord
To water the valley of Shittim.

Amos 9:13
Behold, days are coming, declares the Lord,
When the plowman will overtake the reaper
And the treader of grapes him who sows seed;
When the mountains will drip sweet wine
And all the hills will be dissolved.

Other Words

Chamar, a Chaldean word, is a wine mentioned in Daniel 5 and though it is intoxicating, it is also considered with the blessings of God (Dt. 32:14). *Sobe*, another Old Testament word, is considered a potent intoxicant and is rendered drunkard (Dt. 21:20) and heavy drinker (Pr. 23:20).

While there is strong drink and many different wines in the Bible, some sweet and some robust in flavor and color, there is no evidence that supports a two-wine theory where fermented beverage is evil and grape juice is blessed by God. In fact, quite the opposite is true. In moderation, fermented drink is a blessing from the Creator that can bring enjoyment. On the other hand, its abuse is expressly condemned. The only limitation on fermented drink is for priests and kings while on duty and those fulfilling a Nazarite vow.

New Testament

Having examined the significant words for wine and strong drink in the Old Testament, our attention now turns to key words in the New Testament. The twenty-seven books of the New Testament are thought to have been written within one hundred years of Christ's death. In stark contrast, the thirty-nine Old Testament books cover a much broader period of time. Despite the difference in writings, length, and historical timeframe, we do not find contradictory teaching about alcohol in the New Testament. Old Testament teaching is not debunked by the New Testament; instead, we find compatibility.

Oinos

This is the most frequently used word for wine in the New Testament (33 occurrences). There are several good reasons for believing that *oinos* in the New Testament is fermented wine and not grape juice:[55]

Oinos in the New Testament is the equivalent of the Old Testament *yayin*.

If *yayin* is fermented wine and *oinos* is its equivalent, then *oinos* must be fermented as well. We know that *oinos* is the equivalent of *yayin* because it is translated as such in the Septuagint, the Greek translation of the Old Testament that became the Bible of the New Testament Church during its early days. Translating *yayin* as *oinos* in Greek is purposeful. A Greek reading the Old Testament in his own language would see the following:

> . . . wine (*Oinos*) made Noah and lot drunk (Gen. 9:21; 19:33–35). He would learn that the priests were forbidden, under the law of Moses, to drink this wine while on duty (Lev. 10:9). He would learn that a Nazarite was not to use it during the time of a vow (Nu.. 6:3). He would also find examples of (1 Sa. 25:37) and warnings against drunkenness (Prov. 20:1; 23:29–35). But he would also read that wine (the same *oinos*) is a blessing from God (Ps. 104:15 (103:15 in LXX)), and a wholesome aspect of life (Eccles. 9:7; Deut. 32:14; Prov. 3:9,10), even though it was the strongest kind of wine (Deut. 14:26; Jud. 9:13; Isa. 25:6, 49:26).[56]

Oinos is used of fermented drink in classical Greek.

Classical Greek is the language from which biblical Greek arises. The New Testament is written in Koine Greek, a more simplistic language reflecting the common vernacular of the day, whereas its forerunner, classical Greek, is a bit more complex and nuanced. It is the difference between classical music and country music. Well, that's a stretch, but you get my point. Classical Greek uses *oinos* as a fermented drink:

> The Liddell and Scott Greek-English Lexicon defines *oinos* as "the fermented juice of the grape." Interestingly, classical Greek apparently uses *oinos* as a functional equivalent for "fermented juice" of all sorts.[57]

New Testament linguists affirm its alcoholic content.
"No major New Testament lexicon disputes the fermented character of *oinos*."[58]

The scriptural context of *oinos* points toward its alcoholic content.
Oinos is used in contexts where its intoxicating quality is easy to see. When Paul writes in Ephesians 5:18, "And do not get drunk with wine, for that is dissipation, but be filled with the Spirit," we realize that it is possible to get drunk on *oinos*. Paul further indicates that church leaders and older women are not to be addicted to much wine (*oinos*). Apparently, the fact that one *could* be addicted to *oinos* speaks of its alcoholic content. As far as I know, it is not possible to become enslaved to grape juice.

Nowhere in the New Testament is *oinos* forbidden. Even church leaders are not required or expected to abstain from it. The only requirement is that they not be *addicted* to *oinos*. This makes sense. The kind of leader the church seeks is one controlled by the Spirit of God, not alcohol. Drunkenness has no part in God's kingdom. The issue isn't with an inherently evil substance, but with the misuse of a good gift from God.

Prohibitionists, as expected, disagree with this perspective. Since alcohol is an inherently evil substance in their mind, they attempt to work textual miracles believing that Paul's admonition in Ephesians 5:18, "And do not get drunk with wine, for that is dissipation, but be filled with the Spirit" supports *their* view:

> "Be not drunk with wine in which is debauchery." Some commentators say that the words "in which" refer to the whole phrase, "Be not drunk with wine," and not just to "wine." The wish not to accept the idea that debauchery is "in" wine makes them reject this obvious sense, and choose instead the idea that it lies in being drunk."[59]

But this is dealt with quite handily:[60]

> . . . why did not Paul simply command: "Drink no wine, wherein is excess"? Why does the apostle consistently add such limiting notions to the act of drinking, such as "be not drunk," "not addicted to," and "not enslaved to"?

> Further, I would point out that no commentators or lexicographers suggest Reynolds' interpretation.
>
> The contrast is not between the instruments but between the states—between two elevated states, one due to the excitement of wine, the other to the inspiration and enlightenment of the Spirit.

The contrast is between being drunk, which leads to the state of excess, and being filled with the Spirit, which leads to the state of speaking to one another in psalms, hymns, spiritual songs, and singing and making melody in our heart (Eph. 5:18–19). Drinking in moderation is never condemned.

Gleukos

Gleukos only occurs once in the New Testament (Acts 2) on the day of Pentecost when the apostles are gathered together in Jerusalem. It is here that they are filled with the Holy Spirit and witnesses suggest they are drunk for speaking in tongues:

> Acts 2:1–4
> When the day of Pentecost had come, they were all together in one place. And suddenly there came from heaven a noise like a violent rushing wind, and it filled the whole house where they were sitting. And there appeared to them tongues as of fire distributing themselves, and they rested on each one of them. And they were all filled with the Holy Spirit and began to speak with other tongues, as the Spirit was giving them utterance.

> Acts 2:11–13
> . . . we hear them in our own tongues speaking of the mighty deeds of God. And they all continued in amazement and great perplexity, saying to one another, "What does this mean?" But others were mocking and saying, "They are full of sweet wine."

Based on the response of the crowd, "They are full of sweet wine," we might be tempted to think *gleukos* refers to fermented drink, but in reality this word probably refers to freshly squeezed juice from the grape. According to linguists, it *could* possibly refer to fermented wine, but if it doesn't, the crowd is mockingly saying, "You are only drinking grape juice but you are acting like you are drinking fermented wine." The surprise is that this is the only instance of the word *gleukos* in the New Testament. If it does refer to unfermented grape juice, why is it not specifically presented as the biblical alternative to drinking the sinful substance of *oinos*? The answer is obvious. While grape juice did exist during the Old and New Testament (all you have to do is squeeze a grape), that juice is never presented as the safe, sinless alternative to drinking the inherently evil substance of *yayin* or *oinos*. That's because *yayin* and *oinos* are *not* inherently evil substances, but good gifts from God for His people to enjoy with moderate use.

Having examined key words in both the Old and New Testaments, we concur with the following statement: ". . . wine is clearly shown to be an intoxicating drink in the Bible. It is a thing that man can easily abuse to his own destruction. Yet Scripture says it is also a blessing when it is properly used by those who understand and believe truth."[61] The clever invention of the two-wine theory lacks biblical support for serious consideration.

Summary: There is no biblical support for a two-wine theory (positive references refer to grape juice while negative references speak of fermented drink) because the biblical words in both the Old and New Testaments, and the contexts in which the words are used, refers to alcoholic drink.

JESUS AND ALCOHOL

This chapter examines Jesus' use and perspective of wine. After all, He lived in a land filled with vineyards. What does He drink? How does He view wine? Does His life and teaching reveal anything about the subject?

A biblical study on alcohol is incomplete without examining Jesus' approach to the topic. After all, He is accused of being a drunkard, institutes wine as a symbol of the New Covenant, turns water into wine at a wedding celebration, and speaks of wine, vineyards, and drunkenness in His parables—familiar concepts with the audience.

Jesus is an example of holiness—a life pleasing to the Heavenly Father. The Corinthians are encouraged to mimic Paul because he imitates Christ: "Be imitators of me, just as I also am of Christ" (I Cor. 11:1). According to Peter, Christ left us an example to follow: "For you have been called for this purpose, since Christ also suffered for you, leaving you an example for you to follow in His steps, who committed no sin, nor was any deceit found in His mouth" (I Pt. 2:21–22). Since Jesus is our example, His life may yield interesting information regarding His perspective on fermented beverage.

For Christians, Jesus is the sinless sacrificial lamb whose substitutionary death on the Cross of Calvary reconciles us to the Father. He is holy and "committed no sin, nor was any deceit found in His mouth," and "He made Him who knew no sin to be sin on our behalf, so that we might become the righteousness of God in Him" (I Pt. 2:22; 2 Cor. 5:21). The representative for humankind is both human and sinless at the same time. A flawed sacrifice is worthless, but the blood of an unblemished human representative releases us from the bondage of sin. We are bought with a price—the precious blood of our Lord (I Cor. 6:20; Acts 20:28; Rev. 5:9).

While this doctrine is Basic Christianity 101, it becomes a stumbling block for prohibitionists. Since they believe alcohol is inherently evil, they cannot fathom a holy, sinless Christ drinking alcohol or condoning its use in any shape or form, let alone turning water into wine or elevating it as the symbol of a New Covenant. This perceived impossibility creates interpretive obstacles for them. If it is *impossible* for Jesus to condone, drink, or make alcohol, then any scriptural text affirming that He does must be reinterpreted in a manner that upholds their predetermined viewpoint. Rather than changing their perspective, they modify Scripture.

Not once does Jesus condemn wine as intrinsically evil, a wicked substance to be avoided at all costs. Instead, we find Him following the biblical perspective of moderation. But since moderation isn't an option for prohibitionists (it is impossible), they believe Jesus turns water into nutritious grape juice at the Cana wedding and the "fruit of the vine" at the Last Supper is nothing more than harmless grape juice. They engage in exegetical gamesmanship in arriving at their predetermined conclusions.

Did Jesus Drink?

Does Scripture tell us what Jesus drinks? Not explicitly. There is no verse that expressly says, "Jesus lifts His cup of wine to His mouth and takes a big gulp." Sorry, it just isn't there. Don't get too excited over this fact, for there isn't one verse that tells us that He explicitly drinks water, milk, tea, grape juice, or anything else. While there is no smoking gun, it is implied that He drinks wine during the Last Supper and at His crucifixion. We know He drinks *something*, for He can't survive without some form of hydration.

In order to discover what Jesus drinks, we look to what is culturally available, the contexts where He is present with wine, and inferences about what He might be drinking. Wine is a plentiful, common, and daily household drink during the time of Jesus. The culture of His day and the history of Israel inform us of this. There is no pasteurization to slow microbial growth, no safe filtration system for purifying drinking water, and no preservatives or refrigeration for keeping grape juice. But there are numerous wine presses for producing wine, the everyday drink of Jesus' day.

Wine is common and plentiful during the life of our Lord, but He never condemns wine as an inherently evil substance. In His eyes, inebriation crosses a line into sin (Mt. 24:48; Lk. 12:45; 21:34), but drinking wine itself is permissible. This, of course, is in keeping with Old Testament teaching. If Jesus had taught otherwise, He would have upended centuries of biblical instruction.

The accusation that Jesus is a drunkard indicates that He consumes wine (Mt. 11:19; Lk. 7:34). In fact, the contrast is with John the Baptist, who doesn't drink. Calling Jesus a drunkard is intended to slander and injure His reputation and ministry. It is precisely *because* Jesus drinks that He is accused of drunkenness. If He abstains from fermented drink like John the Baptist, the accusation becomes absurd. But since He is drinking in moderation, the slander is that He crosses the line into what is prohibited—intoxication. The religious elite of Jesus' day are difficult to please. If Jesus is happy, they want Him sad. If He spends time with sinners, they want Him to separate from them. They constantly seek to trap Him with their many, and oftentimes, silly questions. Jealousy burns within, and they seek His downfall with spurious accusations.

Prior to his birth, an angel announces in Luke 1:13–15 that John the Baptist will abstain from wine and strong drink:

> But the angel said to him, "Do not be afraid, Zacharias, for your petition has been heard, and your wife Elizabeth will bear you a son, and you will give him the name John. You will have joy and gladness, and many will rejoice at his birth. For he will be great in the sight of the Lord; and he will drink no wine or liquor, and he will be filled with the Holy Spirit while yet in his mother's womb."

That John abstains from wine and strong drink is understandable to the people of his day, especially if he is a Nazarite as many scholars believe (Num. 6:1–4). Whether or not John is a Nazarite is debatable and nonessential; the contrast involves the drinking of alcohol. Jesus' lifestyle is totally different than John's, as seen in the slanderous accusation of Luke 7:33–35:

> For John the Baptist has come eating no bread and drinking no wine, and you say, "He has a demon!" The Son of Man has come eating and drinking, and you say, "Behold, a gluttonous man and a drunkard, a friend of tax collectors and sinners!"

In direct contrast to John, Jesus eats normal food and drinks wine. Nowhere in Scripture is Jesus ever portrayed as being drunk, yet the disparaging accusation is a good indication that He actually drinks wine. The contrast is between John not eating bread or drinking wine, and Jesus, who arrives on the scene doing both.

One can eat bread without being a glutton, and one can drink alcohol without being a drunkard. In other words, if Jesus is a known abstainer like John, no drinking accusation can be made for there is no basis for contrast, and the absurdity of such a statement is exposed to all. However, Jesus doesn't correct them on the fact that He imbibes. His accusers watch Him consume wine and enjoy a merry time in the presence of despised tax collectors and sinners. This becomes their opportunity to portray Him as going too far—crossing the line from moderation to drunkenness. How can anyone follow Jesus or desire His association when He drinks to excess and hangs around the wrong kind of people?

But, as one author notes,

> But when they heard that Jesus, in contrast to John, came both "eating and drinking" (Lk. 7:33) it would not offend them. Though our Lord was accused of being "a gluttonous man and a drunkard" (Lk. 7:34) they knew, from the teaching of the Old Testament, that one could lawfully eat without being a glutton and drink without being a drunkard. It would not offend them to hear that their Lord made wine for a wedding feast (John 2:1–11) because they already knew from Scripture that wine is a blessing that God provides for His people (Deut. 14:26). They did not attempt to rewrite Scripture so as to make the word wine stand for grape juice, since they knew from Scripture that even strong drink was permitted.[1]

Both culture and context indicate that Jesus drinks what everyone else drinks—wine. He drinks wine while John the Baptist doesn't touch the stuff—fulfilling his birth pronouncement. The false accusation of drunkenness indicates that Jesus moderately consumes the common drink of His day without overindulgence.

Turning Water into Wine

A colossal bombshell for prohibitionists is John 2:1–11, where Jesus turns water into wine at a wedding celebration in Cana of Galilee:

> On the third day there was a wedding in Cana of Galilee, and the mother of Jesus was there; and both Jesus and His disciples were invited to the wedding. When the wine ran out, the mother of Jesus said to Him, "They have no wine." And Jesus said to her, "Woman, what does that have to do with us? My hour has not yet come." His mother said to the servants, "Whatever He says to you, do it." Now there were six stone waterpots set there for the Jewish custom of purification, containing twenty or thirty gallons each. Jesus said to them, "Fill the waterpots with water." So they filled them up to the brim. And He said to them, "Draw some out now and take it to the headwaiter." So they took it to him. When the headwaiter tasted the water which had become wine, and did not know where it came from (but the servants who had drawn the water knew), the headwaiter called the bridegroom, and said to him, "Every man serves the good wine first, and when the people have drunk freely, then he serves the poorer wine; but you have kept the good wine until now." This beginning of His signs Jesus did in Cana of Galilee, and manifested His glory, and His disciples believed in Him.

According to prohibitionists, wine is a wicked substance; and yet, here is Jesus actually manufacturing the beverage. He isn't just making a few glasses of wine; He turns six jars full of water (about 120–180 gallons) into wine. This is a considerable amount, but then again, it is a wedding celebration with many guests.

The manufacturing of wine by Jesus is impossible in the mind of a prohibitionist, leading to outlandish statements like these:

> To think that Jesus would turn water into alcohol is preposterous; and eliminates all he stood for. Jesus did change water into a grape mixture that day but one that was unfermented. Sure it was the best wine because it was the most nutritious.[2]

> I am absolutely incredulous when I hear Bible "experts" suggest that our blessed Saviour used His supernatural powers to turn water into at least 120 gallons of intoxicating wine (six pots at twenty to thirty gallons each, according to the Revised Standard Version of the Bible) to restock a bar at a wedding reception. How could the sinless Son of God miraculously fabricate a wine which His own Holy Word denounced as "the poison of a serpent"?[3]

While we admire their quest to uphold the holiness of our Savior, prohibitionists fail to link reason with common sense. When a particular result is considered impossible, facts are either discarded, trivialized, or manipulated toward a preferred conclusion. Is it possible that Jesus actually did turn water into fermented wine? If so, does the amount He produces make a difference, whether 20, 100, 180, 2,000 gallons? Must there be tension between Jesus making or using fermented drink and the biblical prohibition against drunkenness? Why must holiness and consuming wine be at odds with one another when it isn't in Scripture? Do we manufacture new presumptions and twist the plain meaning of Scripture to ensure that the "impossibility" doesn't become possible?

To some, the creation of such a large quantity of wine by the holy Jesus is simply unbelievable. But why is this so difficult to believe? Jesus isn't producing evil or violating Scripture. Wine is the blessing of God, and now the Son of God is blessing others with the Father's good gift to humankind. In the Old Testament, Israel is distinguished as God's vine and vineyard while God Himself is the master vintner.

Jesus will go on to do many other miracles, such as bestowing sight to the blind, feeding 5,000 people with five loaves of bread and two fish, and raising the dead. Turning water into wine is not an unusual miracle or display of His power. Jesus simply honors the Old Testament teaching that wine is a gift from God to His people, and creates the customary beverage on this joyous wedding occasion. Drinking wine or enjoying its pleasure is not immoral and never has been.

Weddings in our culture only last a short time. I performed the marriage ceremony for my nephew; the ceremony lasted thirty minutes, pictures took forty-five minutes, and the after-dinner celebration took us through the evening. At the time of Christ, wedding celebrations could take days. With so many guests over such a long period of time, running out of wine was a real possibility that could lead to an embarrassing situation for the wedding host.

Prohibitionists, however, have their own take on this miracle at Cana. Many of their arguments are listed below:

Argument 1:
Jesus turns water into grape juice, not fermented wine.

Here we go again with the erroneous two-wine theory. Jesus obviously changes water into something; that cannot be denied. Since fermented wine is ruled out in the prohibitionist's mind, the only remaining option for them is grape juice. But the two-wine theory is debunked in Chapter 6.

Argument 2:
Fermented wine is decayed juice and doesn't reflect the holiness and purity of Jesus.

For prohibitionists, grape juice best represents the purity of God and His kingdom, not a juice contaminated with alcohol. This is interesting in light of the fact that Scripture portrays God as a vintner providing wine and making people merry. At the Last Supper, it is a glass of wine (Jesus' choosing) that depicts the holiness and purity of His blood. Besides, the premise that fermented wine is somehow contaminated or decayed is without merit. Here is what one prohibitionist writes:

> . . . to imagine Christ making wine any less than the freshest, purest liquid sustenance is inconceivable. Those who insist to the contrary—asserting the wine Jesus makes is intoxicating—do so against all reason. For the fact is fermented wine is decayed wine; that is wine by its chemical makeup is impure. During fermentation, when the sugar of the grape is exposed to microorganisms, what is produced is gas and alcohol, neither compound of which in inherent to the grape. Alcohol is foreign. Alcohol is an invader. The natural sugar of the grape God creates is absent from fermented wine. Thus, to be fermented wine on all accounts is to be inferior wine. As Creator, Christ Jesus the Lord makes water into the freshest, most delightful grape juice imaginable.[4]

Turning water into fermented wine is "inconceivable" according to the above author. In other words, since it isn't possible, another explanation must arise.

According to this reasoning, any time food or drink alters its original state, it becomes decayed and therefore "foreign" and an "invader." Basically, you cannot heat or boil any food since its composition is altered. Be careful eating a banana that has been sitting on the counter too long! The moment the skin of a grape is cut, even when it is on the vine, bacteria begin to do their work.

Some believe that fermentation is an unnatural process, but this is not true. Any time there is yeast or bacteria, sugars to feed upon, and appropriate environmental conditions, the fermentation process begins. It even occurs in our own bodies to some degree. Yet, it is God who chooses this "inferior wine" to symbolize His blessing upon Israel, represent the blood of Christ, serve as a drink offering to Him, and become one of His many gifts that make our hearts merry. This view goes "against all reason" because it avoids common sense and is diametrically opposed to the clear teaching of Scripture.

The author quoted above includes a remark by Leon C. Field in 1882, noting that if Jesus did indeed use and make fermented wine, it would "prove exceedingly damaging, if not utterly fatal, to the claims of total abstinence" and "If their premises are correct their conclusion is inevitable."[5] Of course, Field doesn't believe moderation premises are correct and supports total abstinence, but what if the premises of moderationists are indeed true, as I believe they are, then the conclusion is obvious. But because the obvious conclusion isn't "conceivable" to prohibitionists, exegetical gymnastics prop up an argument that cannot stand on its own.

Argument 3:
The large amount of wine Jesus produces indicates it is not fermented.

What does the volume of wine Jesus creates have to do with anything? At what volume does the wine cease to be grape juice and turn into fermented wine—1, 5, 20 gallons? Prohibitionists believe Jesus would never encourage drunkenness by producing such a large volume of intoxicating drink for such a small wedding party. Surely, this overabundance is a sign that the liquid must be grape juice! When sound arguments cannot be justified, people often resort to spewing forth many claims, thinking that if they throw everything at us, we will be overwhelmed with the sheer volume of madness and come around to their view. Unfortunately, this argument adds to the growing pile of failed explanations.

This view assumes the wedding party is small. Where in the Bible does it say this? Why must we assume this? There is no biblical support for such an outlook. Could the volume of wine be created *precisely* because the wedding party is large, or that there are days remaining in the celebration? Could Jesus simply be refilling an adequate supply of wine for the number of guests attending?

How do we know an overabundance is actually created? There is no fact to support such a claim. Could the large volume merely reflect the six waterpots available for the miracle? Could the large volume reflect Jesus' large miraculous powers, making a statement with His first public miracle? Why must such volume encourage drunkenness? Wine is a good gift from the Creator, no matter how much is produced. It is the abuse and overindulgence of God's good gift that leads to drunkenness, not the gift itself.

This wedding celebration occurs right before Passover season, when guests are expecting fermented wine. "Furthermore, William Hendriksen comments that due to the season of the wedding—just before Spring Passover (John 2:13)—the wine would naturally be fermented. The grape harvest would have been collected over six months earlier in September. Thus, the wine had ample time to ferment."[6] Guests are not anticipating grape juice during a wedding celebration at this time of the year.

Argument 4:
Scholar Stephen Reynolds makes a four-fold argument advanced by many prohibitionists:[7]

> The situation appears to have been as follows: The wedding party had been indulging in cheap, foul tasting wine, made perhaps partly from diseased grapes, and having a high alcoholic content. The people were drunk and behaving in a manner which moved to righteous indignation our Lord who was and is absolutely and totally pure of mind and body. His mother's sorrow that the party had run out of that sort of wine and her implied suggestion that He provide more of the same caused Him in righteous sorrow to speak stern words to her which have much puzzled Bible commentators.[8]

Reynolds four-fold argument is essentially, A) the unruly celebration displeases Jesus and triggers the rebuke of His mother, B) the wedding party guests are drunk, C) the headwaiter recognizes the newly created wine as the best wine because it is actually grape juice, and D) since drunkenness is involved in this rowdy celebration, it is immoral to produce such a large quantity of fermented wine.

A. Jesus rebukes His mother.
Some believe that Jesus is angry with His mother for bringing Him to a wedding where alcohol is being served and the celebration is getting out of hand. Christians have long debated the reason for such a rebuke, but Reynolds believes Jesus is upset that Mary is tolerating raucous behavior and a sinful substance is present at the celebration. If Jesus is rebuking His mother for such reasons, she apparently

doesn't understand it that way. Just after such a rebuke, she asks the servants to do whatever Jesus commands, expecting some action by Him to alleviate the problem (Jn. 2:5). If the rebuke is against the wedding celebration, guest behavior, or the wickedness of wine, it seems that Mary would be *discouraged* from seeking a solution to the scarcity of wine rather than anticipating a solution and asking the servants to obey.

> Why did he not rebuke those who are drunk, since he regularly confronted sin in the sinner (John 4:17–19; 8:11)? Or the governor of such a feast, since Jesus warned of responsibility inhering in positions of authority (Matt. 23:12; Luke 12:48)? Why did Jesus do anything at all to assist them in their partying, since he overturned the tables of those acting sinfully in the Temple (Matt. 21:12–13)? Why did he stay around until the wine ran out?[9]

Many scholars believe in a different and more reasonable understanding of Jesus' response to His mother: "A more plausible interpretation of Jesus' response relates to the fact that he was just beginning his Messianic ministry (John 2:11). Consequently, it was then time for Mary to cease looking upon him as her son and to begin recognizing him as her Lord and Savior (Mark 3:33–34)."[10] After all, this is the first miraculous sign of His public ministry.

B. The wedding guests were already intoxicated.
The text does not indicate that people were drunk, yet prohibitionists interpret verse 10 to indicate that they were:

> Every man serves the good wine first, and when the people have drunk freely, then he serves the poorer wine; but you have kept the good wine until now. But the headwaiter did not say that those at this particular party were "drunk." Rather, he was stating a general practice among those who host feasts.[11]

It was common practice to serve guests the best wine first. The headwaiter, hired to oversee the feast and familiar with wines, recognizes the quality of Jesus' miracle and wonders why it was not served first as is commonly practiced at wedding feasts.

"Drunk freely" doesn't necessarily indicate the guests were intoxicated. Linguist Herbert Preisker, writes in the *Theological Dictionary of the New Testament* that the Greek word "*Methuskomai* is used with no ethical or religious judgment in Jn. 2:10 in connection with the rule that the poorer wine is served only when the guests have drunk well."[12] Speaking of this word, the Parkhurst lexicon notes its meaning: "To drink freely and to cheerfulness, though not to drunkenness . . . John 2:10. And in this sense the verb is plainly used by the LXX [i.e. Septuagint], Gen. 43:34; Cant.

5:1."[13] In other words, the word can mean to drink wine freely without leading to drunkenness, and the Septuagint (the Greek translation of the Old Testament and Bible of the New Testament church) uses the word in this manner.

C. The headwaiter recognizes the new wine as being grape juice.

It seems odd that a professional headwaiter hired to oversee wedding feasts would not be familiar with various wines and their quality. He is a connoisseur of spirits and knows superior wine from poor wine as Luke 5:39 indicates, "And no one, after drinking old wine wishes for new; for he says, 'The old is good enough.'" Aged wine is often viewed as better wine. "Even Messianic prophecies use the imagery of 'aged' (old, fermented) wine at banquets in illustrating that which is good," as seen in Isaiah 25:6:

> The LORD of hosts will prepare a lavish banquet for all peoples on this mountain; a banquet of aged wine, choice pieces with marrow, and refined, aged wine.[14]

Additionally:

> ... assuming these folks were drunk (Reynolds' analysis), why did they not prefer alcoholic wine? Why would the (allegedly) drunken headmaster declare Jesus' wine "better," since he was in the "partying spirit"? After all, Reynolds argues that "the natural man with corrupted taste" prefers fermented wine. You would think that drunken men at a riotous party would exhibit the "natural man's" preferences for fermented beverage when analyzing Jesus' wine.[15]

The professional headwaiter didn't proclaim sudden astonishment that grape juice wasn't served first. Both the "original wine and the miraculously produced wine are called *oinos*, which means 'fermented grape juice,' or alcoholic wine."[16] The wine Jesus produces is superior because it is aged wine that tastes better.

Some claim the miracle of water to grape juice occurs because the quality of water in those days was so poor. I suppose Jesus could have miraculously turned the jars of contaminated water into crystal clear H_2O and simply avoided this wine controversy altogether. But He doesn't. In fact, the intoxicating properties may make the liquid healthier and safer to drink than unfiltered water.

D. Creating a large quantity of alcohol is immoral with so many intoxicated people at the wedding.

If alcohol is inherently evil, its creation, whether miniscule or extensive, becomes immoral. However, Paul understands that wine is not evil by nature and claims in Romans 14:14, "I know and am convinced in the Lord Jesus that nothing is unclean in itself." Jesus Himself understood this in Mark 7:15: "there is nothing outside the man which can defile him if it goes into him; but the things which proceed out of the man are what defile the man." The quantity of wine produced is irrelevant.

Though wedding guests are drinking freely in celebration of the bride and groom, there is no indication that they are intoxicated or that the celebration is a raucous affair. Everything that Jesus makes is good and when He turns water into wine, the miracle isn't merely a change in substance (water to wine), but also a miracle of quality (water to excellent tasting, aged wine). The trained headwaiter recognizes the excellent quality of the wine and wonders why it is served last instead of following traditional protocol. There is nothing immoral about Jesus' miracle at all. It is in keeping with Old Testament teaching—wine is a good gift from the Heavenly Father. It seems that Jesus not only drinks wine, but also makes fermented beverage.

The Last Supper

Not only does our Lord miraculously produce superior, aged wine from six jars of water with His first public miracle, He also chooses fermented wine to symbolize the New Covenant in His blood (Mt. 26:17–30; Mk. 14:12–25, Lk. 22:7–20). Of course, prohibitionists struggle with this significant fact and interpret "fruit of the vine" to be harmless, nutritious grape juice.

> Luke 22:14–20:
> When the hour had come, He reclined at the table, and the apostles with Him. And He said to them, "I have earnestly desired to eat this Passover with you before I suffer; for I say to you, I shall never again eat it until it is fulfilled in the kingdom of God." And when He had taken a cup and given thanks, He said, "Take this and share it among yourselves; for I say to you, I will not drink of the fruit of the vine from now on until the kingdom of God comes." And when He had taken some bread and given thanks, He broke it and gave it to them, saying, "This is My body which is given for you; do this in remembrance of Me." And in the same way He took the cup after they had eaten, saying, "This cup which is poured out for you is the new covenant in My blood.

The thought of Jesus imbibing or instituting wine as the symbol of His shed blood is unimaginable to the prohibitionist camp. Note their five-alarm panic:[17]

> What about fermented wine at the Passover celebration? At communion? Jesus passed the cup to His disciples and said, "Drink—to remember" (see Matthew 26:27). How could He have served them a drink that causes men

to forget? Ask any alcoholic why he drinks, and he is quick to answer, "I'm trying to forget!"

Alcoholic wine is a sacrilege on the sacrament. It turns the chalice into a kind of hypodermic needle squirt. It turns the cup of remembrance into an opium pipe.

Unfortunately, this kind of rhetoric seems to champion the day and fermented wine is declared an unsuitable representation of Christ's precious blood. It takes courage (and a healthy dose of madness) to dispute the biblical parallel instituted by Christ Himself. It is reminiscent of Peter's stinging rebuke of our Lord for His plan to enter Jerusalem and sacrifice His life. Poor Jesus, He can't even please the prohibitionists as they slap Him on the wrist for using wine to represent the New Covenant in His blood.

The fact that wine (*oinos*) is not used in this passage brings prohibitionists great comfort. Much is made of the phrase "fruit of the vine." The argument goes something like this: Instead of using the typical word for wine (*oinos*), Matthew, Mark, Luke, and even I Corinthians use the phrase "fruit of the vine." This indicates that fermented wine is not in the Passover cup. Had fermented wine actually been in the cup, the word *oinos* would have been used.

This reads far too much into the phrase since the "fruit of the vine" is merely another way of saying fermented wine. It is a figure of speech. If "fruit of the vine" is taken literally it refers to grapes in a cup, not a beverage. The fruit of the vine is literally a solid grape, not juice. But the cup isn't filled with plump, freshly picked grapes; it is filled with the end result of ubiquitous wine presses throughout the land producing the common drink of the day.

Under the heading of "Wine," in *A Religious Encyclopedia of Biblical, Historical, Doctrinal and Practical Theology*, Dunlop Moore writes:

> The fruit of the vine is literally the grape. But the Jews from time immemorial have used this phrase to designate the wine partaken of on sacred occasions, as at the Passover and on the evening of the Sabbath. The Mishna (De. Bened, cap. 6, pars I) expressly states, that, in pronouncing blessings, "the fruit of the vine" is the consecrated expression for yayin . . . The Christian Fathers, as well as the Jewish rabbis, have understood "the fruit of the vine" to mean wine in the proper sense. Our Lord, in instituting the Supper after the Passover, availed himself of the expression invariably employed by his countrymen in speaking of the wine of the Passover. On other occasions, when employing the language of common life, he calls wine by its ordinary name.[18]

A different author offers a similar perspective:

> The "fruit of the vine" has from ancient times been a technical term for the wine drunk by Jews on such solemn occasions as the Passover and the evening of the Sabbath. This custom certainly goes back to the time of the Mishnah. In the tractate containing specific formulas for various types of blessings the rabbis answer the question "What blessing do they say over fruits?" in these words: "Over the fruit of trees a man says, 'Blessed art thou, O Lord, our God, King of the Universe, who creates the fruit of the tree; except over wine, for over wine a man says, 'Blessed art thou, O Lord, our God, King of the Universe, who creates the fruit of the vine'" (Berakoth 6:1). Incidentally, the Jewish prayer book still gives this blessing in Hebrew as the benediction to be recited, and I quote, "before drinking wine."[19]

The "fruit of the vine" is known to refer to wine as "The Greeks also used the term as a synonym of wine which was capable of producing intoxication (Herod I. 211, 212)."[20] The Passover is a celebration and remembrance of a time when the angel of death "passed over" the first-born Hebrew children—the final plague inaugurating release from Egyptian bondage. During Jesus' day, the Passover looked something like this:

> The household was seated around the table and after a blessing had been asked on the feast, the first cup of wine was emptied. Then the father or head of the group would retell the story of the Passover (sometimes in response to the question of the eldest son—Exodus 12:26ff). Then there would be household singing of Psalms 113–114. A second cup of wine was then emptied, to be followed by the actual Passover lamb. When the meal was over, a third cup of wine was drunk. This was most likely the time that Jesus inaugurated the Lord's Supper. After another cup of wine was drunk and Psalms 115–118 were sung, the feast officially ended.[21]

Leaven is not to be eaten or allowed in the house according to Passover requirements (Ex. 12:19–20). The work of leaven in bread is a timely process, whereas the Hebrews were in haste to leave Egypt. The hurried pace reflects the alacrity of their deliverance from Egyptian bondage. The Passover meal, according to Exodus 12:11, was eaten with belts fastened, sandals on feet, and staff in hand. Because fermented wine contains yeast or leaven, some argue that wine is precluded from use during the Passover meal.

The staunch prohibitionist Stephen Reynolds admits, "A modern Jewish Rabbi had advised me that modern Jews make a distinction between ferment, which is permitted at Passover, and leaven, which is not."[22]

If the Jews of Jesus' time knew of this prohibition of ordinary wine during this period, it seems strange that the Mishnah in its six thousand words of directions for the observance of the Passover should contain no allusion whatsoever to it," and "the first evening of the Paschal feast . . . was also invested with peculiar importance . . . It became either a law or a custom to drink four glasses of wine upon this festival of rejoicing.[23]

Notice how Joel McDurmon describes the symbol of the New Covenant as being *in the cup* during the Last Supper:[24]

> Jesus gave us the meal as a New Covenant meal. And He specifically said the covenant was in the cup—not bread, or meat, or water, or anything else, but the cup which He held. It contained "the fruit of the vine"—that is, wine. This wine was "the new covenant in my blood." This is to say, the cup was a new version of the old Ark of the Covenant. Instead of the blood of animals being poured on it, it had the symbol of Christ's blood poured into it—wine. Wine was, therefore, the key symbol for the covenant, a key to understanding the kingdom.
>
> As Passover was eaten in haste with no time for leavened bread, there certainly was no place for fermentation which takes even longer. Wine, therefore—which required lengthy fermentation—is a symbol of stability, patience, endurance, perfection. These are the attributes of a long term Kingdom, not people in a transition of flux.
>
> As a regular covenant meal, the wine of Communion reminds us of God's eternal kingdom. We have not yet arrived at its fullness, but we are given a foretaste of it in the glass of wine.
>
> When Jesus switched the emphasis of the Passover meal, he was saying, "Things have changed." From now on, the focus is not on the types and shadows of God's kingdom, but about the actual arrival of it. From now on, prepare to live life in God's kingdom.

Some contend that we are asked to *remember* at the Last Supper, whereas alcohol is utilized by many to *forget*.

> The unbeliever uses wine to drown his misery, to forget his fellows, and to forget his Creator. Dr. Cornelius Van Til once said that if the unbeliever had the opportunity to forget God altogether by simply pushing a button, he would not hesitate to do so. Wine is often the unbeliever's button. And in

many cases (where wine has enslaved the unbeliever altogether), he not only drinks to forget God, but to forget that he drinks![25]

Some may abuse alcohol to drown their sorrows, but that doesn't mean *we* have to, or that Jesus can't use the good gift of God simply because some have maltreated its true intention. If Jesus is unable to use wine at the Last Supper because some abuse alcohol, then He cannot use bread to represent His body either, for some eat in excess leading to gluttony. We live life according to God's purposes and intention, not how others abuse them.

What does it mean to "remember" Him in drinking the cup and eating the bread? While theological understandings of communion may vary by denomination, at the very least, it is more than merely recalling facts or remembering a past event—Jesus' sacrificial death. During Veteran's Day, for instance, we recall historical events and people in our past, but we also remember in a way that values the significance, sacrifice, and love of the relationship we experienced.

Similarly, when we partake of the cup and the bread, the very act is a moment of recalling, but it is more than that. With grateful hearts we appreciate and value Christ's love for us, the significance of His sacrificial death, and remind ourselves to imitate our Lord's selfless service to others. The best remembering is a life lived for Him. By remembering, we affirm our commitment and look forward to eating and drinking with Him in the future kingdom. Wine, God's good gift to us, is an entirely appropriate symbol for the precious blood of Christ. Jesus and His disciples celebrated the Last Supper together with wine, and with wine we shall celebrate our future kingdom reunion. After all, "Is not the cup of blessing which we bless a sharing in the blood of Christ?" (1 Cor. 10:16).

Some believe the wine in the New Testament and at the Last Supper is a watered-down wine. One of my former New Testament seminary professors wrote an article supporting this view. Though not a proponent of the grape juice theory, he believes the wine we drink today is different from the past and references Homer's *Odyssey* (IX, 208f.) where wine is mixed with a 20 to 1 ratio (20 parts water and 1 part wine).[26] Famous pastor John MacArthur "contends that the wine of biblical days was between 2.25 percent and 2.75 percent alcohol and that 'Even the more civilized pagans of Bible times would have considered the drinking of modern wines to be barbaric and irresponsible.'"[27] But these views are inaccurate:[28]

> Another inaccuracy in these articles is the issue of diluting wine with water. Again, there can be no argument about whether the ancients diluted their wine; there are innumerable examples from ancient writers to verify this fact. The problem is one of emphasis and implication.

There are a few problems with this citation [*Homer's Odyssey*]: first, the characters in Homer's narrative begin by drinking the wine unmixed, then (apparently to make it last longer) they begin diluting it with increasingly greater volumes of water until they reach 20:1. Homer's point in this narrative was that Maronean wine was so robust that it never lost it's flavor! It could also be that by the time they were drinking at 20:1 they were so drunk that they could not taste/notice the dilution (cf. John 2:10). But, there is a second problem: this citation from Homer is like using *The RugRats* as a research tool for understanding toddlers. Homer was the *Star Trek* of the ancient world! Both Pliny and Plato refer to the "legendary" aspects of Homer's wine.[12] Listen to Plato on Homer,

We may assume, then, that all the poets from Homer downwards have no grasp of reality but merely give us superficial representation of any subject they treat.[13]

...to suggest Homer's 20:1 is ridiculous and to put forth Pliny's 8:1 as normal would also be wrong. A 2:1 or 3:1 ratio was not unusual. But it must be remembered that the juice of grapes, under natural circumstances, will have an alcoholic content of 10–17%, thus even a 3:1 ratio would yield a drink of 3–5%, which is similar to an average American beer. The wine in the ancient world was most likely stronger (in flavor, not necessarily alcoholic content) than modern wines to withstand such a dilution. No modern wine could withstand dilution with three parts water. It would taste, well, watered down.

Another author has this to say about mixing water with wine:[29]

While it is true that the ancient Church sometimes mixed a little water with wine (Prov. 9:2,5)—probably to make a good wine "stretch further" and to provide a better refreshment during a scorching day—this was not done because of prohibitionist sympathies, nor to adulterate God's gift, which would have been theft (Isaiah 1:22), much less because drinking the pure fermented juice of the grape was barbarous. Some of the Church Fathers even mixed a little water with the wine for christologocial reasons, that is, the convergence of water with the wine symbolized the union of Christ's human nature with his divine nature. What is more, water was never mixed with "strong drink" (*shekar*) because the "strong drink" God's people were encouraged to receive would cease to be strong.

For the sake of argument, let's say the alcoholic content of wine in ancient days is less than modern-day content, maybe 3%, 5%, 8%, or 10%. What does this prove? The wine still contains alcohol. The biblical warnings and examples of drunkenness aren't suddenly nullified. The biblical teaching on alcohol is not conditioned upon the strength of the beverage. Would it be okay to drink fermented wine at 3% but not at 10%? "By making it a question of quantity instead of quality, the only difference is the size of the glass."[30] Alcohol is permitted as a good gift from God whatever its alcoholic content happens to be, as long as the line into inebriation is not crossed. The limitation is inebriation, not alcoholic content. The Bible recognizes wine (*yayin*) and strong drink (*shekar*) as a blessing from God. Both can be joyfully consumed without leading to drunkenness.

Whatever its alcoholic strength, we know that some Corinthian believers cross the line into inebriation while drinking wine at the Lord's Supper (1 Cor. 11:20–22). Yet, Paul doesn't command them to abstain from wine, but to do their eating and drinking at home "Do you not have houses in which to eat and drink?" (1 Cor. 11:22). Celebrating the Lord's Supper is a time for remembering and examining oneself, not stuffing your belly and drinking to excess. When Jesus lifts the cup as a symbol of the New Covenant, we are confident that the "fruit of the vine" is indeed fermented wine.

The Crucifixion

Wine is present even in the crucifixion narrative. Jesus is offered wine on two occasions during the ordeal. On the first occasion, He refuses the wine mixed with myrrh or gall. Later, with little life left in Him, Jesus thirsts and sour wine is offered to Him, of which He partakes.

> Mark 15:22–23
> Then they brought Him to the place Golgotha, which is translated, Place of a Skull. They tried to give Him wine mixed with myrrh; but He did not take it.

> Matthew 27:34
> And when they came to a place called Golgotha, which means Place of a Skull, they gave Him wine to drink mixed with gall; and after tasting it, He was unwilling to drink.

> John 19:28–30
> After this, Jesus, knowing that all things had already been accomplished, to fulfill the Scripture, said, "I am thirsty." A jar full of sour wine was standing there; so they put a sponge full of the sour wine upon a branch of hyssop and brought it up to His mouth. Therefore when Jesus had received the sour wine, He said, "It is finished!" And He bowed His head and gave up His spirit.

Wine laced with myrrh and gall acts as a narcotic to dull the pain of execution. Whether the offer of spiced wine arises from a common merciful Roman practice or is merely another derision by soldiers who previously whip Him, fight over His clothing, and mockingly place a crown of thorns upon His head is up for debate.

Upon tasting the spiced drink, Jesus knows exactly what it is and refuses it. Apparently, He desires to fulfill the Father's divine plan without the help of pain killers. Prohibitionists, however, interpret Jesus' refusal to drink this mixed wine as proof of His rejection of all alcohol. Jesus is viewed as a High Priest who is forbidden to drink alcohol while performing priestly duties and He "refused both as Priest and as an Israelite to drink the Intoxicant offered to Him."[31]

Jesus isn't from the tribe of Levi, from which priests are required to originate. He is, instead, from the tribe of Judah. Jesus isn't fulfilling temple duties prescribed by the Old Testament and is not seen as a priest by His contemporaries. Instead, He is viewed as the promised Messiah. The long-awaited Messiah offers a sacrifice, but not one of bulls, goats, or birds. He sacrifices Himself, which no priest in the Old Testament ever did. Jesus' death becomes the consummate, ultimate, once-for-all sacrifice the Old Testament sacrificial system points toward (Heb. 10). He is the fulfillment of the Old Testament: "Do not think that I came to abolish the Law or the Prophets; I did not come to abolish but to fulfill" (Mt. 5:17). John the Baptist recognizes Him as the sinless, sacrificial Lamb of God, "The next day he saw Jesus coming to him and said, 'Behold, the Lamb of God who takes away the sin of the world!'" (Jn. 1:29).

Jesus isn't against alcohol, for He produces fermented wine with His first miracle, institutes it as a symbol of the New Covenant in His blood, and refers to wine and vineyards in His teaching parables. He refuses laced wine not because He abhors alcohol or is fulfilling an obligation *not* to drink; He refuses the narcotic because He doesn't want His senses dulled in any way during this momentous event. To suggest that we must abstain from wine because Jesus refuses this medicinal gesture implies that we must also abstain from modern-day pain killers.

Jesus appears to drink the second wine offered to Him, sour wine, in fulfillment of Scripture. If Jesus has any obligation at all, it is to drink wine in fulfillment of Scripture.

> When our Lord suffered his death on the cross, he was offered two wines. The first he refused—it being a drug that would deaden his pain and make him less conscious of his redeeming work. But the sour wine or vinegar was received by Christ. According to Eerdman's *The New Bible Dictionary*, the posca of the Romans was an acidic wine and formed part of the soldier's rations. "It was this which was offered to the crucified Christ as refreshment ... and was different from the myrrh-flavored anodyne which he had refused earlier ..."[32]

In His dehydrated state, Jesus says, "I am thirsty," and receives sour wine. Wine vinegar is fermented wine made from grape juice and yeast. That Jesus "received" this sour wine is the closest we come to an outright verse indicating that a beverage touches His lips, and it happens to contain alcohol.

> The "sour wine" here is essentially vinegar—wine that has been exposed to oxygen too long and has soured.
>
> We are told specifically that Jesus received some of it, and that He did so in order to fulfill the Scriptures—in other words, to fulfill prophecy.[33]

The two prophecies referring to His thirsting and the giving of sour wine include Psalm 22:15 and Psalm 69:20–21:

> Psalm 22:15
> My strength is dried up like a potsherd,
> And my tongue cleaves to my jaws;
> And You lay me in the dust of death.

> Psalm 69:20–21
> Reproach has broken my heart and I am so sick.
> And I looked for sympathy, but there was none,
> And for comforters, but I found none.
> They also gave me gall for my food
> And for my thirst they gave me vinegar to drink.

Jesus not only produces fermented wine for a wedding celebration, He also commands His disciples to drink the Passover wine instituted as a symbol of the New Covenant in His blood. Even in His final hours, we find Him drinking a fermented beverage to fulfill Scripture:

> While Jesus was clearly not drinking for pleasure here, it is interesting that in this only explicit reference to Jesus drinking anything in Scripture, that drink is alcoholic. And in this instance, it was mandatory that He drink it, so that prophecy could be fulfilled.[34]

The Teaching of Jesus

Jesus also references wine and vineyard images in His teaching ministry. Our purpose here is not to exegete those teaching passages, but to identify them as notable elements in Christ's didactic word choices.

Parable of the Landowner

A vineyard owner builds a wall and tower to protect his winepress and vineyard in Matthew 21:33–46. He hires vine-growers to oversee the vineyard and when harvest time arrives, servants are dispatched to gather the produce. After several attempts to secure his crop, the owner finally sends his own son, but the vine-growers kill him. The vineyard owner is the Heavenly Father and His son is Jesus, the stone which the builders rejected. The chief priests and Pharisees realize the parable is about their rejection of Him and would have seized Jesus had it not been for the crowd believing Him to be a prophet.

> Listen to another parable. There was a landowner who PLANTED A VINEYARD AND PUT A WALL AROUND IT AND DUG A WINE PRESS IN IT, AND BUILT A TOWER, and rented it out to vine-growers and went on a journey. When the harvest time approached, he sent his slaves to the vine-growers to receive his produce. The vine-growers took his slaves and beat one, and killed another, and stoned a third. Again he sent another group of slaves larger than the first; and they did the same thing to them. But afterward he sent his son to them, saying, "They will respect my son." But when the vine-growers saw the son, they said among themselves, "This is the heir; come, let us kill him and seize his inheritance." They took him, and threw him out of the vineyard and killed him. Therefore when the owner of the vineyard comes, what will he do to those vine-growers? They said to Him, "He will bring those wretches to a wretched end, and will rent out the vineyard to other vine-growers who will pay him the proceeds at the proper seasons."
>
> Jesus said to them, "Did you never read in the Scriptures,
>
> 'The stone which the builders rejected,
> This became the chief corner stone;
> This came about from the Lord,
> And it is marvelous in our eyes'?
>
> Therefore I say to you, the kingdom of God will be taken away from you and given to a people, producing the fruit of it. And he who falls on this stone will be broken to pieces; but on whomever it falls, it will scatter him like dust.
>
> When the chief priests and the Pharisees heard His parables, they understood that He was speaking about them. When they sought to seize Him, they feared the people, because they considered Him to be a prophet.

Vineyards grace the landscape of Palestine, and wine production is commonplace. A vineyard parable is something everyone understands, since wine is the prevailing drink of the day. Vineyards are worth protecting as seen in the building of a wall and tower. The necessary winepress is present, as well as workers to tend the vineyard. God is the owner of the vineyard who expects produce from the harvest.

Ready for His Coming

Jesus teaches His disciples to live in readiness for His coming (Lk. 12:35–48). The disciples want to know if He is addressing the parable to them. He responds by indicating that those who are faithful at His return are blessed. He contrasts a faithful servant with one not anticipating his master's return. Instead of being faithful, the unwise servant drinks toward drunkenness and irresponsibility. Both servants know what the master requires of them, but only one is faithful. Punishment awaits the irresponsible, drunken servant.

> Be dressed in readiness, and keep your lamps lit. Be like men who are waiting for their master when he returns from the wedding feast, so that they may immediately open the door to him when he comes and knocks. Blessed are those slaves whom the master will find on the alert when he comes; truly I say to you, that he will gird himself to serve, and have them recline at the table, and will come up and wait on them. Whether he comes in the second watch, or even in the third, and finds them so, blessed are those slaves.

> But be sure of this, that if the head of the house had known at what hour the thief was coming, he would not have allowed his house to be broken into. You too, be ready; for the Son of Man is coming at an hour that you do not expect.

> Peter said, "Lord, are You addressing this parable to us, or to everyone else as well?" And the Lord said, "Who then is the faithful and sensible steward, whom his master will put in charge of his servants, to give them their rations at the proper time? Blessed is that slave whom his master finds so doing when he comes. Truly I say to you that he will put him in charge of all his possessions. But if that slave says in his heart, 'My master will be a long time in coming,' and begins to beat the slaves, both men and women, and to eat and drink and get drunk; the master of that slave will come on a day when he does not expect him and at an hour he does not know, and will cut him in pieces, and assign him a place with the unbelievers. And that slave who knew his master's will and did not get ready or act in accord with his will, will receive many lashes, but the one who did not know it, and committed deeds worthy of a flogging, will receive but few. From everyone who has been given much, much will be required; and to whom they entrusted much, of him they will ask all the more."

Future Kingdom Wine

In the Last Supper accounts found in Matthew, Mark, and Luke, Jesus specifies that He will not drink wine again until He does so with His disciples in the future kingdom. The same wine He commands His disciples to drink at the Last Supper and institutes as a symbol of the New Covenant in His blood is the same wine He will partake of with joy and celebration in the future kingdom with His followers. Matthew 26:26–29 says,

> While they were eating, Jesus took some bread, and after a blessing, He broke it and gave it to the disciples, and said, "Take, eat; this is My body." And when He had taken a cup and given thanks, He gave it to them, saying, "Drink from it, all of you; for this is My blood of the covenant, which is poured out for many for forgiveness of sins. But I say to you, I will not drink of this fruit of the vine from now on until that day when I drink it new with you in My Father's kingdom."

Laborers in the Vineyard

In Matthew 20:1–16, Jesus compares the kingdom of heaven to a landowner hiring laborers for his vineyard. Some laborers are hired early in the morning and others late in the day. When time for compensation arrives, the landowner pays them all the same amount, even those who arrive late in the day. Dissension surfaces with the early workers at the perceived injustice, since they have been working longer. But God can do what He desires with what He owns, and pays them the agreed-upon wage. Are they jealous of His generosity? In God's kingdom, the last shall be first and the first shall be last. Though the parable isn't particularly about wine, it is yet another occasion in which vineyard images are used in Jesus' teaching ministry.

> For the kingdom of heaven is like a landowner who went out early in the morning to hire laborers for his vineyard. When he had agreed with the laborers for a denarius for the day, he sent them into his vineyard. And he went out about the third hour and saw others standing idle in the market place; and to those he said, "You also go into the vineyard, and whatever is right I will give you." And so they went. Again he went out about the sixth and the ninth hour, and did the same thing. And about the eleventh hour he went out and found others standing around; and he said to them, "Why have you been standing here idle all day long?" They said to him, "Because no one hired us." He said to them, "You go into the vineyard too."
>
> When evening came, the owner of the vineyard said to his foreman, "Call the laborers and pay them their wages, beginning with the last group to the first." When those hired about the eleventh hour came, each one received a denarius. When those hired first came, they thought that they would receive more; but each of them also received a denarius. When they received it, they grumbled at the landowner, saying, "These last men have worked only one hour, and you have made them equal to us who have borne the burden and the scorching heat of the day." But he answered and said to one of them, "Friend, I am doing you no wrong; did you not agree with me for a denarius? Take

what is yours and go, but I wish to give to this last man the same as to you. Is it not lawful for me to do what I wish with what is my own? Or is your eye envious because I am generous?" So the last shall be first, and the first last.

Vine and Branches

Jesus points out in John 15:1–11 that He is the true vine and the Heavenly Father is the vinedresser. Of all the things Jesus could have compared Himself with, He chooses vineyard metaphors. As branches connected to the vine, we are to produce fruit. In fact, it is by the production of fruit that we confirm our connection to the vine. Once again, Jesus selects familiar images (grapes, vineyards, vine, vinedresser) for instructional purposes.

> I am the true vine, and My Father is the vinedresser. Every branch in Me that does not bear fruit, He takes away; and every branch that bears fruit, He prunes it so that it may bear more fruit. You are already clean because of the word which I have spoken to you. Abide in Me, and I in you. As the branch cannot bear fruit of itself unless it abides in the vine, so neither can you unless you abide in Me. I am the vine, you are the branches; he who abides in Me and I in him, he bears much fruit, for apart from Me you can do nothing. If anyone does not abide in Me, he is thrown away as a branch and dries up; and they gather them, and cast them into the fire and they are burned. If you abide in Me, and My words abide in you, ask whatever you wish, and it will be done for you. My Father is glorified by this, that you bear much fruit, and so prove to be My disciples. Just as the Father has loved Me, I have also loved you; abide in My love. If you keep My commandments, you will abide in My love; just as I have kept My Father's commandments and abide in His love. These things I have spoken to you so that My joy may be in you, and that your joy may be made full.

Good Samaritan Parable

The Good Samaritan parable is found in Luke 10:30–37:

> Jesus replied and said, "A man was going down from Jerusalem to Jericho, and fell among robbers, and they stripped him and beat him, and went away leaving him half dead. And by chance a priest was going down on that road, and when he saw him, he passed by on the other side. Likewise a Levite also, when he came to the place and saw him, passed by on the other side. But a Samaritan, who was on a journey, came upon him; and when he saw him, he felt compassion, and came to him and bandaged up his wounds, pouring oil and wine on them; and he put him on his own beast, and brought him to an inn and took care of him. On the next day he took out two denarii and gave them to the innkeeper and said, 'Take care of him; and whatever more

you spend, when I return I will repay you." Which of these three do you think proved to be a neighbor to the man who fell into the robbers' hands?" And he said, "The one who showed mercy toward him." Then Jesus said to him, "Go and do the same."

Jesus points out that those who should have demonstrated both the compassion and capacity to help an injured man didn't lift a finger. Though they see the helpless stranger, they intentionally pass by on the other side of the road to avoid helping him. Yet, a lowly Samaritan feels compassion, bandages up his wounds, and pays for the injured man to receive a night of rest and recuperation. Wine is used medicinally by pouring it upon wounds as a disinfectant. Sugary grape juice isn't going to help, but the alcohol in wine serves as a disinfectant.

New Wine into Old Wineskins

Possibly the most famous of Jesus' statements about wine is found in Matthew 9:14–17 regarding new wine in old wineskins.

> Then the disciples of John came to Him, asking, "Why do we and the Pharisees fast, but Your disciples do not fast?" And Jesus said to them, "The attendants of the bridegroom cannot mourn as long as the bridegroom is with them, can they? But the days will come when the bridegroom is taken away from them, and then they will fast. But no one puts a patch of unshrunk cloth on an old garment; for the patch pulls away from the garment, and a worse tear results. Nor do people put new wine into old wineskins; otherwise the wineskins burst, and the wine pours out and the wineskins are ruined; but they put new wine into fresh wineskins, and both are preserved."

Various interpretations exist regarding the meaning of this parable. Is Jesus contrasting old ways with new ways, Old Testament law with New Testament grace, legalism of the Pharisees with the grace of Jesus, that Christianity is something Judaism cannot contain, or some other viewpoint? To pursue the meaning of the metaphor is beyond the scope of this book, although I do have an opinion on the matter. For our purposes, we are not so much interested in the meaning of the parable, but why old wineskins burst when new wine is put into them. Jesus is likely referring to the fermentation process.

As a master communicator, Jesus utilizes common and familiar metaphors that His audience easily grasps. We argue and deliberate over the concept of putting new wine into old wineskins, but His hearers readily understand exactly what He means.

The grape juice enthusiasts believe this passage supports their view:

> The passage can best be explained if it is understood that the new wine (*neos oinos*) is grape juice specially prepared not to ferment before being poured into the skins. Wine skins, either new or old, were not suitable for the fermentation process.[35]

> The only "new wine" which could be stored safely in new wineskins was unfermented must, after it had been filtered or boiled.[36]

This is a difficult text for prohibitionists to explain, but the issue can be summed up this way:

> It is agreed that "new wine" (onion neon) here means unfermented grape juice, or grape juice in which the process of fermentation is not completed. And the question to be answered is this: Was the "new wine" put into "new skins" because they, being air-tight, would prevent fermentation? Or was it put into them because they, being comparatively strong and elastic, could bear without bursting the pressure of fermentation? The former explanation is given by advocates of the theory of two wines; and the latter by the great body of interpreters hitherto.[37]

So why do old wineskins burst? According to prohibitionists, old wineskins previously housing fermented wine contain leftover ferment that adheres to the inside of the skin and initiates an unwanted fermentation process. Gases produced by fermentation bursts the old wineskins that are intended to hold only grape juice. According to this view, grape juice is placed in new wineskins in an effort to retard fermentation. Is this really what Jesus intends and what the people of Jesus' day would have understood?

> And there is not one of the authorities that uphold the use of "unfermented wine" but give directions as to the manner of keeping the juice of the grape sweet or unfermented. They all admit that something must be done to must or it will ferment and become wine.[38]

> The biblical mention of bursting wineskins (Matt 9:17; Mark 2:22; Luke 5:37) shows that gas-producing fermentation took place in the wines produced in Israel, a chemical action that began within a few hours after the pressing of the grapes. The juice usually had begun to ferment as it stood in the lower pressing vats but was soon poured into jars or into skins...Freshly made wine was put into new wineskins; old skins would burst under the pressure.[39]

When it is fresh, the skin stretches to a degree, but when it is old it becomes stiff and bursts quickly under pressure. People therefore never put new wine, which still ferments and causes pressure, into old, dried-out skins.[40]

With the lack of modern-day preservatives, refrigeration, and pasteurization, it would be nearly impossible to keep grape juice from fermenting, unless it was consumed very quickly after being pressed. Once exposed to the air, however, fermentation is a process to be stopped. Without contemporary preservation methods, merely filling a new wineskin with grape juice does nothing to prevent fermentation, for it is already too late; the juice has already been exposed to bacteria and yeast.

Rather than putting new wine into new wineskins to *prevent* grape juice from fermenting, a better understanding is that new wine is placed into new wineskins for the *very purpose* of fermentation. McDurmon says it well:[41]

> Notice in this passage that the word "wine" (oinos) itself was not sufficient for Jesus to make His point about non-fermented wine. He had to qualify it: new wine—the kind that is fresh-pressed and not yet fermented. And yet this new wine is specifically expected to become fermented: that is why the bottles (skins) are expected to expand. If old, already-stretched-out wineskins are subjected again to the expansion of the fermentation process, they will simply not hold out—they will burst. So, Jesus says, "new wine is put into fresh wineskins, and so both are preserved."
>
> So, new wine is fresh, awaiting fermentation, and old wine has completed the process of fermentation (the wineskins having expanded).
>
> With this in mind, it is interesting that in Luke's version of the same parable, Jesus adds the following statement: "and no one after drinking old wine desires new, for he says, 'The old is good'" (Luke 5:39). Could it really be that Jesus advocated what everyone else knew, and which they all took for granted—that old, fermented wine is "good"?
>
> And there is theology in this as well: this "good" that we taste in old wine is the same Greek word used to say "taste and see that the Lord is good" (Ps. 33:9; see 1 Pet. 2:3). This very goodness of God leads us to repentance (Rom. 2:4), and is itself a fruit of the Spirit we should manifest (Gal. 5:22). In other words, it does not just taste good, it is good.

With the peppering of vineyards along the countryside, Jesus makes a point of using metaphors people easily grasp. Everyone understands that if an unshrunk patch is put on an old garment, it eventually pulls away and a worse tear results. In like manner, old wineskins burst when new wine is placed in them because they lack the needed elasticity for the fermentation process. Job 32:18–20 notes the needed stretching of new wineskins:

> For I am full of words;
> The spirit within me constrains me.
> Behold, my belly is like unvented wine,
> Like new wineskins it is about to burst.
> Let me speak that I may get relief;
> Let me open my lips and answer.

Summary: Jesus makes wine, drinks wine, institutes wine as a symbol of the New Covenant in His blood, commands His disciples to drink wine, promises to drink it again in the future kingdom, and uses wine and vineyard images in His teaching ministry.

PERCEIVED PROBLEM PASSAGES

This chapter looks at several Scriptures purportedly prohibiting alcohol consumption. These passages are frequently championed by zealous, but uninformed opponents, to prove that God prohibits alcohol use. Upon closer examination, however, we discover the passages offer no support for the prohibition of alcohol.

This chapter focuses on oft-quoted Scripture passages allegedly supporting the belief that fermented drink is prohibited by God. Anything less than total abstinence is sacrilege. With a great deal of exegetical liberty, these passages are taken out of context and slaughtered on the altar of good intentions. Of course, without a context, the text merely becomes a pretext for predetermined conclusions. Key prohibitionist passages are examined with a view toward correctly understanding their context.[1]

Leviticus 10:8–11 Priests & Kings

The LORD then spoke to Aaron, saying, "Do not drink wine or strong drink, neither you nor your sons with you, when you come into the tent of meeting, so that you will not die—it is a perpetual statute throughout your generations—and so as to make a distinction between the holy and the profane, and between the unclean and the clean, and so as to teach the sons of Israel all the statutes which the LORD has spoken to them through Moses."

Prohibitionists believe we must abstain from wine or strong drink because we are called "kings and priests" in the New Testament (1 Pt. 2:5, 9; Rev. 1:6). Since "kings" were not allowed to drink in the Old Testament (Pr. 31:4–5), the abstention requirement remains the same for New Testament "kings." Because New Testament believers fall under the doctrine of the priesthood of all believers, they must also abstain from alcohol just like Old Testament priests.

These arguments, however, are extremely precarious.[2] First, Jesus Himself undermines this very argument as He drinks wine at the Last Supper and during His last hours on the cross. Second, Peter handpicks concepts originally designed for Old Testament followers of Yahweh and applies them to New Testament Christians in I Peter 2:9–10:

> But you are A CHOSEN RACE, A royal PRIESTHOOD, A HOLY NATION, A PEOPLE FOR God's OWN POSSESSION, so that you may proclaim the excellencies of Him who has called you out of darkness into His marvelous light; for you once were NOT A PEOPLE, but now you are THE PEOPLE OF GOD; you had NOT RECEIVED MERCY, but now you have RECEIVED MERCY.

In a similar vein, Exodus 19:5–6 says,

> Now then, if you will indeed obey My voice and keep My covenant, then you shall be My own possession among all the peoples, for all the earth is Mine; and you shall be to Me a kingdom of priests and a holy nation. These are the words that you shall speak to the sons of Israel.

The words "holy nation, chosen race, royal priesthood" exclusively applied to Old Testament Israel, but Peter notes that New Testament Christians (both Jew and Gentile) partake of the same status once reserved for Old Testament followers. It is interesting to note that this Old Testament "kingdom of priests and a holy nation" made wine, drank wine, sold wine, and utilized wine in religious offering and celebration. For them, wine is a good and gracious gift from God.

Third, limitations of priestly abstention are only in effect "when you come into the tent of meeting." The prohibition against kings imbibing is also limited: "It is not for kings to drink wine, or for rulers to desire strong drink, for they will drink and forget what is decreed, and pervert the rights of all the afflicted" (Pr. 31:4–5).

> The perversion of rights could only come about with official sanction, i.e. while acting magisterially or judicially. God prohibits wine-drinking in these limited contexts in order to prevent the frequent corruption of justice brought about by kings who function magisterially while intoxicated (Is. 28:7). Biblical law does not forbid wine to kings permanently and universally (Gen. 14:18–20).[3]

The limited abstention for priests only applies while they are engaged in priestly duties. Priests are permitted to drink when they aren't performing their official duties. The first century historian Josephus observes,

> ..."as for priests, [Moses] prescribed them a double degree of purity" (Antiquities 3:12:1). This special purity includes the following: "nor are they permitted to drink wine so long as they wear those garments" (Antiquities 3:12:2). The priests only wore their "sacerdotal garments" (Antiquities 3:12:2) while ministering—"when he enters the holy place" (Ex. 28:2-4,29), "when he goes in before the Lord" (Ex. 28:30), "when he ministers" (Ex. 28:35), "when they approach the altar to minister in the holy place" (Ex. 28:43).[4]

Nadab and Abihu offer strange fire before Yahweh in Leviticus 10:1, a fire He had not commanded. Careless in their service and lax in attentively following His commands, Nadab and Abihu forfeit their lives (Lev. 10:2–3). It is only after this incident that a prohibition against drinking wine or strong drink during formal service is enacted. Could it be that Nadab and Abihu are drunk when they offer strange fire to Yahweh? The Lord wants no more Nadab and Abihu incidents during times of holy service as Aaron and his descendants minister before Him. Since we are not sons of Aaron or in the Aaronic priesthood, this limited prohibition doesn't even apply to us today (Heb. 9–10).

Fourth, if it is true that we are priests of Aaronic order today and must abstain from all drink, how do we interpret New Testament passages allowing church elders to imbibe, as long as they are not addicted to alcohol (1 Tim. 3:3, 8; Titus 1:7)? Why doesn't Paul command Christians *not* to drink wine instead of commanding them not to be *drunk* on wine (Eph. 5:18)?

The "no-drink" proponents fail to adequately consider the context. This passage doesn't support total abstention at all times. The prohibition is limited to Aaron and his sons (Aaronic priesthood in the Old Testament), and only while they are serving the Lord in their official priestly capacity. Outside of drinking "while on the job," they are allowed to enjoy fermented beverages like everyone else. "In this passage a directive is given specifically to Aaron and his descendants not to consume wine or 'strong drink' before ministering at the tabernacle. This is a prohibition on alcohol at a specific time and for specific persons only."[5]

The Aaronic priesthood, Tent of Meeting, and Jerusalem Temple no longer exist. Since the context reveals a limited prohibition for a limited time to a limited group of persons during limited religious duties, we are not limited to the limiting prohibitions. I know, too many "limited" words in that last sentence, but it was purposeful—to help us understand that the priestly prohibition on alcohol during official service in the tabernacle has absolutely no bearing on us today.

Numbers 6:1–6 Nazarite Vows

> Again the Lord spoke to Moses, saying, "Speak to the sons of Israel and say to them, 'When a man or woman makes a special vow, the vow of a Nazarite, to dedicate himself to the Lord, he shall abstain from wine and strong drink; he shall drink no vinegar, whether made from wine or strong drink, nor shall he drink any grape juice nor eat fresh or dried grapes. All the days of his separation he shall not eat anything that is produced by the grape vine, from the seeds even to the skin. All the days of his vow of separation no razor shall pass over his head. He shall be holy until the days are fulfilled for which he separated himself to the Lord; he shall let the locks of hair on his head grow long. All the days of his separation to the Lord he shall not go near to a dead person.'"

While a Nazarite vow forbids the consumption of alcohol, it is not a generalized absolute prohibition for all persons at all times as some would have us believe. The context (which prohibitionists seem to conveniently overlook) clearly indicates to whom the restriction applies. Notice that abstaining from alcohol applies only "when a man or woman makes a special vow, the vow of a Nazarite, to dedicate himself to the Lord" (Num. 6:2). Once this public vow of separation is made before the Lord, individuals must provisionally refrain from alcohol, but when the temporary vow has been fulfilled, consumption may resume: "Then the priest shall wave them for a wave offering before the Lord. It is holy for the priest, together with the breast offered by waving and the thigh offered by lifting up; and afterward the Nazarite may drink wine" (Num. 6:20).

Not only do Nazarite vow-takers abstain from alcohol, they must also abstain from *anything* made from grapes "nor shall he drink any grape juice nor eat fresh or dried grapes. All the days of his separation he shall not eat anything that is produced by the grape vine, from the seeds even to the skin" (Num. 6:3–4). Vow-takers also abstain from cutting their hair (vs. 5) and coming in contact with a dead body (vs. 6). To view alcohol as a *permanent prohibition* in this context means that we must also permanently abstain from grape juice, fresh grapes, dried grapes, anything produced from the grape vine, its seed or skin, cutting our hair, and coming in contact with a dead body.

Nazarite vows are pledges of separation and dedication unto the Lord for a special, limited time. Once the time period passes and the vow is fulfilled, the temporary abstention from alcohol, grape juice, fresh grapes, dried grapes, anything produced from the grape vine, its seed or skin, cutting hair, and coming in contact with a dead body is lifted. This passage does bar drinking alcohol as prohibitionists trumpet, but the context clearly delineates the *temporary* nature of such restrictions.

Once the vow is completed, the prohibition is removed. Furthermore, we are no longer under the Old Covenant and its vows. "When He said, 'A new covenant,' He has made the first obsolete. But whatever is becoming obsolete and growing old is ready to disappear" (Heb. 8:13). If you lived under the Old Covenant in Old Testament times and voluntarily took a Nazarite vow, you were expected to abide by its restrictions until the vow was fulfilled, at which time the restrictions were lifted. This no longer applies to Christians living under the New Covenant.

Judges 13:3–5 Samson

> Then the angel of the LORD appeared to the woman and said to her, "Behold now, you are barren and have borne no children, but you shall conceive and give birth to a son. Now therefore, be careful not to drink wine or strong drink, nor eat any unclean thing. For behold, you shall conceive and give birth to a son, and no razor shall come upon his head, for the boy shall be a Nazarite to God from the womb; and he shall begin to deliver Israel from the hands of the Philistines."

By lifting the phrase "Now therefore, be careful not to drink wine or strong drink" from its context, this verse becomes the ideal ethic of what it means to be a really good Christian. Really good Christians don't drink—period. When verses are severed from their anchoring context, however, faulty interpretations freely surface. Would really good Christians abstain from eating "any unclean thing" also noted in this passage? We know what an "unclean thing" is for those under Old Covenant law (pig, rabbit, owl, camel, water creatures with no fins or scales, etc.), but what does an "unclean thing" mean for Christians living under the New Covenant where the law no longer applies?

By carefully examining the context, we discover that God's angel exclusively addresses Manoah's wife, who is barren. The angel announces wonderful news that she will indeed conceive and give birth to a long-awaited son, Samson. He is to be totally separated unto the Lord under a Nazarite vow for his entire life, per divine instructions. In this special instance, the length of his vow is from birth to death, reflecting the Lord's hand in healing a barren womb. According to the lifelong Nazarite vow, Samson is never to cut his hair (Num. 6:1–6). Finally, having grown into a strong and mature adult, Samson meets Delilah and after multiple attempts, she finally discovers the secret to his power. When she shaves off seven locks of his hair, Samson not only loses his strength but his lifelong Nazarite vow is broken (Judg. 16).

The angel of the Lord, in this context, addresses Manoah's barren wife regarding the birth of her son, Samson. Since she now conceives under the blessing of the Lord, Samson is to be under a perpetual Nazarite vow his entire life. This is not a *prescriptive* passage, that is, a command for all Christians at all times, but a narrow, limited directive for Samson during his lifetime.

Proverbs 20:1 Mocking & Brawling Potential
> Wine is a mocker, strong drink a brawler,
> And whoever is intoxicated by it is not wise.

Because wine is a mocker and strong drink a brawler, this verse is offered as proof that we must not consume alcohol. As discussed earlier in this book, just because good gifts from God *can* be abused or *are* abused doesn't mean the gift itself is corrupt. It is a mammoth mistake to equate the *abuse* of alcohol with the *use* of alcohol. This verse isn't commanding us to abstain from alcohol consumption; it is warning us of the dire consequences of *immoderate* use leading to intoxication. We know that alcohol abuse is in mind here because the phrase "and whoever is *intoxicated* by it is not wise" underscores the problem as one of excessive consumption.

That wine has the *potential* for intoxication is not in dispute any more than food has the potential for gluttony. Paul makes a similar claim in the New Testament when it comes to knowledge: "Knowledge makes arrogant, but love edifies" (I Cor. 8:1). We know that knowledge isn't intrinsically evil and doesn't necessarily make one arrogant, but it can. We don't encourage folks to avoid arrogance by pursuing ignorance and forfeiting the acquisition of knowledge in a quest for growth and maturity. But we do understand Paul's point, which is the same one being made in Proverbs 20:1. "The point of Proverbs is that wine has the *potential* to mock, just as the point of Paul is that knowledge has the potential to make 'arrogant.' Neither do all who partake of wine become 'mockers' or 'brawlers.'"[6]

This particular verse cannot be detached from the entirety of scriptural teaching on alcohol. As pointed out in previous chapters, the whole of Old Testament Scripture portrays wine as a good gift from God to His people—to make hearts happy. Just as knowledge has the potential to puff one up, so wine has the potential to become a mocker and brawler when excessively consumed.

Proverbs 21:17 Balance & Perspective
> He who loves pleasure will become a poor man;
> He who loves wine and oil will not become rich.

This is one of those "See, I told you so" verses for "no-drink" proponents. They look at the ills of society, gush over statistics on drunk driving and alcohol-related crimes, examine all sorts of cultural and sociological reports and boldly declare, "Look at how alcohol negatively affects society. See, I told you the Bible doesn't want us touching alcohol." I call this the Ida Syndrome (remember my friend from

Chapter 1?) where the actual consequences of abuse are used to condemn all use, even moderate use permitted by Scripture. All consumption is denied because of *some* abuse—see, I told you Christians should not drink!

Once again, context is waylaid by the ugly face of personal agenda. When pleasure is loved so much that everything else is placed on the back burner, that kind of singular focus impacts life. Always pursuing pleasure at the expense of responsible living is problematic. When all you want to do is play all day, it is easy to see how balanced perspective is lost and becoming poor is a real possibility. We see a loss of balance all the time in many different ways among many different people concerning many different items. It is a matter of perspective. The same thing can occur with an unrestrained thirst for alcohol.

I once pastored a church in Northern Minnesota where summertime outdoor living was nearly as popular as their beloved wintertime hockey. Surrounded by immense beauty, people addicted to walleye fishing are outdoors every chance they get. In fact, some slack on their jobs, neglect family responsibilities, and fudge on their obligations in order to fulfill their singular thirst for walleye fishing. Nothing wrong with walleye fishing in the land of ten thousand lakes (it is good eating by the way), but when it takes over your life, interferes with your work and marriage, you know you have a problem.

You get the drift of this passage. The proverb is addressing balance and perspective. Similarly, money is the root of all evil according to 1 Timothy 6:10, but we don't abstain from money, do we? Of course not, but we do maintain a healthy and proper perspective about it. This proverb warns against a love of "wine and oil" but we don't abstain from all oil, do we? Of course not, especially noting that oil is a gift from God (Ps. 104:15) and makes the heart glad (Prov. 27:9). The issue is one of perspective. When life lived without responsibility and balance is exchanged for the sole pursuit of pleasure (whatever that pleasure happens to be), everything else falls by the wayside except that which tickles our fancy. Elsewhere, this same concept is acknowledged:

> Proverbs 23:21
> For the heavy drinker and the glutton will come to poverty, and drowsiness will clothe one with rags.

> Isaiah 5:11
> Woe to those who rise early in the morning that they may pursue strong drink, who stay up late in the evening that wine may inflame them!

The "I told you so" of Proverbs 21:17 is not "I told you this is what happens when alcohol is consumed," but rather "I told you this is what happens when you *abuse* alcohol and *thirst* for alcohol in a way that controls your life and takes away your perspective."

Proverbs 23:29–32 An Absolute Prohibition

> Who has woe? Who has sorrow?
> Who has contentions? Who has complaining?
> Who has wounds without cause?
> Who has redness of eyes?
> Those who linger long over wine,
> Those who go to taste mixed wine.
> Do not look on the wine when it is red,
> When it sparkles in the cup,
> When it goes down smoothly;
> At the last it bites like a serpent
> And stings like a viper.

If there is one passage of Scripture prohibitionists proudly parade through the town square, it is this one. Though seen as both solid support for their own view and the motherload of problems for moderationists, their parade is about to experience an early demise. Proverbs 23:29–31 is touted as an absolute prohibition against drinking alcohol. Did you get that—an *absolute prohibition!* Maybe this is their smoking gun, a dagger in the heart of alcohol consumption that lays the issue to rest for all generations. If you are tempted to believe Proverbs 23 nails the coffin of moderation shut, you are sorely mistaken. The only thing being placed in a grave is the dying theory that this passage absolutely prohibits the consumption of alcohol.

Dr. Samuele Bacchiocchi, a strong opponent of alcohol consumption states,

> Solomon...admonishes in a categorical way to refrain from even looking at wine: "Do not look at wine" (Prov. 23:31). The reason for this absolute prohibition is no doubt the fact that gazing at something attractive is the first step towards partaking of it.[7]

The purpose of one article by Dr. Stephen M. Reynolds, a prohibitionists of great repute, is to prove that Proverbs teaches an absolute prohibition against all alcohol use:[8]

> It is the intent of this essay to prove that Proverbs teaches an absolute prohibition against the beverage use of alcohol and that as soon as a Christian becomes convinced of this meaning he should abstain and not seek excuses for indulging his unnatural taste. He should not conceal the true reason for abstaining, as some are tempted to do in order to escape the scorn of drinkers, or to seek to win their favor.

Reynolds goes on to say the following:[9]

> We all know television commercials and magazine advertisements do their best to get everyone to look at beautiful representations of liquor and then drink the products so favorably shown. God says not to gaze at the sparkling stuff. This is the plain command! Bible believers ought to obey this command and not take the opposite course of saying that God has given it for us to enjoy. Ought we to let vipers bite us to enjoy the effect of their poison?

Finally, a staunch supporter of a Proverbs 23 "no-drink" stance is Peter Lumpkins:[10]

> Without the least hesitation . . . without doubt . . . without embarrassment whatsoever Solomon says this *yayin* is the substance whose presence only the fool would offer a glance toward. He plainly offers this bit of Inspired Wisdom, a divine call to holiness—"Look not thou upon the wine [*yayin*]." "Look not" is neither difficult to understand nor does it require special knowledge to grasp the meaning—Do not look on the *yayin*.
>
> Once again noticeably absent is the mention of moderately looking at the wine. Nor is the mention here of drinking but not being drunk. No limitation to a single glass of wine is instructed. No mention of quantity, measure, or amount. Yet some see the solution to be in the abuse of *yayin* and not the use of *yayin*. Does Solomon mention abusing the wine? Using the wine? Does he not clearly demand that people not even look on the *yayin*?

It is easy to understand the initial euphoria behind their parade; after all, Proverbs does say, "Do not look on the wine when it is red, when it sparkles in the cup." I can picture a gifted orator in front of television cameras wrenching this verse out of its contextual environment and spewing forth convicting rhetoric. As the saying goes, "This passage will preach."

Desirous of obeying Scripture and fearful of disappointing God, we fall prey to the preacher's sway, believing we can't even look at the stuff. To do so is absolutely sinful. But is this the heart of the passage? Is this really what Proverbs warns us of and asks us to do—not to look at a specific liquid? The passage may be good preaching, but it is better to ask if it is *accurate* preaching. This view, we will shortly see, is deficient and incorrect when considered in its context—something prohibitionists often downplay or conveniently ignore. Let's begin deconstructing this flawed approach to Proverbs 23.

Close Your Eyes

Alcohol is seen as so intrinsically evil that God instructs us not to even look at it. In parallel thought, Lot is also instructed not to look upon the wicked city of

Sodom as he flees impending doom (Gen. 19:17). That God asks individuals *not* to look at something is biblical, prohibitionists proclaim. Lot's instruction is an absolute prohibition against looking at Sodom, and in like manner God instructs us not to look upon alcoholic drink, or so the argument goes. Fermented wine "is not even to be looked at, no doubt because gazing at something attractive is a first step towards partaking."[11]

Is the one-time exclusion of looking back while fleeing Sodom's destruction the same as an alleged permanent prohibition against consuming alcohol? Is the issue really one of "looking" at alcohol? Can we not gaze upon *anything* beautiful for fear that we might somehow move toward partaking, even if that beautiful thing is from God and for our joy? This means that I won't be able to look at new Gibson guitar models or the latest lineup of Harley Davidson motorcycles. After all, I do find them attractive. In examining the context of Proverbs 23, we will see that much more is involved than merely "looking" at alcohol.

Here is what the account of Lot actually states in Genesis 19:15–22:

> When morning dawned, the angels urged Lot, saying, "Up, take your wife and your two daughters who are here, or you will be swept away in the punishment of the city." But he hesitated. So the men seized his hand and the hand of his wife and the hands of his two daughters, for the compassion of the Lord was upon him; and they brought him out, and put him outside the city. When they had brought them outside, one said, "Escape for your life! Do not look behind you, and do not stay anywhere in the valley; escape to the mountains, or you will be swept away." But Lot said to them, "Oh no, my lords! Now behold, your servant has found favor in your sight, and you have magnified your lovingkindness, which you have shown me by saving my life; but I cannot escape to the mountains, for the disaster will overtake me and I will die; now behold, this town is near enough to flee to, and it is small. Please, let me escape there (is it not small?) that my life may be saved." He said to him, "Behold, I grant you this request also, not to overthrow the town of which you have spoken. Hurry, escape there, for I cannot do anything until you arrive there." Therefore the name of the town was called Zoar.

Lot's do-not-look directive seems to be for the limited time of fleeing destruction. We discover just how wicked Sodom can be when two angels arrive in the city. Sitting at the entrance gate, Lot invites these two strangers to his house in a spirit of hospitality and protection. He knows wicked things may come upon them if they spend the night in the town square.

Later that evening, men from every part of town, both young and old, surround Lot's house seeking to have relations with the two men (angels) enjoying his gracious hospitality. The "relations" the crowd is seeking is not business relations, contract relations, sports relations, hospitality relations, social relations, spiritual relations, but sexual relations, for Lot even offers up his virgin daughters to no avail in Genesis 19:7–8:

> Please, my brothers, do not act wickedly. Now behold, I have two daughters who have not had relations with man; please let me bring them out to you, and do to them whatever you like; only do nothing to these men, inasmuch as they have come under the shelter of my roof.

Why a man would offer his virgin daughters to be raped by a crowd of evil men is an entirely different story, but it is an example of the crowd's dishonorable intentions and the debauched characteristic of the city for which God unleashes His wrath.

With one voice, the crowd rejects the two virgin daughters and are struck with blindness as they attempt to break down the door to Lot's house. As morning dawns, the angels "urged" Lot to quickly flee the city for it was about to be destroyed. He hesitates in Genesis 19:16 so the angels lead Lot and his wife outside the city. Noting the urgency of the situation, one of the angels remarks, "Escape for your life! Do not look behind you, and do not stay anywhere in the valley; escape to the mountains, or you will be swept away" (Gen. 19:17). Fearing that he will not make it to the mountain heights, Lot pleads for refuge in the small town of Zoar instead. His request is granted and the nearby town is spared from certain destruction.

Though commanded to flee the Lord's imminent judgment, Lot hesitated. There is no more room for delay of any sort, and time is of the essence. Lot needs to swiftly make his way to Zoar. He is not to look back, but move with haste in order that he may live. There is no time to watch the unfolding drama. Life is in the balance. The no-look-back prohibition isn't against *ever* looking at Sodom, for we know that Abraham himself looks back on Sodom and Gomorrah to view the resulting destruction in Genesis 19:27–28:

> Now Abraham arose early in the morning and went to the place where he had stood before the Lord; and he looked down toward Sodom and Gomorrah, and toward all the land of the valley, and he saw, and behold, the smoke of the land ascended like the smoke of a furnace.

Comparing Lot's no-look-back directive during Sodom's impending doom with the statement "do not look on the wine" is tremendously strained and compares apples with oranges. In Lot's case, looking back may have cost him his life as the urgency of safety necessitated expedient action. Proverbs isn't an absolute prohibition either, as we shall soon see.

The Color Red

Proverbs 23 instructs us not to look at wine "when it is red." Redness, the argument notes, is a sure indication that this is the bad kind of wine, the kind God absolutely forbids us to even look upon. The fermentation process is seen in the terms "red," "sparkling in the cup," and "goes down smoothly."

According to McDurmon, equating "red" with fermented wine and the fermentation process is based on the old King James version of this passage:[12]

> The common argument is based upon the King James Version: "Look not thou upon the wine when it is red, when it giveth his colour in the cup, when it moveth itself aright." The argument says that the wine here has changed color and is moving itself. The change in color is supposedly caused by fermentation, and in the process of fermentation wine releases bubbles … and could create a stirring within the vat. The wine thus "moves itself."

> Unfortunately, most of this is based on a poor translation. Admittedly, the Hebrew is difficult here (as poetry sections often are), but hardly any other English translation follows the erroneous King James on this passage. Here are just a couple of points at which it is really bad: the phrase "giveth his colour" literally means "gives its eye." The word for "eye" never refers to color in Hebrew. In this case it likely refers to something about wine in the glass that catches the eye. Almost all modern English translations call it "sparkle." The other bad phrase is "moveth itself aright." The modern English attempts are better: they almost all say something like, "goes down smoothly." Even the old Geneva Bible says "goeth down pleasantly," and this was translated fifty years before the King James.

> The better translation helps clarify the meaning. The wine is not moving itself in the sense that it is acting upon itself, stirring itself up. Rather, it is moving itself smoothly from the cup and down the throat. The redness, the sparkle, and the smoothness are not signifying that some change has taken place in the juice itself, but rather are the basic characteristics of wine that allure people who love wine.

That wine is red, sparkles, and goes down smoothly isn't describing the fermentation process (although the wine spoken of is indeed fermented); rather, it is simply describing the alluring *appearance* of wine to those who are ruled by it, lust for it, and relentlessly thirst for it. Even if "red" did refer to the fermentation process as some believe, a perspective of moderation is in no way undermined and the very context of Proverbs 23 destroys any hope of an absolute prohibition stance.

Nature of a Proverb

We have seen how prohibitionists downplay context, even when it so obviously undermines their position. Yet, Proverbs 23 is but another example of contextual separation skewing the passage toward a preferred interpretation.

Of first importance, it is essential to understand the nature of a proverb. The Bible contains various types of literary genres (poetic, historical, law, prophecy, apocalyptic, etc.). Interpreting poetry (Song of Solomon) is different than interpreting law (Deuteronomy), and we don't approach apocalyptic literature (Revelation) in the same way we approach historical passages (Joshua). Take note, the alleged absolute prohibition is a proverb.

"Proverbs and other proverbial literature are not absolutes. They are ancient 'sound bites,' not cohesive and complete arguments."[13] During a seminary class on wisdom literature, I raised this very point using Proverbs 22:6 as a case in point: "Train up a child in the way he should go, even when he is old he will not depart from it." I asked the professor if this was an absolute truth or a general rule of thumb. The class, of course, became a hotbed of strong opinions. I wanted to know exactly how to approach Proverbs; is it a book of absolute sayings or a book of inspired pithy truisms and sage advice for wise living?

Whenever a question like this is raised, one's commitment to God and scriptural veracity comes under attack. In my experience, some folks don't handle questions like this very well and refuse to adequately reason that an approach to wisdom literature like Proverbs might differ from an approach to the law in Deuteronomy. I once tried to engage a federal judge in a dialogue about the problem of evil and the nature of God, thinking that of all people, this adroit Christian man could handle such a difficult topic often brought up by nonbelievers in their consideration of Christianity. Though he allowed his brilliant mind to work wonders with complex legal theories, to my surprise, he was unwilling to think deeply about his faith. If we merely view the Bible as a manual of legislative rules to be blindly obeyed, we may miss the very heart of God and the deeper excavations of truth.

I am often asked if I take the Bible literally. Knowing there is often a polarizing agenda behind the inquiry, I ask clarifying questions and ensure that my answer contains something like, "I literally take a metaphor to be a metaphor, hyperbole to be hyperbole, and literal meanings literally, etc." I want to recognize that God uses various literary genres and writers across history to give us a picture of Himself and how we should live. If I interpret every word literally, there can be no poetry, no prophesy, no wisdom literature—for everything would have to be literal even when dealing with symbolism, hyperbole, poetry, and figures of speech.

When wine is spoken of as a mocker and strong drink a brawler (Prov. 20:1), we understand that wine doesn't literally mock and strong drink doesn't brawl; it is a substance that cannot speak or fight. Yet, if we interpret it literally that is how we must understand the phrase. Instead, we know this text is speaking about the behavior of the person drinking too much wine and strong drink, not the behavior of the liquid beverage itself.

If we took every word literally we could never reconcile God having nostrils, ears, eyes, hands, and arms, when in fact we are told He is a spirit. To be a spirit is by definition to be immaterial, yet we understand references to physical body parts as tools for describing Him in ways we can comprehend. The fancy theological term for this is anthropomorphism. But if every word must be taken literally, then God actually possesses these physical human features and is also an immaterial spirit, thereby placing us in a logical conundrum.

My point is that Proverbs is not a book of law, prophesy, history, narrative, etc., but a book of wisdom. A proverb is a short, pithy statement that reveals a pattern of wisdom and a way of life that is good for us and pleasing to God. Proverbs is not a collection of absolutes, for that would be an incorrect approach to interpreting the literary genre. Is it absolute that if you raise children in the way they should go that in the end, they will not depart from it? Absolutely? Absolutely always? Every time, with every child, in every circumstance? The obvious answer is "no" because we know of parents who raise their children right and in the end they don't turn back, unexpectedly die before turning back, or continue arrogantly defying God. It won't suffice to always blame parents when a child doesn't return, for sometimes parents do things right and the child remains rebellious. This doesn't mean God's Word is wrong, but that an inspired proverb is doing exactly what it is designed to do—provide pithy nuggets of wisdom.

As a truism, a general rule and saying of wisdom, it is *generally, most often* true that if you raise children with certain values, beliefs, morals, expectations, etc., they often make their way back to the strong moral teaching of their Christian parents, even though they may go their own way for a season. Not absolutely and in every instance, but generally. This isn't by any means a denial of the inspired Word of God, but an acknowledgement that proverbs are short, pithy statements and sayings inspired by God to provide wisdom, advice, and a pattern of living that is both wise and pleasing to Him, not absolutes with coherent, organized arguments. To say that Proverbs 23:29–31 is an absolute prohibition is a serious misunderstanding of the nature of a proverb and fails to recognize the proverbial context of the saying.

The Immediate Context

Pulling certain verses, phrases, or words from their immediate context is a sure sign that magic tricks are about to be performed, tricking us to watch the left hand while the right hand functions without scrutiny. However, an examination of the immediate context makes it abundantly clear that overindulgence is condemned here, not alcohol itself.

We can pull out "do not look on wine when it is red" as an absolute, but to do so not only defies the nature of a proverb, it also defies the immediate context addressing the one who lingers over wine and who, despite his pitiful condition, still seeks another drink:

> How could a context be any clearer? Here Proverbs specifically and carefully describes the person whom it admonishes. This person exhibits all the emotional, social, and physical characteristics of the drunkard: depression (v.29a), a contentious spirit (v. 29b), and telltale physical appearance (v. 29c). Here we have before our view those who "longer long over wine" (v. 30). These drunkards have developed alcohol-induced delusions (v. 33), disorientation (v. 34), and detachment (v. 35a,b). But despite all this, such an addict to wine refuses to give it up (v. 35c).[14]

The Surrounding Context

Moving from the narrow focus of verses 29–35 to the surrounding context of Proverbs 23, we discern that it is the drunkard and the immoderate use of alcohol that is being addressed, not an absolute prohibition against alcohol.

Proverbs 23: 20–21 helps us understand the "do not look" phrase of verse 31:

> Do not be with heavy drinkers of wine,
> Or with gluttonous eaters of meat;
> For the heavy drinker and the glutton will come to poverty,
> And drowsiness will clothe one with rags.

It is "heavy drinking" that is in mind. If verse 31 (do not look upon wine) is to be interpreted as an absolute prohibition, we must also interpret verses 4–5 in the same manner—prohibiting wealth:

> Proverbs 23:4–5
> Do not weary yourself to gain wealth,
> Cease from your consideration of it.
> When you set your eyes on it, it is gone.
> For wealth certainly makes itself wings
> Like an eagle that flies toward the heavens.

Gentry correctly understands this dilemma:[15]

> But this [Prov. 23:31] no more universally and absolutely prohibits wine drinking than verse 4 of the same chapter universally and absolutely forbids wealth accumulation . . . After all, the Lord grants his obedient people "the power to make wealth" (Deut. 8:18) and promises economic abundance for covenant faithfulness (Deut. 28:1:14; Gen. 13:2; Job 1:1–3). We must understand Proverbs 23:4 contextually. He warns against a wholesale thirst, a driving ambition to gain wealth, which is much like the alcoholic who gives his life over to a wholesale thirst for alcoholic drink.

Seeing the entirety of Proverbs 23 as the surrounding context for the "do not look" phrase, McDurmon identifies the theme of the chapter as the dangers of lust.[16] According to McDurmon, Proverbs enlightens us to the perils of following our foolish lusts while self-control and discipline lead us to wisdom and a life pleasing to God.

This theme is detected early in Proverbs 23:

> Proverbs 23:1–3
> When you sit down to dine with a ruler,
> Consider carefully what is before you,
> And put a knife to your throat
> If you are a man of great appetite.
> Do not desire his delicacies,
> For it is deceptive food.

> Proverbs 23:6–7
> Do not eat the bread of a selfish man,
> Or desire his delicacies;
> For as he thinks within himself, so he is.
> He says to you, "Eat and drink!"
> But his heart is not with you.

A man of "great appetite," or "given to appetite" as one Bible version puts it, becomes the basic theme of Proverbs 23:

> The key phrase here is "given to appetite." "Given" means completely given over to—totally invested in. The Hebrew literally means something closer to "ruled by appetite." This is not about the food and drink itself, it is about an absence of self-control. The situation here is a microcosm of human life: there are lusts to be avoided, for lusts pervert judgment and lead to destruction.[17]

> Notice that the Proverb does not forbid the "delicacies" or wine or meat altogether. It does not even condemn them in themselves at all. The warning, rather, is about two things: 1) an uncontrolled appetite, and 2) the evil intentions of the tempter. Be warned of both.[18]
>
> Now the entire chapter 23 goes on to elaborate this theme in many examples, highlighting different things upon which our lusts can focus. Without going through a complete exposition, here is the short version: beware of your soul being ruled by food (vv. 1-3, 6–7), riches and wealth (vv. 4–5), an audience (v. 9), envy (v. 17), sex (vv. 27–28), and finally, wine (vv. 29–35).[19]

Even with good gifts from God, Satan tempts us to move beyond clearly established boundaries so our insatiable and unrestrained thirsts control us. When this happens, we become men and women "given to appetite" rather than the things of God. Used properly, wine is a good gift from God that makes us merry, but for someone "given to appetite," whose ruling lust is excessive drinking, it is far better to not even look at the stuff if that's what it takes to withstand lust's alluring temptation. Jesus said something similar in Mark 9:43: "If your hand causes you to stumble, cut it off; it is better for you to enter life crippled, than, having your two hands, to go into hell, into the unquenchable fire."

If you have a problem, whether it is with alcohol, sex, money, etc., it is better for you to take great precautions than to succumb to its temptations. Do what it takes to avoid stumbling. As McDurmon aptly notes, "Once you embrace a life of self-control, you will be on the road to maturity. A mature Christian knows how to enjoy God's gifts without absolute fear of them, and yet also knows when and where to stop."[20]

The Greater Context

Moving from specific context to broader contexts, we now consider a global perspective involving Scripture in its entirety. In other words, the teaching on alcohol in Proverbs 23 must be interpreted in light of the biblical teaching on alcohol as a whole. If the rest of Scripture informs us that fermented beverage is a good gift from God for moderate consumption, do we now find an absolute prohibition nullifying the whole of Scripture? In light of the fact that both Old and New Testaments clearly teach that drunkenness crosses a line, should we interpret Proverbs to absolutely forbid *all use* of alcohol? Which view best fits Scripture as a whole?

Unfortunately, the Proverbs 23 firecracker turns out to be a dud. When the least bit of contextual analysis is applied to the "do not look" line of reasoning, the absolute prohibition stance crumbles like a stale cake donut.

Isaiah 5:21–22 Drinking Heroes
>Woe to those who are wise in their own eyes
>And clever in their own sight!
>Woe to those who are heroes in drinking wine
>And valiant men in mixing strong drink,

To be a hero in the drinking of wine and the mixing of strong drink is no compliment. In fact, it reminds me of a past schoolmate whose father was a well-known local attorney. After graduating from high school, my schoolmate attended the large state university and became a party animal, drinking excessively and acting foolish. He became a hero in drinking alcohol on the campus of a big-time university. What an accomplishment! The hero was eventually expelled—nothing at all to be proud of. He wasn't a moderate drinker by any means, but an abuser, someone "given to appetite" when it came to alcohol. He is a "hero" in a sarcastic sense.

This passage isn't condemning all alcohol consumption, and it isn't contradicting the whole of Scripture that permits the moderate use of fermented drink. Rather, it is a sarcastic condemnation of those who overindulge. According to Isaiah 5:11, this is exactly the kind of person the writer has in mind: "Woe to those who rise early in the morning that they may pursue strong drink, who stay up late in the evening that wine may inflame them!" These early rising heroes are further described in Isaiah 5 as men who . . .

>5:18 "drag iniquity with the cords of falsehood"
>5:20 "call evil good, and good evil"
>5:23 "justify the wicked for a bribe"

Isaiah 5 isn't prohibiting alcohol consumption, but condemning the kind of individuals who rise early in the morning to pursue their unwholesome appetite. It is also interesting to note the following:

>. . . we find these verses set in a larger judgment context, where the prophet condemns other normally acceptable practices. For instance, verse 8 calls down woe upon those who "join house to house." Is multiplying real estate holdings always sinful? In verse 12 we learn that the Jews are attending banquets where music is produced "by lyre and harp, tambourine and flute." Are public festivities involving music necessarily evil?[21]

Context and common sense often go together, and this passage is no exception.

Jeremiah 35:5–6 The Rechabites
>Then I set before the men of the house of the Rechabites pitchers full of wine and cups; and I said to them, "Drink wine!" But they said, "We will not drink

wine, for Jonadab the son of Rechab, our father, commanded us, saying, 'You shall not drink wine, you or your sons, forever.'"

These verses are viewed as further proof that alcohol is absolutely forbidden by God. But it is clear that no absolute prohibition exists when the verses are considered in their contextual environment. If this is a universal absolute prohibition on drinking wine, then we are also absolutely forbidden to also own houses:

Jeremiah 35:7–9
You shall not build a house, and you shall not sow seed and you shall not plant a vineyard or own one; but in tents you shall dwell all your days, that you may live many days in the land where you sojourn. We have obeyed the voice of Jonadab the son of Rechab, our father, in all that he commanded us, not to drink wine all our days, we, our wives, our sons or our daughters, nor to build ourselves houses to dwell in; and we do not have vineyard or field or seed.

There you have it—we are forbidden to drink alcohol and forbidden to build or live in houses. We must live in tents, even those Christians dwelling in Alaska or Siberia during the middle of winter. And why would we do this? Because we are to obey the voice of Jonadab, the son of Rechab. Do you see the issue here? Jonadab the son of Rechab is not our father, and we are not a Rechabite. This isn't a universal command by our Heavenly Father, but a specific Rechabite practice passed down from generation to generation through Jonadab's family. The decree to not drink wine and live in houses is Jonadab's call to Rechabites obeying their earthly father's voice, not God's call to Christians everywhere obeying their Heavenly Father's voice.

Universalizing for all people a specific and peculiar command to a few is a huge mistake. If we are allowed to universalize specific family practices, "we would all dedicate our children to temple service, as did Samuel's mother (1 Sam. 1:11, 20–22) and commit our children to Nazarite holiness, as did Samson's mother (Judg. 13:5)."[22]

This passage may also be a form of prophetic theater as noted by Gentry:

...this obligation swerves as a prophecy acted out against sinful conditions. For instance, Hosea lives out prophetic theater when God commands him to marry a harlot (Hos. 1:2, 3:1) as a symbolic portrayal of God's love for unfaithful, idolatrous Israel (Hos. 1:2, 4–11). Here in Jeremiah 35 the sons of Jonadab portray a spiritual truth by keeping this vow. By obeying this obviously unnecessary and unreasonable command of their father, they serve as a testimony against faithless Israel for her refusal to obey God's good and reasonable law (Jer. 35:12–19).[23]

Hosea 7:5 The Poison of Wine

> On the day of our king, the princes became sick with the heat of wine.

Some folks, like Dr. Stephen Reynolds, argue that the word "heat" should be translated "poison," turning the words "heat of wine" into "poison of wine." By translating the word as "poison," this verse is linked back to the viper's bite of Proverbs 23:32 which says of wine, "At the last it bites like a serpent, and stings like a viper." But, as Gentry points out, "though Reynolds prefers the translation 'poison,' no modern translation committee does. And for good reason: The context all around it crackles with flames."[24] The word "heat" is apropos for the context of Hosea 7:4–7 noting all of the terms associated with heat (bolded):

> They are all adulterers,
> Like an **oven heated** by the baker
> Who ceases to stir up the **fire**
> From the kneading of the dough until it is leavened.
> On the day of our king, the princes became sick with the **heat** of wine;
> He stretched out his hand with scoffers,
> For their hearts are like an **oven**
> As they approach their plotting;
> Their anger **smolders** all night,
> In the morning it **burns** like a **flaming fire**.
> All of them are **hot** like an **oven**,
> And they consume their rulers;
> All their kings have fallen.
> None of them calls on Me.

Gentry goes on to say of this passage,

> Furthermore, the imagery Hosea presents is of rulers who are drunk on wine. They are "sick with . . . wine," which is a familiar problem with those who drink too much of it (Is. 19:14; 28:8; Jer. 25:27; 48:26). This abuse of wine by men in positions of authority is a common problem that the prophets confront— and which explains Proverbs 31:4–5—as we may discern from several references (Is. 5:22–23; 19:14; 28:7; 56:12).[25]

Twisting Scripture so it says what we want it to say doesn't make it so, no matter what view we hold. After examining several passages allegedly deemed problematic for moderationists, we discover just how important context is to interpreting God's Word. It is easy to flippantly yank a verse from its contextual environment, quote it with great vigor, and offer it up as proof of argument. Without a context, however, it merely becomes a pretext for what we want it to say. This is an unacceptable practice in determining what the Bible actually says and means. Basic to Bible Interpretation 101 is the idea that context matters and is fundamental to a proper understanding of Scripture. It doesn't take a degree from MIT to figure this out. When these alleged problem passages are examined under contextual light, we discover what the Bible has said all along—that consuming alcohol in moderation is permitted while intoxication is condemned. There is no absolute prohibition of alcohol.

Summary: *Believing the Bible portrays alcohol as evil and absolutely forbids its consumption is a false conclusion and divorces specific verses from their contextual environment, for a text detached from its context becomes nothing but a pretext in support of a predetermined conclusion.*

ABSTINENCE IN THE BIBLE

This chapter examines alcohol abstinence in the Bible. Often elevated as sterling examples that all good Christians should emulate, we must ask if the examples are universal commands or limited to specific situations. This chapter explores whether abstinence is applicable for today.

To support their view, promoters of total abstinence confidently cite Bible passages where individuals abstain from consuming alcohol. Elevated to spiritual heights, they serve as sterling examples of how really good Christians should behave. It is true—abstinence does occur in the Bible, but not for the reasons many assume. In Scripture, abstaining from alcohol is the exception, not the norm. Abstinence never occurs as a universal and absolute decree from God for the ages. The Bible portrays wine and strong drink as the Heavenly Father's blessing, one of His many good gifts to be enjoyed in moderation. Abstinence, however, is limited in scope and always tied to contextual boundaries. Though some of this material occurs in previous pages, gathering abstinence passages into one chapter helps focus the issue and becomes a healthy reminder that scripture-twisting always undermines biblical truth.

We get our current bearings on how abstinence fits into the whole of Scripture from Whittington's study (previously discussed) of 247 Scriptural passages dealing with alcohol. We discover that of those 247 passages, 59% are positive references (145 out of 247), negative references account for 16% of the verses (40 out of 247), and 25% fall into the neutral category (62 out of 247).[1] This means that 84% of the references to wine and strong drink in the Bible are either positive or neutral. Of the sixty-two neutral references, twenty-one refer to vows of abstinence (both partial and total)—that's 8.5% of 247 passages. To counter this overwhelming positive portrayal of alcohol in Scripture, a convoluted and nonsensical two-wine theory is invented (debunked in Chapter 6), and now, prohibitionists desperately hoist limited instances of abstention upon a divine pedestal of model behavior. But abstaining from alcohol in limited cases for a limited time does not equate to the condemnation of all alcohol use, all the time.

Priestly Abstention During Service

Priestly abstentions are explained in the previous chapter, but the central passage is found in Leviticus 10:8–11 and later repeated in Ezekiel 44:21. Here are some key points to keep in mind regarding the priestly abstention:

1. The mandate to abstain from wine and strong drink comes only after Nadab and Abihu offer strange fire unto the Lord which He did not direct. Though no official reason is given for the abstention command, many scholars believe Nadab and Abihu were inebriated while ministering in the tabernacle, hence, the prohibition against drinking during tabernacle service.

2. The prohibition is only applicable during times of official service "when you come into the tent of meeting" and is not an absolute prohibition against consuming alcohol, for priests may imbibe when they are not engaged in solemn service (Num. 6:20).

3. The prohibition is limited to Aaron and his sons. The Aaronic priesthood no longer exists under the New Covenant and does not apply to Christians today.

Nazarite Vow of Separation

In addition to priests abstaining from wine and strong drink during times of official service, Israelites taking a vow of separation were called Nazarites, which means "consecrated" or "separated." This practice became known as the "Nazarite vow" or the "vow of a Nazarite." This is a vow of separation unto the Lord for a specific period of time—from one hour to a lifetime. Through a solemn dedicatory vow, the Nazarite "cut himself off from the normal ways of life by abstention from certain things, and so put himself at the disposal of the deity as a special instrument."[2]

Voluntarily choosing a Nazarite vow involves the following restrictions: 1) abstaining from anything made of grapes, including grape juice, wine, strong drink, dried grapes, its seed or skin, 2) abstaining from cutting one's hair, and 3) abstaining from contact with a dead body (Num. 6:1–6, 20; Judg. 13:5,7).

Prohibitionists often view the Nazarite vow as a mark of elevated holiness. According to one author, if we want to obtain the Lord's favor we must abstain from wine and strong drink like the Nazarites:

> Jeremiah's description of the Nazarites might fairly be used to describe these holy people. They "were purer than snow, whiter than milk, more ruddy in body than rubies" (Lam. 4:7). These people were all abstainers from intoxicating drink, and were in much favor with the Lord. Surely it is not possible that the Lord of life would cause all these people, who were the cream of society in that day in Jerusalem, to violate their consciences by forcing upon them the intoxicating cup.[3]

Not everyone in Israel adopts a Nazarite vow. In fact, it is the exception, rather than the norm. There is nothing wrong with abstaining from certain activities for a specified time as a means of focusing solely on the Lord. It is certainly not anti-biblical, but neither is it commanded or expected. These Old Testament restrictions only applied "when a man or woman makes a special vow, the vow of a Nazarite, to dedicate himself to the Lord" (Num. 6:2). If you choose a Nazarite vow, the restrictions apply. If you choose not to partake, the restrictions don't apply. It is a "vow of separation" for those Old Testament Israelites selecting participation (Num. 6:5). This is not a universal expectation for all believers, but a restriction upon Old Testament vow-takers.

Portraying Nazarites as shining examples of what it means to be exemplary Christians cannot be supported. If Jeremiah describes Nazarites as "purer than snow, whiter than milk, more ruddy in body than rubies" (Lam. 4:7) and this becomes the standard for genuine holiness, then must we also be white and ruddy? I guess that leaves out a whole lot of people who don't possess white skin and ruddy bodies. So much for diversity in the kingdom of God!

And why focus on only one aspect of the Nazarite vow? In other words, if we are to permanently abstain from wine and strong drink as prohibitionists indicate, would we also permanently abstain from all grape products, cutting our hair, and contact with dead bodies? This means we can't attend funerals, even if a loved one passes. "If the Nazarite rule is a rule that applies to New Testament believers, then surely the rule must stand as a whole. Yet the common practice is to arbitrarily select one aspect only, while ignoring the rest."[4] If this was a permanent and universal rule for all Christians, it is interesting that not everyone actually had the right to partake of a Nazarite vow and pursue elevated levels of holiness. "Women and slaves, who did not have full rights before the religious law, could take the

Nazarite vow, but only with the consent of their husbands or owners, while the vow was not valid among the heathen (Naz. iv. 1-5, ix. 1, *et passim*)."[5]

Notice that the Nazarite vow is one of separation and dedication. It is a voluntary abstention from the *normal* activities of life. The vow isn't a declaration against the items of abstention, for they are normal, typical, expected aspects of life. The reason for abstaining is not because wine, strong drink, short hair, or attending funerals is inherently evil; it is simply a means of denying some of the normal things of life for a time of purposefully focusing on the Lord. My point is that vow-takers are abstaining from approved, permitted, good things, not because they are evil, but because vow-takers want to make a noticeable separation unto the Lord.

When Old Testament Israelites, for various reasons, desired to voluntarily separate unto the Lord, there was a prescribed way to go about it so all would know of their intention. We are no longer under Old Testament law, and there is no rule or expectation for New Covenant Christians to abide by Old Testament prescriptions of the Nazarite vow.

Rechabite Family Vow

Displaying the Rechabite family's abstention as a universal moral example of our need to also abstain from alcohol is filled with so many holes it is like trying *not* to get wet when taking a shower. We discover the Rechabites in Jeremiah 35 and realize they are a devoted group of individuals—devoted to the wishes of their founding father's desire that they follow a certain way of life, which they did for nearly three hundred years after his death.

Jeremiah speaks highly of them but not for the reason many think. At a time when Jerusalem was under siege, a group of Rechabites enter the city. They are examples of staying true to the commands and ideals of Jonadab, their founder. Jeremiah invites the Rechabites into the house of the Lord and offers them wine to drink. Now keep in mind that this is the house of God and wine is present for drinking. At the command of the Lord, Jeremiah invites them to consume alcohol. The Rechabites decline the offer citing their loyalty to the cause and commands of Jonadab, their founding father. Their devotion and steadfast commitment is impressive, even to the Lord, and He uses them to make a point to faithless Israel.

God is not impressed that they refrain from drinking, farming, or living in houses, for Jonadab could have easily commanded that they not fight in war, abstain from eating meat, or refrain from participating in some social or cultural festival, etc. The issue really isn't about wine, farming, or living in houses; it is an issue of loyalty and obedience. This is seen in Jeremiah 35:13–13 when the Lord says,

> Will you not receive instruction by listening to My words? declares the LORD. The words of Jonadab the son of Rechab, which he commanded his sons not to drink wine, are observed. So they do not drink wine to this day, for they have obeyed their father's command. But I have spoken to you again and again; yet you have not listened to Me.

The Rechabites become an authentic example to Israel of loyalty and obedience to their founder at a time when Israel pays no attention to their own founder, Yahweh Himself.

Who were the Rechabites and why did their father, Jonadab, command abstention?

> Apparently they were a seminomadic group who lived in the Judean wilderness. They likely intended by their way of life to protest the corrupting influences of Canaanite life in Israel. They refused to live in houses, till the soil, plant vineyards, or drink wine. Such practices as these were regarded by the Rechabites as an accommodation to Canaanite sedentary civilization and thus a threat to the purity of Israel's ancestral faith as represented in the wilderness period. Although the group survived for more than 250 years, it was likely never large in numbers.[6]

Another author states it this way:

> Obviously, Jeremiah does not mean for his demand for Israelite imitation of the Rechabites to be all-inclusive, since elsewhere, in contradiction of their nomadic life, he advises Israelite captives in Babylon to build houses and settle down (29:5). Therefore, lest we want to expose ourselves to the charge of guilt by association, we had better go slow in our use of the Rechabites as a moral example. As a matter of fact, their prohibition of wine did not spring from moral considerations; their opposition to it did not even stem from intoxicating effects. They objected to it because, and only because, to them it symbolized a settled and civilized mode of life.... they abstained from the produce of the vine for the same reason they refused to build houses—as a protest against the agricultural civilization of the Canaanites. Anxious to restore the good old days and ways of their nomadic ancestors, they cultivated a rigorous type of sociological primitivism as a solemn reminder that they must never "get above their raisin'." They abstained from wine not so much because of its alcoholic contents as its agricultural connections. Therefore, unless we stand ready to refuse potatoes because they grow on the farm and tear down our houses in protest against civilization, maybe we

had better go slow in claiming spiritual kinship with the Rechabites because they practiced abstinence.[7]

Jeremiah's Rechabite example contrasts the faithfulness of a band of followers obeying their founding father without deviation, even when tempted to do so, against the faithless Israelites who disobey Yahweh at the drop of a dime. Yahweh is far greater than Jonadab, and yet it is the Rechabites who exemplify loyal obedience.

One final observation must be made regarding the nature of their abstinence:

> The real heroism of the Rechabites consisted not in their denying themselves sinful things; rather, they denied themselves what was, and still is, supremely good. Agriculture, houses, vineyards, and wine are things supremely good. John Calvin made a classic understatement, when he wrote "that the Rechabites obeyed the command of their father in not drinking wine: this is hard..."[8]

The purpose of this account in Jeremiah is not to prohibit the consumption of alcohol but to "show the amazing contrast between the faithfulness of the Rechabites in keeping an *unreasonable* commandment of an earthly father, while the Israelites disregarded the *reasonable* law of their Father in heaven (Jer. 35:16–19)."[9] The restrictions on alcohol, houses, and farming Jonadab passed down to his sons have no bearing upon Christians today.

Kingly Abstention While Officiating

According to Proverbs 31:4–5, kings should not drink wine or strong drink, "For they will drink and forget what is decreed, and pervert the rights of all the afflicted." This is not a universal, absolute prohibition wherever Christians reside and in whatever age they live. It is limited to kings who were the political and governmental rulers of their day.

The limitation is further restricted since it is only applicable during times of official activity. If the king consumes strong drink in his chambers at night, enjoys a glass of wine during a meal, or desires a drink while traveling, there is no restriction or prohibition. However, when making governmental or political decisions in his official capacity as king, wine is forbidden. The king could only "pervert the rights of all the afflicted" while functioning in an official capacity.

This limited abstention is much like the priestly abstinence—no alcohol while on the job. It makes sense. If one overindulges during magisterial duties, injustices can occur, rights can be affected, perceptions can be dulled, and judgments can be forgotten or skewed. To protect the rights of those coming before the king, alcohol consumption is forbidden.

Similar expectations are made of airline pilots, boat captains, train operators, etc. where judgments are so critical to the lives of others that drinking is strictly forbidden while on the job, not because alcohol is inherently evil, but because overindulgence can drastically affect the lives and rights of others. There is to be no chance of inebriation influencing the king during official duties where the lives and rights of others are so paramount. Drunkenness and overindulgence is always condemned in Scripture, whether on the job or not. This particular abstention is only in effect while kings engage in their official duties.

> The Scripture records occasions of kings becoming drunk and causing political catastrophes: Elah (1 Kin. 16:9) and Ben-hadad (1 Kin. 20:16). It warns of drunkenness among the leadership of Ephraim (Is. 28:1,3) and threatens drunkenness among the kings of Judah (Jer. 13:13) and of Babylon (Jer. 51:57). We also read of blessings upon kings not given to drunkenness: "Blessed are you, O land, whose king is of nobility and whose princes eat at the appropriate time—for strength, and not for drunkenness" (Eccl. 10:17). We should note that God does not send the blessing because of abstinence, but sobriety.[10]

No one should go to work wasted. Drunkenness in any vocation is wrong because the overindulgence of alcohol is wrong. This doesn't mean we cannot and should not *ever* drink alcohol, but that sobriety is positive and drunkenness is negative. To be inebriated while on the job endangers others. It is drunkenness that is condemned, not moderate consumption. However, if you were a priest or king in Old Testament days, you were prevented from drinking on the job in an effort to eliminate any possibility of overindulgence affecting temple service or political and governmental decisions. Consuming alcohol is permitted outside of official service.

Daniel, John the Baptist, and Paul

After Nebuchadnezzar captures Jerusalem, Daniel, known for his wisdom, is transported to Babylon to learn the literature, language, and culture of the Chaldeans. After three years of education, he will enter Nebuchadnezzar's personal service. During this time, "Daniel made up his mind that he would not defile himself with the king's choice food or with the wine which he drank; so he sought permission from the commander of the officials that he might not defile himself" (Dan. 1:8).

We are not told why Daniel feels the king's food and wine will defile him. There is no Old Testament law or practice dictating that captives cannot eat or enjoy their captor's food. But Daniel, as a wise and holy follower of Yahweh, realizes what has just occurred. A foreign king has just invaded Jerusalem, the city is fallen, and God's chosen people are captured and carted off to live and work in a distant city to serve a foreign king. The unthinkable happens, brought about by Israel's repeated and continual disobedience to Yahweh. They were warned of this day and instead of repenting and changing their ways, judgment arrives in the form of Nebuchadnezzar's invading army.

Since there is no law against eating the captor's food, the idea of Israel being conquered by foreigners with no respect for the Lord may be repugnant to Daniel. Here he is in captivity, living well, being educated in literature, culture, and language, and eating the king's choice food, while his brethren don't fare so well. This situation may be so incompatible in his mind—so repulsive—that eating the king's choice food would, in his conviction, entail a total capitulation to the enemy and acquiescence to the very things that felled Israel. Despite his captivity, he will still follow Yahweh, and denying choice food from a godless king is one small way of showing it.

This is a limited abstention, for a limited time, for a very specific situation. Later we discover that Daniel does drink wine on occasion, but it must have been wine not furnished by the king. If Daniel's refusal to drink the king's choice wine is somehow a universal and absolute law by which all Christians must abide, then it seems that we can't eat choice food, either. Additionally, the law would only kick in when we are captured by a king and carted off to Babylon.

Daniel's abstention has to do with Nebuchadnezzar's conquest of Jerusalem, not a defiance of wine itself. He knows that wine is a good gift from God, but to accept choice wine from the hand of one who defies God just doesn't seem right to him. We are not required to abstain from alcohol as Daniel did. In fact, Daniel isn't even required to abstain. In this particular instance, he chooses not to partake of the king's choice food or wine, but there is no command for us to do the same.

John the Baptist also abstains from alcohol. The account of John's birth is found in Luke 1 where we read the following (Lk. 1:13–17):

> But the angel said to him, "Do not be afraid, Zacharias, for your petition has been heard, and your wife Elizabeth will bear you a son, and you will give him the name John. You will have joy and gladness, and many will rejoice at his birth. For he will be great in the sight of the Lord; and he will drink no wine or liquor, and he will be filled with the Holy Spirit while yet in his mother's womb. And he will turn many of the sons of Israel back to the Lord their God. It is he who will go as a forerunner before Him in the spirit and power of Elijah, to turn the hearts of the fathers back to the children, and the disobedient to the attitude of the righteous, so as to make ready a people prepared for the Lord."

Rather than unearthing a universal command for all believers to abstain, we discover a specific and unique instance where the angel Gabriel informs Zacharias that his wife, Elizabeth, will give birth to a son. Gabriel commands Zacharias to name the boy John, for he will be great in the sight of the Lord, will drink no alcohol, and will be filled with the Holy Spirit while still in his mother's womb. John's unique role is that of a forerunner, a herald in the spirit of Elijah to prepare people for the Lord. Jesus would soon emerge on the scene, and John holds the honored status of preparing the people for His arrival.

This birth is special and comes with an angelic announcement by Gabriel. This baby is filled with the Spirit while still in the womb. This baby has a special mission in life, that of a forerunner, preparing people for Jesus' arrival. This baby is destined to fulfill a role in the spirit of Elijah. He is set apart for life, marked for dedicated service toward a particular, once-in-a-lifetime role. This prohibition for John originates with God, is declared prior to John's birth, and relates to the destined role he fulfills in announcing the Messiah. It is not a universal decree for all believers.

Regarding Paul, we read in Acts 18:18, "In Cenchrea he had his hair cut, for he was keeping a vow." For some, this indicates that Paul is taking a Nazarite vow and as such, he is not to drink alcohol. The text, however, doesn't state that Paul is taking a Nazarite vow or that he in any way abstains from alcohol consumption. In fact, if he were taking a Nazarite vow he would *not* be cutting his hair because Nazarite vows forbid it. Although, at the expiration of a Nazarite vow, priests would often shave the vow-taker's untouched hair and burn it in the altar fire. Could it be that Paul is not initiating a vow, but completing one?

The biblical text doesn't provide enough information for arriving at solid conclusions as to the nature and reason for this vow. We would merely be playing in the sandbox of conjecture and speculation. But what is the point, anyway? If Paul initiated or completed a vow before the Lord, then good for him. There is nothing wrong with taking a vow if you want to take one. I could vow to no longer watch television or listen to music for thirty days if I desired. Nothing prevents me from doing so, and nothing commands me to do so. For some reason, which we do not know, Paul is either initiating a vow or completing one.

If he is completing a Nazarite vow, then he is free to consume alcohol, for the Nazarite prohibition against alcohol consumption lasted only during the term of the vow. If Paul is initiating a vow, it has nothing to do with alcohol or a Nazarite vow, since shaving one's head is the very thing Nazarite vows prohibit. If reading abstention into Acts 18:18 is a stretch, then seeing a prohibition against alcohol in the passage is the pinnacle of folly.

We must concur with Howard H. Charles' statement in *Alcohol and the Bible:*

> The Old Testament as a whole seems to indicate that abstinence from the use of wine was exceptional rather than normative. The cases of total abstinence were few in number. More common were instances of temporary abstinence. Although certain dangers were recognized in its excessive use, there is no blanket condemnation of wine. Properly used, it was a legitimate part of normal Hebrew life.[11]

If total abstinence is truly the mark of holiness as prohibitionists advance, we should expect the wilderness generation to be the holiest generation of all, for they wandered forty years in the desert without one ounce of alcohol. Yet, they were nothing but a bunch of selfish complainers who cause Moses and God undue heartache: "For forty years I loathed that generation, and said they are a people who err in their heart, and they do not know My ways. Therefore I swore in My anger, truly they shall not enter into My rest" (Ps. 95:10–11).

During the Old Testament, the Lord requires a tithe from the produce of the land. If the amount of that tithe is large and transporting it to the Lord's designated place is burdensome, the tithe can be sold and the money spent on whatever their hearts fancied, even fermented beverage:

> If the distance is so great for you that you are not able to bring the tithe, since the place where the LORD your God chooses to set His name is too far away from you when the LORD your God blesses you, then you shall exchange it for money, and bind the money in your hand and go to the place which the LORD your God chooses. You may spend the money for whatever your heart desires: for oxen, or sheep, or wine, or strong drink, or whatever your heart desires; and there you shall eat in the presence of the LORD your God and rejoice, you and your household (Dt. 14:24–26).

The Hebrew word for "strong drink" is *shekar*, a word already noted as referring to intoxicating beverage. "The people of God are not only permitted to drink *shekar*, but are to drink it 'before the presence of the Lord,' and 'in the fear of the Lord' (14:23)."[12] As we drink *shekar*, we must do so rejoicing. Apparently, it is not sinful to drink alcohol, or to desire an alcoholic drink, nor is it sinful to rejoice in the presence of God while consuming the beverage. However, overindulgence leading to drunkenness is sinful. This passage seems to drive a stake into the heart of the total abstinence argument.

Some argue that leaders in the church should practice "leadership abstinence" as Timothy did in the New Testament. But there is no such thing as a required or preferred "leadership abstinence." Where does it say that Timothy engaged in "leadership abstinence"? It sounds spiritual enough, doesn't it, to say that godly leaders abstain from fermented drink. But where does it say this in the Bible? Where is the command for New Testament church leaders to abstain from consuming alcohol? Look all you want, it isn't there. Is it better for leaders to rightly divide the Word of God or follow a socially pressured agenda? Is it more appropriate for leaders to stand up for what the Bible *actually* teaches or skew its meaning to fit a particular theological viewpoint?

If there is such a thing as leadership abstinence, then all of the New Testament church leaders, including Timothy, could not participate in the Lord's Supper, which Jesus institutes with a cup of fermented wine. This invented "leadership abstinence" is contrary to scriptural teaching regarding the qualifications for church leaders. Elders must not to be "addicted to wine" (1 Tim. 3:3; Titus 1:7), and deacons must not be "addicted to much wine" (1 Tim. 3:8).

There is no verse in the Old or New Testament requiring total abstinence by the followers of God, let alone church leaders. What is forbidden is the *abuse* of wine as noted in Ephesians 5:18: "And do not get drunk with wine, for that is dissipation, but be filled with the Spirit." Timothy is even encouraged to mix some water with wine to help soothe his stomach ailment. Having well-known preachers call for "leadership abstinence" appears to add credibility to a total abstinence perspective, but in reality, it undermines and cheapens the truth of Scripture. The Bible doesn't mention, promote, expect, or command any type of total abstinence, no matter what we call it. Why can't individuals simply accept Scripture for what it teaches instead of trying to shape it into their own preferred point of view?

Finally, in trying to elevate total abstinence to some overarching moral principle for Christian living, one author believes that the entire Christian life is built upon abstinence.[13] The argument goes something like this: God created abstinence and throughout the Bible asks us to pursue this moral principle. Adam and Eve are commanded to abstain from eating the fruit of the tree, the Ten Commandments are nothing but abstention items, and the dietary laws of the Old Testament require saying "no" to certain types of food. In the New Testament, John the Baptist abstains, and Jesus Himself says "no" when asked to turn stones into bread during His temptation. He even taught that we are to deny ourselves. These all point toward a larger moral principle of abstention, created by God Himself, that leads to the highway of holiness and experiencing abundant life in Christ.

It reminds me of the preacher constantly screaming about what we can't do and what we shouldn't do, holding an entire view of Christianity as one of rules and regulations that must be obeyed. While watching a secular television show years ago about a new Christian couple, I cringed. When asked what difference

Christianity made in their lives, they articulated a litany of things they no longer do. To them, following God meant no longer doing this or doing that. Nothing was ever mentioned about forgiveness of sins, a new redeemed status as child of God, the freedom to please the Heavenly Father, or the inexplicable joy of being in right relationship with the Creator. Instead, their response continued the stereotype that Christianity is a killjoy religion for emotional deadbeats who can't survive in the real world.

By following Christ, we do turn away from such sinful things as lying, cheating, stealing, fornicating, etc., but these are merely the *results* of the internal change within us. Outward changes in lifestyle reflect the transformation inside our heart.

This moral principle view, however, accepts that alcohol is inherently evil and that total abstinence is commanded by God. It accepts as the foundation for its argument the very thing it is arguing for. It is an ingenious sounding moral principle for the followers of God, but, unfortunately, it is wrong.

We have previously shown that alcohol is not inherently evil, for it is a good gift from God to His people. The abundance of wine in the Old Testament is viewed as proof of His blessing, while scarcity is seen as a curse. Old Testament followers drink wine in His presence with joy. What is absolutely forbidden is drunkenness, not moderate consumption.

What we *are* commanded to abstain from is drunkenness. But, because the *use* of alcohol is equated with the *abuse* of alcohol, many forbid what God actually permits. If there is an overarching principle to be followed, it is this: stop adding to Scripture and simply follow its teachings instead of inventing spiritual-sounding ways for squeezing Scripture into a preferred interpretive box.

Summary: There is no universal, absolute command to abstain from alcohol in the Bible and occurrences of abstention are for a limited time, to limited individuals, in limited situations.

THE WEAKER BROTHER

This chapter explores a significant passage about offending weaker brothers. What is a weaker brother? What does it mean to offend, cause to stumble, or destroy another's faith? How does this passage relate to alcohol consumption? Clear understanding of this passage helps us maintain biblical relationships with weaker brothers.

We now come to a section of Scripture that many believe has significant ramifications regarding the use of alcohol by Christians. According to Romans 14–15:13, the church in Rome is divided over scruples of eating specific foods and setting apart certain days above others. Paul categorizes these two factions as either weak or strong in faith. For abstentionists and prohibitionists, Romans 14:21 is a key verse upholding the denial of alcohol consumption: "It is good not to eat meat or to drink wine, or to do anything by which your brother stumbles." In other words, we should abstain from drinking alcohol if it offends other believers or causes them to stumble in their faith. Our conduct is determined by the weakness of another.

A proper understanding of this critical passage is essential if we are to respond to weaker brothers in a biblical manner. Toward that end, I have included Romans 14–15:13 in its entirety:

> Now accept the one who is weak in faith, but not for the purpose of passing judgment on his opinions. One person has faith that he may eat all things, but he who is weak eats vegetables only. The one who eats is not to regard with contempt the one who does not eat, and the one who does not eat is

not to judge the one who eats, for God has accepted him. Who are you to judge the servant of another? To his own master he stands or falls; and he will stand, for the Lord is able to make him stand. One person regards one day above another, another regards every day alike. Each person must be fully convinced in his own mind. He who observes the day, observes it for the Lord, and he who eats, does so for the Lord, for he gives thanks to God; and he who eats not, for the Lord he does not eat, and gives thanks to God. For not one of us lives for himself, and not one dies for himself; for if we live, we live for the Lord, or if we die, we die for the Lord; therefore whether we live or die, we are the Lord's.

For to this end Christ died and lived again, that He might be Lord both of the dead and of the living. But you, why do you judge your brother? Or you again, why do you regard your brother with contempt? For we will all stand before the judgment seat of God. For it is written, "As I live, says the Lord, every knee shall bow to Me, and every tongue shall give praise to God." So then each one of us will give an account of himself to God. Therefore let us not judge one another anymore, but rather determine this—not to put an obstacle or a stumbling block in a brother's way. I know and am convinced in the Lord Jesus that nothing is unclean in itself; but to him who thinks anything to be unclean, to him it is unclean. For if because of food your brother is hurt, you are no longer walking according to love. Do not destroy with your food him for whom Christ died. Therefore do not let what is for you a good thing be spoken of as evil; for the kingdom of God is not eating and drinking, but righteousness and peace and joy in the Holy Spirit. For he who in this way serves Christ is acceptable to God and approved by men.

So then we pursue the things which make for peace and the building up of one another. Do not tear down the work of God for the sake of food. All things indeed are clean, but they are evil for the man who eats and gives offense. It is good not to eat meat or to drink wine, or to do anything by which your brother stumbles. The faith which you have, have as your own conviction before God. Happy is he who does not condemn himself in what he approves. But he who doubts is condemned if he eats, because his eating is not from faith; and whatever is not from faith is sin.

Now we who are strong ought to bear the weaknesses of those without strength and not just please ourselves. Each of us is to please his neighbor for his good, to his edification. For even Christ did not please Himself; but as it is written, "The reproaches of those who reproached You fell on Me." For whatever was written in earlier times was written for our instruction, so that through perseverance and the encouragement of the Scriptures we might have hope. Now may the God who gives perseverance and encouragement grant you to be of the same mind with one another according to Christ Jesus, so that with one accord you may with one voice glorify the God and

Father of our Lord Jesus Christ. Therefore, accept one another, just as Christ also accepted us to the glory of God. For I say that Christ has become a servant to the circumcision on behalf of the truth of God to confirm the promises given to the fathers, and for the Gentiles to glorify God for His mercy; as it is written, "Therefore I will give praise to You among the Gentiles, and I will sing to Your name." Again he says, "Rejoice, O Gentiles, with His people." And again, "Praise the Lord all you Gentiles, and let all the peoples praise Him." Again Isaiah says, "There shall come the root of Jesse, and He who arises to rule over the Gentiles, in Him shall the Gentiles hope." Now may the God of hope fill you with all joy and peace in believing, so that you will abound in hope by the power of the Holy Spirit.

As you might imagine, this passage stirs up spirited differences of opinion, even among scholars, on its meaning and application. If the numerous opinions surrounding any given biblical passage are bewildering for believers, it must be totally perplexing to those outside the faith. After all, there is only one Bible. Is its meaning so obscure that agreement is impossible? This is one reason why so many denominations exist today. In tracing their history, we discover that division and discord typically incubate denominational birth. Imagine that—church growth through church splits!

With so much division in the contemporary church, it is a wonder anyone wants to join. The church in Rome is not so different as believers are judging one another over food and days. I am surprised a new congregation didn't spring up in Rome on the corner of Division Street and Third Avenue called First Church of the Weak, a new church split with a sign out front identifying itself in large letters as "the church that finally gets it right." This kind of division is detrimental to our faith, our outreach, and our unity. It has the potential to undermine the very thing God desires to firmly establish, His church.

R. Kent Hughes shares a humorous story about a father-son conflict that typifies what is happening in the church at Rome:

> The pastor under whom I served for almost ten years liked to tell about a play he saw which portrayed an intense conflict between a father and a son. The point came when the father and son agreed to part. In the middle of the night the son had trouble sleeping, so he went down to the kitchen to fix himself a sandwich, and there was his father, who couldn't sleep either.
>
> After they fixed their sandwiches they began to reminisce about the past—about the years in Little League, about their great hunting expeditions, about their swimming together, about their fishing trips.
>
> As some needed healing was taking place, the son said, "Dad, do you remember the time we were out on the lake in that green boat?" His father said, "The

boat was blue, son." The son said, "No, it was green." The father said, "You are mistaken—it was blue." "Green." "Blue." "Green." "Blue." And his son departed, never to return. Some things just don't matter. May we allow God to give us the wisdom to see what is essential and what is not.[1]

Like a razor-sharp knife in the hand of a reckless individual, this passage can be wielded to hurt, maim, and divide. Without proper context and understanding, the text can be abused much like I Thessalonians 5:22 where we guilt and coerce others to abstain from all sorts of activities we find disagreeable, simply by labeling it "the very appearance of evil." Here, all we have to say is, "Stop it! I am offended," fully anticipating the transgressor to immediately abide by our misgivings. Rather than pressuring others to acquiesce to our preferred perspective, we might actually want to first discover the meaning of this passage so we can apply it wisely, lovingly, and correctly.

Some believe that if a fellow sojourner is offended by something we do, we are obligated to immediately stop doing it. Really? Is that the teaching here? Are we required to stop doing or saying what another finds offensive? This is sheer madness and makes little sense, not to mention its blatant disconnection with the context. If this is how you want to live your life, then I wish you lots of luck—you will need it. Jesus couldn't even please everyone, and He was perfect in all ways. Many were offended at His teaching and practice—so offended they crucified Him. If you are upset that I wear blue socks and your favorite sock color is brown, must I change socks? After all, God deserves our very best and you have determined that brown is the very best sock color.

We readily see the absurdity of such thinking when it comes to sock colors, but what about something more substantive? A former parishioner strongly believed that communion should only be administered during the Sunday morning church hour and that no music should be played during such a holy event. When the congregation celebrated communion together on an ocean beach after baptizing a new believer, complete with acoustic guitars and singing, she was livid. I had caused her to stumble. I offended her and was scolded like a naughty dog who just deposited doo-doo on the living room carpet. Bad pastor! She vehemently complained to church leaders and denomination officials causing all sorts of strife.

Should we refrain from celebrating communion outside of Sunday morning to accommodate this individual—to ensure that she is not offended? In an effort to be biblical, should we maintain absolute silence during communion to meet her preferences? What about those with a preference *for* music. Will they be offended? To appease one is to offend the other. In an effort not to offend, should Jesus have toned down His message, not fraternized with sinners and tax collectors, said nothing of sin, and held His tongue instead of calling the Pharisees a brood of vipers?

The unfortunate term "offense" used in the King James Version of Romans 14:21 and "grieved" in Romans 14:15 has led many to conclude that we cannot engage in any behavior that upsets another. If you do something I don't like, or think is right, such as drinking a glass of wine, then I simply quote Romans 14:21 to you, using the King James Bible of course, and expect you to immediately change your ways. You must not do "anything" that upsets me. Think about it, you must stop doing *anything* that *offends* me. ANYTHING! One writer sums it up pretty well:

> Some denominations believe that watching plays and movies, **any** kind of drama, regardless of rating, is a sin. Will we all agree to never attend a movie or play again, and to watch only the news and educational programs that don't involve dramatizations on the television? If not, what happens when someone who believes it is a sin decides to attend a movie because he saw us doing it? Some denominations believe it is a sin to wear makeup. Will we all agree to forgo makeup? Some denominations believe it is a sin for women to cut their hair or wear jeans. Will we all conform to this regulation on the off chance that we might be imitated by someone who really thinks she shouldn't? What about wearing shorts, mixed bathing, wearing jewelry, buying anything on Sunday, playing cards, playing dominos, listening to James Taylor, using Celtic words for bodily functions instead of Latin words, the list goes on and on.
>
> As we can see, practically every part of our culture which we take for granted is considered a sin by some segment of Christianity. But it is unlikely that those who insist that the proper implementation of Romans 14:21 is total abstinence from alcohol are willing to alter any other aspect of their behavior in deference to weaker brothers who have problems with things they do every day.[2]

Surely we must engage in deeper reasoning than the romper room antics of "What I don't like, no one else can like." Our tendency is to make what we don't like the standard of truth for everyone else. We really do have to examine the context of a passage, the meaning of words, and actually study to understand biblical teaching—or does the thought of that offend you? Maybe we shouldn't study God's Word because you might be offended at its teaching. This is a childish mentality that dumbs down Scripture to such levels of stupidity that a response is hardly necessary. We just shake our heads in disbelief. To be held to the standard of "can't offend anyone" is to ensure complete failure in this life, for surely we can do nothing without someone being upset. This passage must mean something more—something more thoughtful, reasonable, and reflective of the context and intent of the passage itself. To grasp how this text applies to the consumption of alcohol, we must first properly identify what is meant by being weak in faith and causing a brother to stumble.

Weak and Strong

Just who are these weak and strong believers in Rome? Our initial image of a weaker brother may be much different than what the text means by the term. The word "weak" conjures up images of skinny men with no muscles, projecting low self-esteem, and worthy only of picking flowers with us on a sunny afternoon—not someone with the discipline to forego common aspects of life for the kingdom of God. Understanding the nature of both the weak and the strong is essential to comprehending Paul's teaching.

Is this a real-life problem in the Roman church, or is Paul merely reflecting in a more generalized manner what he has already mentioned in 1 Corinthians 8–10 regarding a similar issue? Some feel the weak cannot be identified, others think they are non-believers, and still others believe they are Christians. If they are indeed Christians, are they Jewish Christians living in Rome, Gentile Christians, or a mixture of both?[3] The most common understanding sees weak Christians as Jews struggling to live under the New Covenant. Steeped in Old Testament law and ceremonial ritual, they resist letting go. The strong, on the other hand, are often viewed as Gentile believers who grow up without such attachment to tradition and religious ceremony. We will probably never know for sure the true identity of the weak and strong in the precise terms many would like, but that doesn't hinder us from understanding the text.

What we do know is that Paul identifies at least two warring factions in the Roman church—weak in faith and strong in faith. Since many of Paul's letters address specific situations within recipient churches, it is not out of line to think that these factions truly are a genuine problem Paul confronts. Unfortunately, so far removed from Paul's day, we only get one side of the picture—his letter. This means we have to piece together what is happening in the assembly by looking at Paul's letter itself. It would certainly be helpful to interview those in the Roman church, but we cannot. We can draw upon history and what we know of cosmopolitan Rome and its culture at the time, but for the most part, we look intently to Paul's letter itself. In it, he addresses two groups of people, the weak and the strong, who are at odds with one another.

This sounds all too familiar, doesn't it—different factions within a local church at odds with one another. Sadly, from an outside perspective, this is how the body of Christ is often viewed—as a group of people proclaiming one thing and living another. The proclamation is undermined by incongruent behavior. Robert H. Mounce says it well in his commentary on Romans: "In the long run the validity of faith is established by the quality of life it produces. What people do is the most accurate indicator of what they really believe."[4] Christians in Rome speak of the forgiveness of Christ, His ability to unify, and the change wrought in their hearts, yet they can't get along with one another. Do you see a problem with that? One group judges others as less spiritual than themselves, while the other faction glaringly despises them. Looks like the love of Christ is freely flowing in this church!

Unfortunately, this scenario is more often the norm than the exception and cuts across all denominational boundaries. Adept at criticizing, Christians freely disparage the pastor, the governing board, the sermon, the singing, the color of the carpet, the décor—you name it. Ironic, isn't it, that a place of supposed love and tolerance among the family of God all too often becomes a place of judgment from check-list Christians? With their lengthy list of sin, they check you off as nonconforming and the condemnation begins. You go to the theater? Check. You use make-up and wear slacks as a woman? Check. You play cards and go dancing? Check. You don't own or study from a King James Bible? Check. You listen to music other than hymns? Check. And so on.

The Bible desires unity among God's people and this winsome quality is described in Psalm 133:1–3:

> Behold, how good and how pleasant it is
> For brothers to dwell together in unity!
> It is like the precious oil upon the head,
> Coming down upon the beard,
> Even Aaron's beard,
> Coming down upon the edge of his robes.
> It is like the dew of Hermon
> Coming down upon the mountains of Zion;
> For there the Lord commanded the blessing—life forever.

Earlier in Romans, Paul prompts us toward unity: "If possible, so far as it depends on you, be at peace with all men" (12:18). Realizing that destructive conflict will assail His followers once He is gone, Jesus prays for their unity in John 17:20–21:

> I do not ask on behalf of these alone, but for those also who believe in Me through their word; that they may all be one; even as You, Father, are in Me and I in You, that they also may be in Us, so that the world may believe that You sent Me.

The harmony our Lord desires is not absolute agreement on every aspect of the faith or singularity in gifts, temperament, skills, and passion. Paul clearly articulates this very idea by describing the church as a body in 1 Corinthians 12. We can't all be a hand, a foot, or an eye, nor should we desire to be. Diversity helps us work together as we are intended to function. The blending of unity with diversity is one of the toughest aspects of Christianity we will ever experience, as both seem to be diametrically opposed to one another. Yet, when Christ's love rules the heart, these two aspects of faith can coexist to the glory of God.

If we cannot get along with one another, then what change has Christ actually brought about? But take a group full of differences, sprinkle in a heaping portion of Christian love, and the possibility of unity makes the wondrous love of Christ stand out as a hallmark of faith. Our choices in this life influence those around us. Since the Christian life is lived in community with others, individualistic isolation is not an option and love becomes a necessary ingredient of premium importance.

Unity amidst diversity doesn't come naturally; it takes a great amount of work and sometimes a greater amount of restraint. Unity is based on the primacy of love, something overtly emphasized in Scripture. We are to love our enemies (Rom. 13:8ff), love God with all our heart and love our neighbor as ourselves (Mk. 12:30–31), and love each other as Christ loves us (Jn. 15:12). When strong and weak brothers in the Lord judge and condemn one another, they violate the basic principles of love set forth in Scripture and demonstrated by Jesus.

Those who are weak in faith restrict their diet to vegetables only and observe certain days above others. The strong in faith are comfortable eating all foods and view each day alike. One operates from a restrictive basis, while the other operates from freedom and truth. If the weak are Jews clinging to Old Testament law and ceremonial regulations, we note that there is no biblical requirement limiting one's diet to vegetables only. The weak are hyper-vigilant or simply believe this is a preferred path to spirituality. Their motivation is pure, but their logic and practice is flawed.

The strong, on the other hand, feel exactly the opposite. They see no need to refrain from eating meat or limiting their diet in any way. Adherence to restrictive diets and special days doesn't ensure greater spirituality and neither is required or expected by God. All food is morally and spiritually safe and available for consumption. Every day is created by the Lord, so why elevate one over another? They realize the truth of Psalm 24:1: "The earth is the Lord's, and all it contains, the world, and those who dwell in it."

Imagine yourself at the monthly church potluck in Rome; the strong bring in all kinds of food (even meat) and eat with joy at the Lord's provision. The weak limit their intake to vegetables only. The strong sit on the right side of the fellowship hall despising those missing out on God's bountiful blessings, while on the left side of the hall, weak believers are judging all others as unspiritual and lacking disciplined commitment. "Weak" and "strong" refer to our belief about freedom—what we think we are free to do. Unbridled freedom can breed condescending attitudes while weakness in faith can spawn a holier-than-thou complex. Such attitudes stand in stark contrast to the attitude Jesus demonstrates. What should be done?

A similar situation exists in Corinth over eating meat that may have been offered to idols (I Cor. 10:25–31):

> Eat anything that is sold in the meat market without asking questions for conscience' sake; FOR THE EARTH IS THE LORD'S, AND ALL IT CONTAINS. If one of the unbelievers invites you and you want to go, eat anything that is set before you without asking questions for conscience' sake. But if anyone says to you, "This is meat sacrificed to idols," do not eat it, for the sake of the one who informed you, and for conscience' sake; I mean not your own conscience, but the other man's; for why is my freedom judged by another's conscience? If I partake with thankfulness, why am I slandered concerning that for which I give thanks? Whether, then, you eat or drink or whatever you do, do all to the glory of God.

The person whose conscience is not functioning properly is not someone who fails to realize he is sinning, but someone who thinks he is (or others are) when he isn't.[5] "The man who has problems with his conscience is the one who is worried about eating the meat, not the one who realizes there is no sin in eating meat."[6] Martin Luther says, "This, however, does not mean that we should bear the superstitious piety, or rather the show of piety of our own time, simply because it flows from weakness of faith. Those who do these works of piety do them because of their gross ignorance."[7]

"In perhaps the most severe passage, Paul tells Timothy that people whose consciences have been seared abandon the teaching of the faith and start to teach a legalistic abstinence."[8]

> But the Spirit explicitly says that in later times some will fall away from the faith, paying attention to deceitful spirits and doctrines of demons, by means of the hypocrisy of liars seared in their own conscience as with a branding iron, men who forbid marriage and advocate abstaining from foods which God has created to be gratefully shared in by those who believe and know the truth. For everything created by God is good, and nothing is to be rejected if it is received with gratitude; for it is sanctified by means of the word of God and prayer (1 Tim. 4:1–5).

Another prominent passage is Titus 1:15, indicating that to the pure, nothing is corrupt: "To the pure, all things are pure; but to those who are defiled and unbelieving, nothing is pure, but both their mind and their conscience are defiled." "The weaker brother is the one who sees prohibitions where God has not placed them. Legalism is actually the result of a weak conscience, not a strong conscience developed from spiritual maturity."[9] It sees impurity where there is no defilement.

Weaker brethren are often presented as having truth on their side, when in reality, their weakness is due to the very fact that they do not understand or follow truth with regard to food and days. If these were simply two equally valid options, then why the big discussion and why refer to individuals as weak and strong? They are called strong and weak for a reason—one is correct and the other is not. If the meat eaters walk up to the vegetable eaters' only lunch table and call them weak Christians, I doubt it will be well received. There is a good chance weak believers will become indignant, believing they are actually the strong ones. After all, look at the things they forbid and say "no" to for the sake of the kingdom. Surely, God is pleased with their restrictive endeavors and notices their level of discipline and commitment.

It is the strong who possess a correct understanding of food and days, not the weak. That is why they are called strong. Even Paul sides with them in Romans 15:1: "Now we who are strong ought to bear the weaknesses of those without strength and not just please ourselves," and Romans 14:14: "I know and am convinced in the Lord Jesus that nothing is unclean in itself." It is a statement of certitude, not mere opinion, and is underscored with the stamp of approval "in the Lord."

Jesus said it Himself in Matthew 15:10–11: "Hear and understand. It is not what enters into the mouth that defiles the man, but what proceeds out of the mouth, this defiles the man." The correct view of days and food is that of the strong. We are indeed free to eat all food without a vegetables only restriction and each day is given by God for His glory and our joy. There is no obligation to set apart one day above another. Lest we think these are two equally viable options reflecting mere differences in personal preference, we remember that one position is correct (the strong) while the other is incorrect (the weak).

Even though only one group holds the correct perspective regarding food and days, theological conviction and doctrinal truth have little *practical* value if the behavior surrounding that conviction is incompatible with Christian love. Falsely believing themselves to be strong, the weak are actually immature, mistaken, and on the wrong side of truth. Yet, they judge others as less spiritual than themselves. The strong, while in possession of truth, despise those who have not yet obtained their level of understanding and freedom. Though the motivation of both groups is to honor the Lord, one group is correct in its theological understanding and the other is not. But it is the unacceptable and unloving behavior of each group that Paul focuses on. The following chart may be helpful in understanding the situation in Rome:

THE ROMAN SITUATION

Faction	Issue	Behavior	Motivation	Result
Weak	Eat vegetables only and observe special days above others	Judge strong as being unspiritual, lacking disciplined commitment	To please and honor the Lord	Division
Strong	Eat all food and view all days alike	Despise weak for their unfounded scruples	To please and honor the Lord	Division

The weak hold a restricted view of food and days unsubstantiated by biblical teaching. While their motivation is pure, their understanding is flawed since nothing in itself is unclean as Paul, Jesus, and others testify. Their weak (incorrect) belief leads them to restrictive action (no meat/observing special days). When the weak engage in what they believe to be morally unacceptable, for them it is sin, not because the act itself is evil, but because they violate their own conscience when they participate. The sin is not *partaking* of something inherently sinful or biblically restricted (for nothing is unclean in itself), but participating in something they *think* is sinful, even though it isn't. Why is it sinful? Because they violate their own conscience and belief. "But he who doubts is condemned if he eats, because his eating is not from faith; and whatever is not from faith is sin" (Rom. 14:23).

Paul's point is that sin is not located in the material item itself, but in the mind of the weak individual. "We must be careful not to generalize on the principle expressed in this teaching. Paul was not saying that sin is a matter of personal opinion. He was not teaching that as long as we think something is okay it is okay for us. Scripture clearly teaches that certain things are wrong."[10] Murder is wrong whether one thinks it is or not, but believing something is sin when it isn't doesn't make it wrong. Sin is not a matter of personal opinion or found in any material item. The weak sin when they violate their misinformed conscience about an object or action, believing it to be sin when it isn't. It is not a sin of participation but a sin against conscience.

A fictitious example may help us better understand this concept. Let's say that I believe technology is inherently sinful (thank goodness it isn't, for I am writing this book on a laptop and I certainly don't want to go back to the good ol' days of manual typewriters). For me, technology steers us away from God, numbs our spiritual senses, and becomes a quick and accessible conduit for sin, or so I believe. I love the Lord dearly and desire nothing more than to honor Him in thought, word, and deed. I don't own a computer, a cell phone, and will not participate in social networking, all to His honor. God instructs us to avoid evil, and I see technology as inherently evil. But in my zeal for purity and holiness, I begin judging fellow believers as undisciplined with no zeal for holiness. If they were half as committed as me, they would clearly see how the Bible forbids participation in the ubiquitous onslaught of technological evils.

My local church utilizes a big screen and projector during the worship service, software for creating slick graphics, computers in the sound booth, and the pastor even owns a cell phone, along with most others in the congregation, and to top it off, he brings his sermon notes to the podium on his portable computer. Don't these folks understand the evils of technology? Don't they grasp how this pains the heart of God? Don't they recognize the slippery slope they are on and the negative example set for future generations? If they are truly committed to holiness, separation from the world, and remaining true to God's Word, they will do away with all technology and simply focus on the Lord.

THE TECHNOLOGY ISSUE

Faction	Issue	Behavior	Motivation	Result
Weak	Do not participate in technology	Judge strong as being unspiritual, lacking disciplined commitment	To please and honor the Lord	Division
Strong	Participate in technology	Despise weak for their unfounded scruples	To please and honor the Lord	Division

My restrictive views on technology make others feel uncomfortable, especially the board of elders, as my judgmental attitude creates division. A small group of us holier-than-thou anti-technologites remain in the local church, but we are marginalized, undervalued, and not genuinely accepted. Those supporting the sin of technology within the church despise us, down us, and view us as troublemakers.

While out shopping at a local big-box retail store, I run into a couple technologites from the church. One is an elder and both are strong supporters of technology. They see this "chance" meeting as the providence of God and pressure me to utilize the blessed wonders of technology and discover for myself the freedom they claim to possess. They know where I stand, yet they work me over pretty good with a tag-team, rapid-fire approach. In fact, they walk me over to the computer aisle, give me a sales pitch, and offer to buy one for me, believing that if I just put my misgivings aside and try technology, I will become a firm believer in its ability to enhance godliness. I take home the computer they purchase for me, give it a try, and all along feel guilty for doing something I believe is morally wrong. Have I sinned?

Is computer ownership immoral? Is using technology during the worship service fundamentally wrong? Does the Bible condemn technology as intrinsically evil? The correct answer is no, technology is not inherently sinful. My perspective is incorrect and therefore I am weak in my faith because I extend the boundaries of biblical truth in an untruthful way. This incorrect belief persuades my conscience that to own, utilize, or support technology is wrong. My sin is not in the use of technology (for nothing is inherently evil and the Bible doesn't forbid its use), but in violating my own conscience—willfully doing something I believe to be sinful.

What about the role of the technologites? Are they in any way culpable for pressuring me into trying technology, purchasing the computer, and encouraging me to violate my conscience? Absolutely! They are not acting in love and instead of accepting me with my weakness of faith, they cause me to stumble (violate my conscience). This crosses a line. The hallmark of the Christian faith, the law of love, has been violated. When it comes to these kinds of issues—issues that are not critical to the foundational core of Christianity, we can accept one another in love, even if someone is on the weak side of truth. These issues don't equate to denying the faith, nor are they fatal flaws to being received as sons and daughters of the king. Instead, they reflect a misinformed conscience that incorrectly extends biblical teaching beyond its appropriate boundaries regarding ancillary issues. But if one denies such pillar doctrines as the death and resurrection of Christ, the mistake is a blatant denial of a fundamental issue of the Christian faith that is central, not ancillary; essential, not optional.

Romans 14:13–17 is a good summary of Paul's teaching:

> Therefore let us not judge one another anymore, but rather determine this—not to put an obstacle or a stumbling block in a brother's way. I know and am convinced in the Lord Jesus that nothing is unclean in itself; but to him who thinks anything to be unclean, to him it is unclean. For if because of food your brother is hurt, you are no longer walking according to love. Do not destroy with your food him for whom Christ died. Therefore do not let what is for you a good thing be spoken of as evil; for the kingdom of God is not eating and drinking, but righteousness and peace and joy in the Holy Spirit.

Breaking the passage down might assist our understanding:

Therefore let us not judge one another anymore,
Judging and despising one another is the unloving and unaccepting behavior occurring in Rome that brings about division. Paul says, "Stop it. Genuinely accept one another as fully Christian, not for the purpose of working each other over." By judging and criticizing one another, we insert ourselves into the role of God and wrongly reject what God rightly accepts.

but rather determine this—not to put an obstacle or a stumbling block in a brother's way.
Instead of spending time and energy judging each other, sincerely accept one another in love by not causing your brother to violate his conscience.

I know and am convinced in the Lord Jesus that nothing is unclean in itself; but to him who thinks anything to be unclean, to him it is unclean.
Nothing is unclean in itself and that includes meat, special days, and even alcohol. But when the weak in faith (the one with incorrect thinking), engages in what he believes is sin, he violates his misinformed conscience.

For if because of food your brother is hurt, you are no longer walking according to love. Do not destroy with your food him for whom Christ died.
By causing a weak brother to violate his conscience, we undermine the preeminence of love, a winsome hallmark of our faith. Our criticism of weaker brothers is tempered when we realize how much Christ values them. He died to save them, and since Christ accepts them, we cannot exclude them. Instead of enticing the weaker brother to sin against his conscience, accept and love him fully.

Therefore do not let what is for you a good thing be spoken of as evil; for the kingdom of God is not eating and drinking, but righteousness and peace and joy in the Holy Spirit.
There is nothing evil in itself, but why allow this truth to become something ill-spoken of by judging one another and causing a weak brother to violate his conscience? Eating and drinking are ancillary issues, not the heart of the kingdom of God. The priority is love and acceptance, just as Christ loves and accepts us.

This is how the chart looks when love and acceptance enter the picture:

LOVE AND ACCEPTANCE

Faction	Issue	Behavior	Motivation	Result
Weak	Eat vegetables only and observe special days above others	Stop judging and start accepting each other	To obey God and love as Christ loves	Acceptance
Strong	Eat all food and view all days alike	Stop judging and start accepting each other	To obey God and love as Christ loves	Acceptance

Loving and accepting a weaker brother does not mean we are obligated to take on his hesitation or agree with his erroneous perspective. That would make us weak in faith, and God wants us to be strong and mature in our belief. "No man can bind the conscience of another on an issue that is not condemned by Scripture either expressly or implicitly."[11]

Stumbling and Offending Others

Considerable debate exists regarding what stumbling means in Romans 14:21–23:

> It is good not to eat meat or to drink wine, or to do anything by which your brother stumbles. The faith which you have, have as your own conviction before God. Happy is he who does not condemn himself in what he approves. But he who doubts is condemned if he eats, because his eating is not from faith; and whatever is not from faith is sin.

Stumbling, according to some, means offending the senses of weak Christians. As a follower of Christ, you simply cannot do things others do not like. But as we have already noted, this is nothing but an exercise in futility. It is impossible to please everyone; not even Jesus could do it. The practical outworking of this view is that we can't do anything and should probably just lock ourselves inside our homes and have as little contact with the outside world as possible. What? You find that idea offensive? It also means that the weakest link in the chain (the person/group with the most qualms) actually runs the church. Inconceivable! It is no longer Christ's church led by the Holy Spirit, but a church extending its ministry only as far as the scruples of the weakest link. This is nonsense, or as we say in Iowa, hogwash.

Faith Abandonment

Others believe stumbling refers to a complete abandonment of the faith. In other words, feeble Christians are so weak that to engage in any activity they believe is wrong, even when the Bible permits it, is so offensive that they may turn their back on Christ and relinquish their faith. We don't find much practical application in our modern age since this rarely, if ever, happens. Are you really going to lose your faith, cast aside Christ, and jettison your Christianity because a fellow Christian drinks a beer when you don't think he should? The behavior of the strong would have to be so egregious that it causes complete abdication of the faith. Would denying the faith really occur over such issues of meat and special days?

What does Paul mean when he says, "Do not destroy with your food him for whom Christ died" (Rom. 14:15)? Is the complete abandonment of the faith leading to eternal damnation in mind? Obviously, "destroy" is a strong word and reveals the seriousness of using a food issue to hurt someone whom Christ loves, values, and dies for. The word reveals the fragility of their thinking, but it seems entirely unreasonable to abandon the kingdom of God because someone eats meat.

Fellow Christians do a lot of things we don't like or agree with, but we don't completely walk away from Christ because of it. The destruction Paul has in mind is not merely being offended that another is doing something we don't like, for that wouldn't be much of a stumble and could hardly be considered destroying someone. Eating meat and viewing all days alike are not even sins. The destruction Paul refers to is *causing* the violation of one's misinformed conscience. In Paul's mind, it is serious business. "Whatever is done without the conviction that God has approved it is by definition sin."[12]

Violating Conscience

Another option, and one that seems to best fit the context, is to interpret "stumbling" as a reference to a misinformed conscience. In other words, by causing one to violate his or her conscience, we become an accomplice to sin as an initiating factor. Though the weak may be immature, judgmental, and incorrect in their view on ancillary issues, it is never acceptable to entice them to sin against their conscience. Eating meat and viewing all days alike is indeed the correct perspective as the strong understand, but it is never an excuse for sinful enticement. The inducement is not the act of eating meat and observing special days, for neither of these are inherently sinful.

We become complicit when we *willfully* and *intentionally* cause the weak in faith to violate their conscience—go against what they believe to be sin. To do this is unloving and doesn't reflect Christ's acceptance of both the weak and the strong. Acceptance has the greater chance of encouraging the weak to become strong—to understand truth and therefore enlighten their mistaken conscience. Not everyone has reached the freedom of the strong as Paul notes in 1 Corinthians 8:4,7, "Therefore concerning the eating of things sacrificed to idols, we know that there is no such thing as an idol in the world, and that there is no God but one . . . However not all men have this knowledge."

It is clear from Romans 14:13 that we must stop judging and initiate a mindful determination not to cause a brother to stumble: "Therefore let us not judge one another anymore, but rather determine this—not to put an obstacle or a stumbling block in a brother's way." There is a play on words occurring here according to Dr. John Stott:

> Instead of passing judgment on one another, Paul writes, "make up your mind not to put any stumbling-block or obstacle in your brother's way" (13b). There is a play on words in the Greek sentence, which contains a double use of the verb "krinein, to judge". 'Let us therefore cease judging one another, but rather make this simple judgment . . .' (NEB). The judgment or decision which we are to make is to avoid putting either a hindrance (proskomma) or a snare (skandalon) in our brother's path and so causing him to trip and fall."[13]

In other words, instead of judging, make this judgment—not to cause your brother to stumble. As irritating as weak consciences can be, and as wrong as they are on the issue of food and days, they are indeed brothers, individuals for whom Christ dearly loves. If any judgment is to be made by the strong, it is a judgment unto themselves; a judgment in their own mind to assign high value to the weak and place no obstacle or trap before them. To *intentionally* cause a weaker brother in Christ to go against his conscience violates the demands of love Christ asks us to demonstrate toward one another. This is not an easy thing to do for the strong who correctly understand truth and freedom regarding such issues.

This produces a dilemma for the strong in faith. Food is not unclean in itself, but for the weak it becomes unclean. When strong consciences bump into weak consciences, what is the proper response? The strong must not place an obstacle before the weak or create a trap to ensnare them. To do so means we no longer walk in love: "For if because of food your brother is hurt, you are no longer walking according to love" (Rom. 14:15). Scripture doesn't say it is sinful to eat meat or drink wine as the prohibitionists advance, only that it is not good to do so in the context of causing a brother to stumble.

> When Paul says, "it is good for a man not to touch a woman" (1 Cor. 7:1) he does not mean that sexual intercourse is inherently wrong. To the contrary, in order to avoid sexual immorality he recommends it—by telling us that each man is to have his own wife and each woman her own husband, if they do not have the gift of continency.[14]

For the strong, the issue is one of loving weaker brothers despite their error, hoping they will "grow in the grace and knowledge of our Lord and Savior Jesus" (2 Pt. 3:18). Remaining in error is nothing to be proud of. Living in alignment with scriptural truth and growing toward maturity is the expected route "until we all attain to the unity of the faith, and of the knowledge of the Son of God, to a mature man, to the measure of the stature which belongs to the fullness of Christ" (Eph. 4:13).

It should be pointed out that although we are not to violate our conscience, our conscience is not the final arbiter of what is right and wrong. In other words, it is not infallible as Paul states in I Corinthians 4:4: "For I am conscious of nothing against myself, yet I am not by this acquitted; but the one who examines me is the Lord." Additionally, the obstacle or trap placed before the weak is one that is deliberate and intentional. It is something *intended* to seduce them toward violating their conscience, not merely irritating their senses. Must we never do anything that others find offensive, or is the issue one of intentional enticement?

I happened to be downtown one day and ran into a fellow parishioner. As we stood on the sidewalk talking, I turned my head to spit. Sometimes men do that, just like we often stand with our hands in our pockets and jingle our keys. Just as I turned my head to jettison my saliva to the sidewalk, unbeknownst to me, a female parishioner happens to drive by and notices my action. She is grieved, takes offense at my spitting, and later gives me an earful. Everyone knows pastors are not allowed to spit!

It wasn't like I had a mouthful of chewing tobacco or half of my sinuses in my mouth. Must I refrain from ever spitting on another sidewalk for fear of offending someone who believes this behavior is sinful, especially for the pastor of a church? There is no spitting sin. There is nothing inherently sinful about saliva or evacuating it from your mouth. But in her mind, I sinned and she was offended. She judged me and elevated her weak conscience as the standard by which all others must adhere.

That she didn't like or agree with my awesome spitting abilities isn't the kind of thing Paul is talking about at all. However, if I was visiting with her on a public sidewalk, knew of her weak conscience on the issue, and intentionally encouraged her to spit, or provided proper spitting lessons, then I have crossed a line. I am not required to accept her scruple as my own, but I am required to genuinely love and accept her in the Lord, even if she is a non-spitter.

Years ago, I interviewed an author who wrote a book on this very subject. When I began asking probing questions of a serious nature, he commented, "You actually read my book and have thought about this. This is so different than most of my interviews. How refreshing." One question I asked was, "Isn't it just simpler if weak believers establish their own congregation and strong believers do the same? This way, the weak and strong can believe and do their own thing without the disharmony caused by two different factions in one local church."

His response, I believe, is spot-on: "First, creating two congregations is not an option for us in Scripture. Instead, we are told to accept one another. Second, creating two congregations would be extremely difficult since we are all weak in some things and strong in others." We all have our idiosyncrasies about the faith—a mixture of weak and strong qualities running through our lives. I would add that togetherness and community, however uncomfortable, become the fertile environment for living out our Christianity. Faith in the midst of similarity is easy, for it requires little of us. There is no stretching of acceptance, love, and patience. Our faith is tested and honed as we live in community with others who are different. This is where the rubber meets the road and the love of Christ shines brightly for the world to see.

In today's world, a weaker brother is often seen as someone with a tendency to overindulge in alcohol. For instance, an alcoholic trying to maintain sobriety is considered a weaker brother. But how can this be? Utilizing Paul's analogy, the weak in faith isn't someone who overindulges, but rather, someone who doesn't consume alcohol at all, believing it to be sinful. He is weak because he doesn't understand that nothing is evil in its essence, including alcohol. His inaccurate perception leads to doubts of conscience. If he drinks, he sins, not because drinking is inherently sinful, but because he violates his own misinformed conscience. If he participates in what he *thinks* is sinful, it is a violation of conscience, not a sin of drinking. The weak brother, from Paul's point of view, is not someone who overindulges, but one who forbids alcohol under any circumstances.

Williamson states it nicely:

> From this it can readily be seen that when Paul speaks of causing a brother to stumble, he doesn't mean anything like the proponents of total abstinence. When they say that we must not cause our brother to stumble, they simply mean that we must not do anything that they do not like. We must not engage in any behavior that is offensive to other believers. Or in other words we must never do anything that other believers consider to be sin. Now this is not at all what Paul meant. When he spoke of causing a brother to stumble, he meant an act on our part which induces our brother to sin—encourages him to act against this scruple that he has in his conscience. It may well be, of course, that what Paul is saying may—in certain circumstances—dictate that we must not do something that is intrinsically lawful. If a certain Christian has been an alcoholic, and now believes that any use of wine for him would be the path of ruin, then other Christians must not act

in such a way as to encourage him to go against conscience. This does not mean that they must adopt the rule of his conscience as law.[15]

Love in the Family

Can the principles regarding food and days be extended to alcohol? Though alcohol is not intrinsically evil, many do not possess the freedom to imbibe; while their motivation is to live a holy life that honors God, they are yet weak in faith. They prohibit what God allows and their understanding of freedom is yet immature. Is it appropriate to apply weak and strong principles to this situation? Many believe we can, and should: "This passage deals with the question of the weak and the strong in a way that applies to every instance in which religious scrupulosity arises in connection with such things as those exemplified in this chapter."[16]

One's view on alcohol is not a pillar doctrine of the faith. You can still be a lover of God and not understand your freedom in this matter. You can be dead wrong in your belief that alcohol is intrinsically evil and still be a brother or sister in Christ. Your particular view on alcohol may not be correct, but it is not determinative of your status as a child of God.

A Weak and Strong Mix

The church is like a great big family, and families contain old and young, mature and immature, babies and great-grandparents. Invariably, a local body of believers contain Christians at various stages of their faith. Some are deep and strong, while others are shallow and weak. Some have great freedom of understanding, whereas the conscience of others forbids participation. It would be wonderful if everyone matured at the same rate and in the same way, but that just isn't reality.

Recognizing the varying levels of spiritual maturity helps us accept one another, for at one time we too were immature and weak, and may still be in some areas. In fact, we are all a mixture of weak and strong, depending on the issue. On one subject we are strong while on another we may be weak. We all have work to do in becoming more like our Lord. In the meantime, we accept one another until that future day when we reach full maturity and perfection.

Love Means Acceptance

Those with freedom to moderately imbibe and those with precluding consciences must accept one another just as Christ accepts all who come to Him in faith. Jesus died for both the weak and the strong. We are members of one family—the family of God whose spiritual gene pool extends to the Creator Himself. Is it possible to genuinely care for one another, accept one another, and love one another in this spiritual family, or will this topic divide us to the point where we dishonor our Lord's desire?

In judging one another like we do, we ultimately place ourselves in the seat of God, for only He is able to rightly judge; it is to Him that we ultimately stand or fall. While the strong understand that alcohol is neither intrinsically evil or unspiritual with moderate consumption, they do not have the right to disavow, belittle, or look down upon an immature conscience. While the weak are unable to grasp their full freedom in Christ, they do not have the right to judge others as less spiritual and less committed. Love must flow in the family, and that means acceptance of all who are God's beloved.

Love Can Mean Restraint

Occasions may arise where the strong, on a temporary and voluntary basis, abstain from drinking alcohol, or anything else for that matter (such as eating meat) that would cause a weaker brother to violate his conscience and participate in what he believes to be sin. Obviously, consuming alcohol, eating meat, and observing all days alike are not sinful activities. But using freedom to purposefully entice a weaker brother into activities he believes are sinful becomes a cause of stumbling, a sin for the strong. For the weak, sin is not in the activity itself, but the violation of a misinformed, weak, and incorrect conscience—intentionally going against what is believed to be wrong.

Love is not merely a theological construct limited to seminary classroom discussions, but a practical extension of the very nature of Christ. Genuine acceptance is not mere tolerance, but caring so deeply about another that we wouldn't dare intentionally cause someone to violate their own conscience. Helping the weak grow and mature is much more likely in an atmosphere of love and acceptance.

Summary: Weak Christians erroneously believe alcohol consumption is sin when it is not, and violate their own conscience when they do something they believe God forbids, while the strong who think accurately about the matter must not intentionally entice weak believers into violating their conscience, since that would disregard the demands of love.

TYING UP LOOSE ENDS

This chapter covers additional concepts such as Paul's "lawful but not profitable" comment, the body as a temple of the Holy Spirit, the Jerusalem Council, etc., that help to tie up loose ends. Think of it this way, the show is nearly over, and in this chapter we sweep the floor, empty the trash, and clean up. In the next chapter, the final chapter, we turn the lights off, lock the door, and go home.

A verse often used to deny alcohol consumption is I Corinthians 6:12: "All things are lawful for me, but not all things are profitable. All things are lawful for me, but I will not be mastered by anything." The inference is that alcohol isn't helpful, so Christians shouldn't associate with it.

Lawful But Not Helpful

Contemporary statistics and damaging data are produced revealing just how *unhelpful* alcohol is, thereby bolstering this "not-helpful" rule. Since alcohol has the *potential* for harmful effects, it should be avoided altogether. But this is a slippery-slope mentality:

> This is classic fallacious slippery-slope argumentation: it leverages fear of what might happen rather than promoting maturity and responsibility.
>
> Besides, the qualifications for elders also require that they be "not a lover of money" (1 Tim. 3:3). Since money in itself can possibly lead one to become a "lover of money" (covetous), should we therefore abstain from it totally? Yet, I don't see any of these pastors preaching "money is lawful, but not

beneficial." Does a single one refuse his paycheck because of what might possibly happen to him spiritually? Can you now see why this type of argument is a fallacy when applied to alcohol as well?"[1]

As is so often the case, context is ignored to the detriment of scriptural truth. Earlier in 1 Corinthians 6, Paul writes, "Or do you not know that the unrighteous will not inherit the kingdom of God? Do not be deceived; neither fornicators, nor idolaters, nor adulterers, nor effeminate, nor homosexuals, nor thieves, nor the covetous, nor drunkards, nor revilers, nor swindlers, will inherit the kingdom of God" (1 Cor. 6:9–10). Are these behaviors lawful, but simply not helpful? Is hooking up with a prostitute in verses 15–16 lawful, just not helpful? Is idolatry lawful, just not helpful?

Not *everything* is lawful, since there are many boundaries we are not to cross. But Paul just said, "All things are lawful for me, but not all things are profitable. All things are lawful for me, but I will not be mastered by anything." How can Paul claim everything is lawful knowing full-well that many things are not permitted and violate the law of God? The explanation lies in the context.

Prior to his statement that all things are lawful, Paul lists several things that are unacceptable to our Lord (1 Cor. 6:9–10):

> Or do you not know that the unrighteous will not inherit the kingdom of God? Do not be deceived; neither fornicators, nor idolaters, nor adulterers, nor effeminate, nor homosexuals, nor thieves, nor the covetous, nor drunkards, nor revilers, nor swindlers, will inherit the kingdom of God.

He also notes in 1 Corinthians 6:13 that "the body is not for immorality, but for the Lord." Why provide a list of unlawful items that bar entrance into heaven if indeed all things are lawful? Could it be that Paul is *not* advancing the argument that all things are lawful, but is actually debunking this belief held by the Corinthian Christians?

> In short, Paul is refuting antinomianism—the view that Christians have no law as a guide to their living, and thus are free to do whatever as long as they "believe." This "lawful but not helpful" passage, therefore, does not apply to the practical issues of areas in which God has clearly already given us freedom, it applies to the false belief that God has given us freedom in every area.[2]

Is Paul really teaching that everything is lawful—everything, and that the real problem lies in the fact that some things just aren't helpful? How can this be? To live as though there are no laws of God, as the Corinthians were doing, is to live with faulty thinking. Surely there are sins that violate biblical teaching and drunkenness is one of them. The logic of the Corinthians, however, is that God forbids nothing, when in reality He clearly does. What God forbids is both *unlawful* and *unhelpful*. Paul is not denying Christians the freedom God already grants them, like the moderate consumption of alcohol, rather, he is denouncing the expression of forbidden and excessive sins that cross established boundaries. Paul himself becomes an example:

> That the saying "but not helpful" should not be used as a guide for determining behaviors that God has already qualified as free strengthens when we see Paul apply it to himself—and then ignore it. In 2 Corinthians 12:1, Paul begins a passage about his experience of being caught up to "the third heaven," receiving unutterable revelations from God, and then being given a "thorn in the flesh" to keep him humble. Paul begins this mysterious passage by saying this: "I must go on boasting. Though there is nothing to be gained by it, I will go on to visions and revelations of the Lord." The phrase, "there is nothing to be gained by it," is the equivalent Greek phrase to "not all things are helpful" (1 Cor. 6:12). Boasting about his experiences, in other words, was lawful but not helpful—yet Paul did it anyway. Why? Because, first, "lawful but not helpful" is not a binding guide to Christian freedom to begin with; and second, because there was a deeper lesson to be learned through the humility that came with Paul's reason for boasting. There was a level of maturity to which the Corinthians needed to advance.[3]

If Paul is saying that all things are lawful, he is erasing centuries of scriptural understanding and promoting life without boundaries (antinomianism), the very thing he is arguing against as the Corinthians attempt to jettison all laws and do whatever they like. Corinth is a bustling city filled with boundless opportunities for sin. This young Corinthian church contains fornicators, drunkards, adulterers, self-promoters, and the like. Some are getting drunk at the Lord's Supper, one is sleeping with his stepmother, some are calling upon prostitutes, and others are visiting pagan meat markets. The whole city seems to be a hotbed of raucous and promiscuous activity. Can't the young Corinthian Christians do whatever they like now that they believe?

Paul confronts their flawed reasoning by listing some established boundaries, such as fornication, adultery, stealing, coveting, lying with a prostitute, etc. He is addressing their lawless mindset, not refuting the liberty God has already given, as in the enjoyment and consumption of moderate alcohol use. When this passage is used to prevent the consumption of alcohol, it becomes "an argument of fear, masquerading as charity. It creates a back door to let in the very prohibition these guys know the Bible does not teach. It's a way of using the Bible to ignore the

Bible."[4] We do not live unrestrained lives without boundaries. Though God forbids drunkenness, we *are* free to moderately enjoy what God permits—even fermented drink.

The Body is a Temple

Many point to I Corinthians 6:19–20 in denying the moderate use of alcohol: "Or do you not know that your body is a temple of the Holy Spirit who is in you, whom you have from God, and that you are not your own? For you have been bought with a price: therefore glorify God in your body." Since our body is the temple of the Holy Spirit, the argument goes, defiling it with alcohol is revolting.

Christ's atoning death purchased us from the marketplace of sin so that we might become redeemed children of God. The Holy Spirit of God now indwells us (2 Cor. 1:22; Eph. 1:14; 2 Tim. 1:14) and we "become partakers of the divine nature" (2 Pt. 1:4). Our body houses the Spirit's presence.

If the precious blood of Christ purchased our salvation and our body is now indwelt by the Holy Spirit, we should indeed glorify God with our body. This makes all the sense in the world, especially in light of Romans 12:1: "Therefore I urge you, brethren, by the mercies of God, to present your bodies a living and holy sacrifice, acceptable to God, which is your spiritual service of worship." What *doesn't* make sense is that we are restricted from glorifying God in what He permits—the moderate consumption of alcohol. One of the best ways to honor our Lord is to abide by His written Word in its freedoms and prohibitions. Instead, what is being said is this:

- Because our body is the temple of the Holy Spirit:
    - We must *not* do what God *restricts*, and
    - We must *not* do what God *permits.*

The first point is fine, for it aligns with Scripture. The second point, however, is problematic because it denies to us what God already allows. It usurps the authority of God's written Word and supplants it with a man-made rule in contradiction to the Bible.

Because alcohol is labeled as intrinsically evil, its presence in the temple becomes unthinkable, like a cancer in an otherwise healthy body. We should be working hard to keep our bodies pure from such defilement. But the context of I Corinthians 6, as previously discussed, deals with the violation of clear boundaries of sin, such as fornication, adultery, and prostitution that misuse the temple-body. A sin of excess, drunkenness also misuses the body. But how does engagement in the things God freely permits, like moderately consuming alcohol, defile the temple, for God has already given us freedom in this area. For Him to now label such freedom as a defiling act is confusing and contradictory.

If the moderate use of alcohol is a defilement of the temple-body, then Jesus Himself is guilty of sin, for He drank wine and encouraged its use during the Lord's Supper. How can the Old Testament look upon wine as a blessing from God if it is such a contaminated object? Paul instructs Timothy to "No longer drink water exclusively, but use a little wine for the sake of your stomach and your frequent ailments" (I Tim. 5:23). Do Paul's instructions encourage Timothy to defile his temple-body? If so, then Paul contradicts himself.

Our bodies are fearfully and wonderfully made by the Creator, and using them to cross clear boundaries of sin does not glorify God. We are to "flee immorality" (I Cor. 6:18). We honor God when we live within His boundaries. Drunkenness is outside the line while moderation is within the boundary.

How far do we go with temple defilement? If I don't work out three times a week, have I defiled my body? If I am overweight by ten pounds, have I defiled the temple? Am I able to enjoy hot tea despite the fact that it contains caffeine? Am I even allowed to breathe knowing the air is filled with pollutants? It reminds me of the legalistic Pharisees. Jesus tells them to love their neighbor and instead of just loving their neighbors, they begin justifying, quantifying, and defining "neighbor." They take a simple command of God and extrapolate it into a million pieces, analyze it to death, and in the end love no one but themselves, all the while failing to realize how unloving they are.

If we took the temple-body analogy too far, we couldn't even live life; yet, Jesus came that we "may have life, and have it abundantly" (Jn. 10:10). Life is to be lived in His presence with joy, blessing, and a smile on our face, for it is God who gives "wine which makes man's heart glad" (Ps. 104:15). Our temple-bodies honor God when we obey Him. That means being careful not to cross established boundaries, but also not to call what God permits a sin when it isn't. Our temple-body is to be under the Spirit's control which moderate alcohol consumption doesn't impede. Drunkenness, intimacy with a prostitute, adultery, and the like all cross clear boundaries of sin as the Spirit's control is lost to the excess of lust.

The Jerusalem Council

Circumcision was God's covenantal sign for Old Testament Israel. After Christ's death, a dispute arises in Jerusalem over the role of circumcision in the Christian faith (recorded in Acts 15). Is circumcision still a necessary requirement for New Testament believers, or does the arrival of the Messiah and the New Covenant negate the Old Covenant sign? A council gathered to discuss the matter and issued the following decree: "For it seemed good to the Holy Spirit and to us to lay upon you no greater burden than these essentials: that you abstain from things sacrificed to idols and from blood and from things strangled and from fornication; if you keep yourselves free from such things, you will do well" (Acts 15:28–29). Local churches were expected to abide by the council decision. Since the decree was binding on local churches, some argue that church leaders today can issue similar restrictions on alcohol to be obeyed by churches. If the Jerusalem Council can do it, why can't we?

However, the ruling is not a universal, all-encompassing, forever-decree for humankind. It is a ruling for a specific dispute, during a specific time, about a specific issue. The transition to the New Covenant is taking shape and circumcision, the physical sign of the Old Covenant so important to Jews, is being replaced with circumcision of the heart: "But he is a Jew who is one inwardly; and circumcision is that which is of the heart, by the Spirit, not by the letter" (Rom. 2:29). The Gentiles have no history, tradition, or connection to circumcision whatsoever. How do Gentile and Jewish Christians survive together during this season of transition? It will take time for the conversion of covenants to occur in the mind of Jewish Christians. The Council's requirements were temporary and necessary in deference to those unable at this point to fully realize the implications of the New Covenant.

The temporary nature of the decree is seen in what Paul later says about stumbling blocks. He advises Christians to "take care that this liberty of yours does not somehow become a stumbling block to the weak" (1 Cor. 8:9). The strong believer obviously has this liberty if he is asked to give it up. In other words, how can there be a right to eat meat sacrificed to idols if the Council decree of Acts 15 is in effect as a universal command to be obeyed by everyone in all circumstances?

> Paul himself, in this passage, clearly teaches that circumstances will determine the use of the believer's right or liberty. Hence it is evident that the Jerusalem Synod also had in mind certain circumstances. It did not make any universal rule. As far as we know, no one has ever disputed this fact.[5]

The situation for which the decree is designed to alleviate no longer exists. Intended for a specific time, place, and situation, the decree fulfills its intended purpose. Elevating it to a universal standard violates Paul's later teaching on the matter.

No Material Thing Unclean

The fact that no material thing is evil in itself is a very difficult concept for some Christians to accept. Viewing items used for sinful purposes as being evil in their material essence is a tendency that nullifies biblical teaching. Paul declares in

Romans 14:14, "I know and am convinced in the Lord Jesus that nothing is unclean in itself." He merely expresses what the Lord Jesus Christ taught in Mark 7:14–15: "Listen to Me, all of you, and understand: there is nothing outside the man which can defile him if it goes into him; but the things which proceed out of the man are what defile the man."

Esteemed theologian Dr. John Murray notes,

> This principle is the refutation of all prohibitionism which lays the responsibility for wrong at the door of things rather than at man's heart. The basic evil of this ethic is that it makes God the Creator responsible and involves both blasphemy and the attempt to alleviate human responsibility for wrong.[6]

He further states,

> Sin is not a material thing, but a "moral condition operative in free moral agents.[7]

If both Jesus and Paul teach that sin is not a material thing but something that arises from within the heart of humankind—a moral condition directly opposed to the intention of God—why are we so willing to disregard it? It is far easier, I suppose, to blame a "thing" than to blame our own blemished desires and actions.

G. I. Williamson believes an important distinction must be made:

> If a certain material thing is dangerous, and potentially harmful, to man, then it is assumed that it must be sinful to use it. Hence the slogan of the proponents of total abstinence defining temperance as "a moderate use of things that are good and total abstinence from things that are harmful." If a thing is harmful or dangerous to man then it is thought of as evil. Yet the truth is that the two are quite distinct. The one does not automatically follow from the other. It is not true that it is always a sin to use something that may be harmful or dangerous. It is not the nature of a thing that determines whether or not its use is sinful, but the way in which it is used.[8]

Williamson goes on to quote J.G. Vos from his work titled *The Separated Life*:

> Beyond doubt it is sinful to commit suicide by drinking carbolic acid. This, however, is not because the use of carbolic acid is sinful in itself, but because it is used with suicidal intent. In such a case, the sin committed is the sin of suicide, not the sin of drinking carbolic acid. Carbolic acid being a material thing cannot be sinful in itself. If its use were sinful in itself, that use would be sinful regardless of the quantity used. If one drop of carbolic acid were to be dissolved in a thousand gallons of water, and one drop of the resultant solution drunk, the drinking of that one drop would be a sin deserving the punishment of eternal death, provided the use of carbolic acid is sinful in itself.

> Let no one say that this is simply a reduction ad absurdum and therefore not worthy of serious consideration. Scripture does teach that sin has an absolute character, and that any sin, even the least, is a violation of the whole moral law and therefore deserving of the judicial sentence of eternal death.[9]

Just because something is harmful or has the potential to be harmful doesn't mean that it is also sinful. In fact, virtually every material object can be utilized in some harmful manner. Water is necessary for life, but too much of it and we drown. A button keeps our shirt on, but if swallowed by a baby, an obstructed airway may cause death. Computers may be used to write blessed sermons or surf pornographic images on the internet.

Let's choose something really wonderful, like the Bible. It can be read to transform lives or wielded to beat children over the head when they don't obey. If sin resides in material objects themselves, how can sin be my responsibility if I use them? After all, God is the one who allows their creation. He is to blame for sin! If sin is in the material object, I cannot wear clothes, sit in a chair, or come in contact with water. It becomes ridiculous, yet that is how many think.

It is wise and biblical to make a distinction between a material object and the use of that object. Alcohol is a material substance without intrinsic evil. We can look at it, touch it, smell it, feel it, and drink it without sin, because it is not evil in itself. Moreover, when we use that material object beyond the boundaries God permits, its use becomes sin. Moderate and responsible drinking of alcohol is permitted, but crossing the line into inebriation is wrong. Sin lies not in alcohol itself, but in its wrongful use in the face of God's directives against such behavior.

Setting Off Potential Alcoholics

Opponents of moderation worry that one sip of alcohol, even at the communion table, could inflame the lust of those with an innate propensity toward alcoholism. In light of this worry, abstention becomes the means of avoiding this potential dilemma and prohibitionists see it as yet another reason God forbids the consumption of alcohol.

In the Bible, drunkenness is not portrayed as a set of genetic defects or predisposed physiological scripts, but something for which we take personal responsibility:

> The Bible clearly condemns drunkenness as a moral failure and a spiritual sin, showing that it is a matter of personal responsibility (Gal. 5:19–21). In fact, chronic drunkenness effectively bars entrance into the kingdom of God, showing that men must turn from it (1 Cor. 6:9–10).[10]

If we cannot moderately imbibe in light of the many potential alcoholics lurking in the shadows waiting to be set off by one drop of alcohol, then we condemn our Lord. After all, He drank wine, manufactured the substance, encouraged His disciples to imbibe, utilized wine as the symbol of the New Covenant in His blood, and informs His disciples that He will drink wine with them again in the future kingdom. Is Jesus guilty of striking the match that causes multitudes of genetic propensities to go up in flames of overindulgence?

Alcoholism is a serious problem that shouldn't be discounted. It was a problem in Jesus' day as well, and we find numerous admonitions against its misuse in Scripture. But when we are precluded from doing something God permits simply because of its potential danger to others, we misunderstand and misapply biblical teaching. We are hard-pressed to find anything that has a zero chance of harming others. We can't drive a car for fear the exhaust is harming others. We can't have friends over for dinner, fearing they may somehow become gluttons. We can't enjoy sexual intimacy, fearing that others might become sexually perverted.

While we are not to intentionally induce weaker brothers to violate their misinformed conscience, that doesn't preclude us from enjoying the freedom God permits simply because someone might possibly, unbeknownst to us, develop a weak conscience by watching us enjoy our freedom. This is living in slippery-slope fear rather than the joy and freedom of the Lord.

Defining Moderation

Another criticism has to do with defining what is moderate and what is immoderate use. Where is the line drawn? How much alcohol is safely in the moderation zone and what quantity crosses into inebriation? Obviously, drunkenness is condemned, but why focus only on alcohol? Where is the line between a hearty appetite and gluttony? Where is the line between responsible stewardship and being too generous? Where is the line between looking and lusting?

The line is different for different people. Does gluttony equate to four pieces of chicken, eight, sixteen, twenty? Just because we cannot define how much is too much for each person doesn't mean that we shouldn't eat or that gluttony is not a sin.

> The moral problem of alcohol consumption is not defining quantity of alcohol consumed (in ounces), but its effect (in moral impact). The danger level will certainly differ from person to person; nevertheless, a difference exists between someone drunk and someone not drunk. After all, how could Scripture condemn "drunkenness" if we cannot tell the difference?[11]

I doubt we will ever arrive at a universal quantity applicable to every person. The issue is not so much one of quantity, but effect. Whenever the effect is drunkenness, we know it is wrong.

Our Christian Testimony

Abstentionist Gleason Archer believes Christians should abstain from alcohol as a means of bolstering their Christian witness:

> If we really care about the souls of men, and if we are really in business for Christ rather than for ourselves, then there seems (to this writer, at least) to be no alternative to total abstinence not as a matter of legalism, but rather as a matter of love.[12]

Being an example to others is a good and godly cause, one the Bible supports (I Tim. 4:12; I Cor. 4:16; 11:1; Phil. 2:15; Titus 2:8; I Pt. 2:11–12). No one in his right mind would disagree. But why is abstinence the example we must set when it is not even a biblical standard? Why is moderate alcohol consumption, permitted by Scripture and exemplified by Christ and His disciples, contrary to a good witness?

Isn't it better to set an example of following Scripture in both its freedoms and its prohibitions? Wouldn't requiring abstinence in something God permits actually diminish our testimony? In a world where drunkenness is often a rite of passage and a badge of honor, isn't moderate consumption and sobriety setting a positive example? If we always avoid what Scripture allows, we send mixed messages about God and undermine the authority of His written Word. We should never encourage a weaker brother to violate his conscience, but disallowing what God permits is never a good witness. It is Pharisaical.

Man-Made Rules

When the fear of alcohol's *potential* danger becomes the focal point, slippery-slope thinking creates a fertile environment for the invention of man-made rules. We love our rules. Instead of thinking things through, being responsible, and living in communion with our Heavenly Father, we often prefer rules to a relationship. Just give us a list to follow of can and can'ts, should and shouldn'ts, sin and sin-nots. God has already given us *His* list, but it doesn't appear long enough or cover all the areas many would like, so we augment the Bible with man-made rules in an effort to avoid the slippery-slope of sin. Man-made rules, however, are of little value in preventing sin from rising in our heart.

The Pharisees are good examples of man-made rules gone awry. For instance, when God commanded a Sabbath rest instead of work, legalists created all kinds of rules and definitions for what constituted work. One author presents some man-made rules legalists followed for resting on the Sabbath:[13]

- You should not look in a mirror on the Sabbath because it might tempt you to pluck out a grey hair and that would be reaping.
- You could only eat an egg which had been laid on the Sabbath if you killed the chicken for Sabbath-breaking.
- A donkey could be led out of the stable on the Sabbath, but the harness and saddle had to be placed on him the day before.
- An egg could not be boiled on the Sabbath, either by normal means or by putting it near a hot kettle or by wrapping it in a hot cloth or by putting it in the hot sand outside.
- If the lights were on when the Sabbath arrived (Sabbath began at sundown), you could not blow them out. If they had not been lit in time, then you could not light them.
- It was unlawful to move furniture on the Sabbath. There was an exception for moving a ladder on the Sabbath, but you could only move it four steps.
- It was unlawful to wear any jewelry or ornaments on the Sabbath, since this might be construed as carrying a burden.
- It was not permitted to wear false teeth on the Sabbath.
- You were allowed to eat radishes on the Sabbath, but you were warned against dipping them into salt because you might leave them in the salt too long and pickle them and this was considered to be Sabbath-breaking. The Pharisees actually had discussions as to how long it took to pickle a radish.
- It was fine to spit on a rock on the Sabbath, but you could not spit on the ground because that made mud, and mud was mortar, and that was work.
- If a woman got mud on her dress, she was to wait until it had dried and then she was permitted to crumple the dress in her hands one time and crush it and then shake it out once. If that did not do the trick, then she had to wear it.

Instead of simply obeying God's standard of Sabbath rest, numerous man-made rules are created as a sin preventative—a hedge to keep individuals from actually breaking God's Sabbath standard. Over time, these man-made rules usurp God's single command. If I look in the mirror on the Sabbath, have I violated God's Sabbath rest or a man-made rule about the Sabbath?

Let's say God told us not to climb a specific tree in the middle of a field. That's it—you can't climb it—got it. What is the *God-made* command? Do not climb the tree in the middle of the field. That is the only rule we need and it is sufficient because it comes from God Himself. But fearful that someone might actually climb the tree, we build a fence around it. Our fear has not subsided, so we build a fence around the fence and so on until there are forty fences around one tree just to keep people from climbing it. One fence is not enough, ten fences are not enough, and many are still unsatisfied with forty fences surrounding the tree.

Over time, instead of God's standard being "Do not climb the tree" it becomes "Do not cross the fortieth fence, the thirty-ninth fence, the thirty-eighth fence," and so on. The forty man-made fence rules displace the one standard God created. Soon, a young lad hops over the fortieth fence in violation of the man-made rule, but nothing happens. He now crosses the thirty-ninth fence and still nothing happens. Breaking the forty fence rules have no consequence, and he thinks less of God and feels free to break all of God's rules, for there are no consequences to fence jumping. But the fence rules are not from God. They are slippery-slope, fear-based, man-made rules, and over time the very thing the forty fences attempt to prevent is enhanced by the creation of so many useless rules. Why not just have one rule, the standard of God, and teach others not to climb the tree? Otherwise, our perspective of God becomes warped and our understanding of His holy standards are diminished.

The same scenario occurs with the consumption of alcohol. God's standard is moderation without drunkenness. Pretty simple, isn't it? Instead of obeying the God-rule, we begin erecting fences to prevent people from consuming alcohol. One fence is called prohibition, another abstention, and so on. In essence, we find the Bible insufficient so we add unnecessary man-made rules, definitions, and standards that more closely articulate what we *wish* the Bible really said. With the greatest of respect, we try to help the Bible out with its many deficiencies. But Scripture is wholly sufficient and needs nothing else added to it—nothing. It is time to identify the man-made fences, call them what they are, and kick them down—for they are without value. It is time to begin living according to the God-standard, realizing that His standard is sufficient.

Colossians 2:20–23 says,

> If you have died with Christ to the elementary principles of the world, why, as if you were living in the world, do you submit yourself to decrees, such as, "Do not handle, do not taste, do not touch!" (which all refer to things destined to perish with use)—in accordance with the commandments and teachings of men? These are matters which have, to be sure, the appearance of wisdom in self-made religion and self-abasement and severe treatment of the body, but are of no value against fleshly indulgence.

G.I. Williamson notes the following:

> Does not the man-made rule of total abstinence agree precisely with Paul's description? Is it not a decree? Is it not one of the commandments and teachings of men? Does it not also have the appearance of wisdom? Yet Paul says that such man-made rules are "of no value against fleshly indulgence." The argument is therefore false. It is not true that man-made laws can promote true godliness.[14]

We obey God's standards because they come from the Creator Himself, not from other humans. The only way we can align our lives with His standards is through the work of the Holy Spirit who indwells and empowers us. This is one reason we are asked to walk in step with the Spirit (Gal. 5: 25) and not become drunk (Eph. 5:18). Obeying God's standard is a matter of the heart which the Holy Spirit moves toward truth (Jn. 17:17). Man-made rules may sound pious, but they are powerless. They merely help perfect the art of fence building and are worthless in helping us enjoy the abundant life in Christ.

Williamson pretty well sums up the inadequacy of man-made rules:

> Our thesis is this, then: the true source for the conquest of sin in the heart is the power of God's Spirit. It is not effected by having other people erect legalistic fences around the believer. It is not promoted by allowing other people to assume responsibility for him. No, it is really promoted when the Church relies upon God's Word and Spirit. It is promoted when the Church teaches the truth of God without addition or subtraction. It is effected as God's people learn to think out the implications of the inspired Scriptures, and then apply these to their own lives in the particular and unique situation in which they find themselves (Ro. 12:2). Those who fear this, in our humble judgment, fail to comprehend the purpose and power of God.[15]

Summary: Sin arises within the heart and does not intrinsically reside within material objects (even alcohol), and we honor God when we follow His written Word in both its freedoms and its prohibitions.

WHAT NOW? A PRACTICAL CONCLUSION

This chapter identifies key biblical principles of application for our life so we can please our Lord and remain faithful to His Word. This is the "so what" part of the book; the final chapter where we turn out the lights, lock the door, and bid each other a fond farewell.

Many principles of application can be gleaned from the salient points of each chapter. The one-sentence summaries become our springboard for concluding this book. Biblical truth is the *foundation* for our actions while practical application is the *expression* of that truth. I often run into people who get this backwards. They hold dearly to particular practices and search the Bible for ways to justify them as biblical.

For example, a young man asked me if he should send one hundred dollars to a television ministry because the preacher promised him a one hundred-fold return. He got bug-eyed thinking about all the money coming his way—and for only one hundred bucks. A lengthy conversation ensued, and I asked this dreamer why the preacher didn't give him one hundred dollars. In other words, if the preacher needs money to expand his television ministry or support a lavish lifestyle, and if he *really* believes his own theology that giving away one hundred dollars will blossom into a one hundred-fold monetary return, why isn't the preacher *giving* away money rather than asking for it?

Enticing individuals to part with their hard-earned cash for a promised financial gain is a lucrative practice. Although it is profitable, milking people out of their money isn't biblical. Without solid grounding in Scripture, we are forced to scour the biblical landscape for strained interpretations, twisted contexts, and the stretching of truth so thin that you can see through it. As long as we can throw in *some* loose connection to the Bible, a veneer of justification is produced and our theology becomes based on a preferred practice rather than accurate biblical understanding.

As we discuss practical application regarding alcohol, it is important to ground our life choices in Scripture rather than man-made rules. This concluding chapter, I imagine, will disappoint those who desire another lengthy list of do's and dont's to augment Scripture. My life is lived by biblical principles rather than extensive lists of rules. I believe that God is alive and well and that He not only communes with us but also invites us to commune with Him. A rule for every circumstance in life doesn't exist. Rather, God desires that we listen attentively to His still, small voice, be led by His Holy Spirit, and apply the principles of His Word. Should you take a new out-of-state job that pays more money? Ask God? The man-made rule book, as extensive as it is, probably doesn't cover this. Why not forget the man-made rules altogether and simply allow God's Spirit to lead you? After all, what's the use of God's Spirit mediating the presence of Christ within us if we are constantly consulting man-made rules that nullify the need for the Holy Spirit? Why not simply go directly to our caring Heavenly Father for guidance and intimately commune with the living God on a daily basis?

We falsely believe the Spirit's role is providing enough energy to survive and obey all of the man-made rules, because after all, they are exhausting. But that is not the Spirit's role. He is not a giant battery that gets us through the labyrinth of man-made rules while our energy is zapped and our joy is drained. I do not create lists of do's and dont's; instead, I provide principles that frame our actions and choices. We are fortunate, in this age, to have the written Word and the Holy Spirit to guide us. But we have more than that; we have the wonderful treasure of coming before His throne of grace and dialoguing with the Lord at any moment.

Below are the one-sentence chapter summaries accompanied by thoughts on practical application:

Chapter 1 Summary:
Though the use of alcohol by Christians is a nonessential issue of faith, the subject is shrouded by confusion, passion, and division, and sound biblical reasoning is needed so the truth of Scripture can be identified, believed, proclaimed, and followed.

Practical Application:
Major on the majors and minor on the minors. Don't elevate non-pillar issues in a way that divides the body of Christ.

God-fearing Christians assume varying positions on the issue of alcohol. I believe moderation most correctly reflects biblical teaching while other views are in some way deficient. One's stance on alcohol is not a matter of division for me. There are wonderful Christians who staunchly support the prohibitionist and abstentionist viewpoint and will do so until the day they die. When we all get to heaven, I will gently elbow them in the side and with a smile on my face whisper, "See, I told you so." But in the meantime, I love them dearly—even though I adamantly disagree with their stance.

After a steady diet of analyzing legal cases in law school, final course exams asked us to decide a legal problem by analyzing fact patterns on such issues as product liability, the commerce clause, breach of contract, etc. Students were required to assess the elements of a case and identify legally significant facts—ones that could make a difference in the outcome. An understanding of law is essential, but knowing the difference between what is legally significant and what isn't may be the greater skill.

In like manner, we do the same with the alcohol issue, not from a legal standpoint, but analyzing what is essential in the kingdom and what is not. Pharisaical outlooks raise every jot-n-tittle issue to the level of foundational status, and great energy is expended in keeping track of minutia and non-essential matters. What we think about alcohol is indeed important and I happen to believe one view excels over all others, but it is not a deal-breaker in my relationship with other Christians who feel differently.

I am not saying that it doesn't matter what you believe about alcohol, for it does. Belief influences our actions and choices, and two dangers are worth noting. First, when a minor issue such as alcohol is elevated to a foundational, pillar-doctrine level, we are in danger of majoring on the minors and minoring on the majors. Like any good attorney worth her salt, separating out that which is necessary and foundational from that which is ancillary focuses our energies on what really matters—loving and accepting one another.

Second, by majoring on the minors, we risk becoming judgmental and the "my way or the highway" mentality takes over. I feel strongly that moderation is absolutely in line with biblical teaching, but I realize this is not a major point in the larger picture of Christian faith. It is not a dividing line drawn in the sand; I can love you, fellowship with you, and accept you because I want to focus on the essentials of faith—those things that really matter.

So, major on the majors and minor on the minors. In matters of ancillary issues we can and should be generous and loving toward one another, see the larger picture, and get off the high horse of legalism.

Chapter 2 Summary:
Alcohol isn't inherently evil simply because it can be abused, and since Scripture sufficiently speaks truth in its own right, we should first seek to understand what a passage means to the original audience in its own culture and time before making application to our own world.

Practical Application:
Scripture speaks truth so seek to understand it and live by its principles.

There are three parts to this notion:

- Scripture speaks truth.
- Seek to understand it.
- Live by its principles.

Deep down, do you really believe the Bible speaks truth? If not, what is the point of following its teachings? This is a serious question. If the Bible is not truth from God, then why follow it at all? Why would the Bible's values be any better than any other value? I have no interest in following falsehood, and besides, if I had to choose between what falsehoods to follow, I would choose those that are more to my liking. If the Bible is the written Word of God, then it becomes authoritative over our lives. In other words, we must pay attention to it, seek to understand it, and live by its principles, precisely because it *is* God's Word to us. This must be firmly settled in our mind.

Understanding some biblical passages can be difficult, but if Scripture speaks God's truth, seeking to understand it is a worthwhile endeavor. While readily agreeing the Bible is God's truthful Word to us, we struggle for time to seriously study it. Though many are gifted teachers within the body of Christ, others are not. Yet, we are not excused from studying it ourselves any more than we are excused from sharing the gospel just because we don't possess the gift of evangelism. Most are unable to attend seminary, obtain a working knowledge of the original biblical languages, and publish scholarly treatises on religious topics. Don't worry, that isn't an expectation. I am merely elevating the importance of personal Bible study, noting that we must first seek to understand what a passage means to its original audience in its own culture and time before making application to our own world. You will be amazed at what a regular time of personal Bible study will do for your mind and your heart.

The third aspect of our practical application principle is that we live by the truth we discover; our lives become aligned with the new knowledge we have gained. What good is believing and understanding if there is no real-world relevance? Truth without real-life application is a one-legged stool that keeps falling down.

Do we believe the biblical teaching on alcohol is true? Have we come to understand its teaching in this area and are we ready to live by its instruction? Why waste time defending or believing what is false? The Lord is pleased with the high value placed on His love letters to humankind. As we begin aligning our life to His Word, God is honored by our commitment to a truth priority.

Along with truth priority and truth understanding comes added strength for saying "no" to pressures that are contrary to biblical teaching, whether they come from the culture around us or within the church itself. We do not have to feel guilty, pressured, or shamed for abiding by Scripture—ever. Biblical truth becomes the spiritual backbone for standing up to all sorts of voices pressuring us to alter our views. When prohibitionists bulldoze you into their camp, stand firm on the biblical record. When abstentionists shame your moderate consumption, stand firm knowing that your behavior and choices are rooted in solid biblical understanding. Scripture speaks truth, and now having studied His Word, we are able to make life decisions based on its teaching.

Chapter 3 Summary:

Recognizing the destructive nature of overindulgence, Scripture clearly condemns the abuse of alcohol whereas a life pleasing to the Heavenly Father is one under the control of the Holy Spirit.

Practical Application:

Do not get drunk under the influence of alcohol, but be under the influence of the Holy Spirit.

I just have to ask, "What part of no don't you understand?" This is the tree in the middle of the field we are not to climb. We don't need fences around it, additional man-made rules, or soliloquies on the prohibition or abstention of alcohol. Instead, we just need to obey. DO NOT GET DRUNK. It doesn't matter if everyone else is inebriated, culture is pressuring you to overindulge, or if the entire Christian youth group is getting plastered on Friday night after the high school football game. God's directive is pretty simple: do not get drunk.

This is the point where different paths are taken. The path of man-made rules desires to supplement God's directive with enhanced standards describing the proper amounts of each alcoholic drink and defining drunkenness to their specifications. Unable to control the rule-making urge, another list is established describing how godly Christians should prevent drunkenness by not entering retail establishments selling alcohol, frequenting restaurants that serve fermented drink, or possessing trace amounts of alcohol in the home. These sin-preventative measures are designed to protect us from the potential danger of drunkenness (fences guarding the tree).

Another path finds the man-made rules too difficult to discern, track, and obey, and simply says, "We should just abstain from alcohol altogether so that we don't have to worry about falling into drunken danger or being associated with such an unpleasant social stigma." This becomes a prudent path to follow in the contemporary milieu.

Still another path decides it is best to embrace personal responsibility for aligning our lives to Scripture. With the backbone of scriptural truth and a solid resolve to follow its teaching, it matters little what culture says and does. This path forbids drunkenness and honors God by not getting drunk. When these folks do imbibe, they do so by honoring God in moderation, as He permits. This is where the rubber meets the road and why I earlier asked if you believe Scripture speaks truth. You will have to take a stand to obey its teaching.

Maybe the issue still brings uncertainty to your mind at this point in your Christian journey, or you are fearful that succumbing to drunkenness might be a real problem for you. Remember, you are not commanded or required to consume fermented beverage. God also allows us to become bakers and bricklayers, but I chose to do neither, and instead, followed another permitted path. Choosing *not* to drink is a valid choice. You should feel no pressure from Scripture or anyone else to imbibe. But if you ever do decide to consume an alcoholic beverage, you must do so with moderation that does not lead to drunkenness.

This is where some yearn for a man-made rule: "I am allowed to drink one and a half drinks at 6% alcohol over a two hour period of time, on Fridays, in the confines of my own home between the hours of 7:00 and 9:00 p.m." Instead, the Bible requires that we take personal responsibility and make Spirit-led decisions in all areas of our life, not just alcohol. But this is a real problem, isn't it—being led by the Spirit of God. We aren't as adept at this as we would like to be. Rather than take the necessary time to develop a communing relationship with our loving Heavenly Father, it is far more palatable to follow a man-made rule—the path of least resistance.

Under the influence of alcohol, we can do some pretty stupid things and become an extreme danger to ourselves and others. The only thing God wants to control us is the Holy Spirit because He always leads in paths of righteousness. Either get drunk under the control of alcohol, do some stupid and dangerous things, and sin against the Creator, or be under the control of God's Spirit and produce the fruit of the Spirit which pleases the Heavenly Father. Isn't the choice obvious? Take responsibility for your actions and intentionally choose to obey God's clear directive.

Chapter 4 Summary:
A consistent view of scriptural teaching on alcohol can be seen throughout Christian history (abuse prohibited—moderation permitted) up until the Temperance Movement of the nineteenth and twentieth centuries when social pressure is brought to bear in the national crusade for total abstinence.

We find great encouragement in knowing that history is on the side of moderation. It is the prevailing view of alcohol throughout Christendom until the Temperance Movement of the nineteenth and twentieth centuries. The gauge of history isn't always accurate, but in this case, we know that from the Old Testament to the landing of European settlers on American soil, moderation was the view accepted and taught by the Christian church. In other words, moderation isn't some fanciful invention for modern times. Instead, it has long been the view of Scripture throughout the centuries. We merely join the ancient choir singing the moderationist chorus.

Chapter 5 Summary:
The Bible teaches, in both testaments, that alcohol is not inherently evil but a gift from God to be enjoyed with thanksgiving, while the abuse of alcohol (drunkenness) is condemned.

Alcohol is not an intrinsically evil substance. In fact, no material item is sinful in its essence (discussed in Chapter 11). The Bible portrays wine and strong drink in positive terms while drunkenness and overindulgence is depicted in negative terms. This surprises many, but they are viewing Scripture from a post-temperance perspective. Prior to the Temperance Movement, alcohol was seen as a good gift from the Creator. If you consume alcohol moderately without overindulgence, then you are within the bounds of scriptural teaching and have the backing of both the Old and New Testaments behind you.

Chapter 6 Summary:
There is no biblical support for a two-wine theory (positive references refer to grape juice while negative references speak of fermented drink) because the biblical words in both the Old and New Testaments, and the contexts in which the words are used, refers to alcoholic drink.

We should follow Scripture rather than invented theories and wild interpretations. The social agenda of the Temperance Movement created a religious viewpoint where alcohol consumption is sinful and prohibition and abstention are commanded by Scripture. To lend credence to such claims, supporters invented a two-wine theory—positive references to wine in the Bible always refer to grape juice while negative references refer to fermented drink. But this malnutritioned view, devoid of biblical support, is nothing more than a boisterous false claim by well-intentioned believers frantically searching to biblicize their skewed perspective. It is only with the rise of the Temperance Movement that this theory gains any sort of traction.

If Christians decide to imbibe in moderation, enjoy a glass of wine during a meal, or drink a beer during a football game, they are permitted to do so without fearing they have violated Scripture. The deciding factor on whether something aligns with Scripture is Scripture itself, not some fanciful theory dreamed up in the minds of those with an axe to grind. Let me say it another way—you have full freedom to obey Scripture. You have full freedom to enjoy what God permits without feeling guilty. His Word is the deciding factor.

Chapter 7 Summary:

Jesus makes wine, drinks wine, institutes wine as a symbol of the New Covenant in His blood, commands His disciples to drink wine, promises to drink it again in the future kingdom, and uses wine and vineyard images in His teaching ministry.

Should you ever decide to exercise your freedom regarding the moderate consumption God permits, you do so while realizing that alcohol is not an inherently sinful substance but something our Lord drank, encouraged His disciples to drink, instituted as the symbol of the New Covenant, and will drink again with us in the future kingdom. Opponents often focus attention on the *moderate* consumption of alcohol, when in reality, it is the *abuse* of alcohol that is so treacherous. Jesus doesn't abuse alcohol and neither do His disciples, for that is not permitted.

Chapter 8 Summary:

Believing the Bible portrays alcohol as evil and absolutely forbids its consumption is a false conclusion and divorces specific verses from their contextual environment, for a text detached from its context becomes nothing but a pretext in support of a predetermined conclusion.

This chapter encourages us to be honest with Scripture. You can't just yank specific verses out of their proper context and apply them in some willy-nilly fashion. Without a strong connection to the context, we can pretty much twist the Bible to say whatever we want it to say. Don't be fooled by spiritual-sounding arguments based on verses detached from their context. It is a charade—a personal opinion all dressed up in religious attire. In our contextual examination of various Bible passages, we discover that God permits moderate consumption of alcohol while drunkenness is condemned. Others may wave their long, bony finger in your face, quote countless Scriptures, and preach up a storm, but it doesn't change a thing. You can divorce Bible verses from their context in a pretty manner or an ugly one—either way, it is still nothing more than a pretext for a predetermined conclusion. Don't be fooled.

Chapter 9 Summary:

There is no universal, absolute command to abstain from alcohol in the Bible and occurrences of abstention are for a limited time, to limited individuals, in limited situations.

    Realize that there is no universal command to abstain from alcohol in the Bible. Scripture is very explicit in its prohibition of drunkenness, but we do not find any such limiting standard with moderate consumption. Why should we allow others to place a prohibition upon us that Scripture doesn't? When shackled with unscriptural, man-made prohibitions, we must be willing to cut loose the fetters that bind us and live according to Scripture alone. The absolute teaching of Scripture is this: you are permitted to consume alcohol, but if you do, make sure you do so in moderation, for drunkenness is not prohibited.

Chapter 10 Summary:

Weak Christians erroneously believe alcohol consumption is sin when it is not, and violate their own conscience when they do something they believe God forbids, while the strong who think accurately about the matter must not intentionally entice weak believers into violating their conscience, since that would disregard the demands of love.

Practical Application:

Do not intentionally entice a weak brother to violate his conscience, for this is unloving.

    We know that Scripture permits the moderate use of alcohol, but weaker brothers erroneously view it as sinful. Instead of simply following their private conviction on the matter, they extend their personal misgivings to all others. While weaker brothers must grow in their understanding of God's Word and move from their present weakness to a strong faith, growth and change best occur in an environment of love and acceptance, not criticism and judgment.

    When we *intentionally* seek to cause weaker brothers to violate their conscience, we no longer act in love. Christ loves both the strong and the weak and calls each one His child. Personal application of biblical teaching means that we do not intentionally cause weaker brothers to violate their conscience.

Practical Application:
Living in community with others means that we have love obligations to one another and our actions should be guided by principles of love.

The church is a spiritual body, connected to one another by our kinship with God. As brothers and sisters in Christ, we have the same spiritual father. We live as family and families live in community. You can pick your friends, but you are stuck with your relatives. Living in community helps us experience God, love one another, and learn to walk in a manner pleasing to our Lord. It is not easy to do and I have a sneaky suspicion that is exactly why God wants us to do it. By living in community we become more like our Savior.

Love becomes a preeminent principle of success when living in community—not the seeking of our own ambitions, but the joy of serving others and desiring their good. Manipulation, guilt-tripping, self-serving actions, accumulation of power and control, my way or highway thinking, and the like are all selfish mentalities that produce friction and division in the body. We can't get around it—being a Christian demands that we actually love one another. Our behavior in the community should reflect the very love Christ has for us—the sacrificial love that caused Him to end His life that we might find ours.

While we are permitted to consume alcohol, the principle of love reaches even to this freedom, just like it touches all of our actions.

> . . . the Christian is careful about how much he drinks and especially with whom he drinks. He does not drink with drunkards, nor drink at all if he easily loses self-control. God has not called us to be hogs or to wallow in the same mire as hogs. God has called us to "drink it [wine] in the courts of my holiness" (Isaiah 62:9).[1]

Brad Whittington shares a story that reveals how maintaining a proper understanding of biblical teaching and love can work together:[2]

> I have another friend who frequently comes to my house for dinner parties. "Gustav" enjoys beer and the occasional margarita, but I've never seen him overdo it, not even at the New Year's Eve parties.
>
> As his son grew older, Gustave became concerned about his son encountering peer pressure at school. When his son turned thirteen, Gustav made a covenant with him that neither of them would drink until his son turned twenty-one. When he told me about it at the next dinner party, I asked if he would prefer I not drink. He said, "No, go ahead. You're not the one who made a covenant. I am." Gustav is still holding strong to his vow, even in situations where his son would never know if he had a beer or not.

> Gustave is a perfect example of the law of love. He has no misconceptions about what the Bible says about drinking, but he chooses to voluntarily deny himself for eight years for the sake of his son.

I really like this story. It shows wisdom, love, and adherence to scriptural truth. This father has loving concern for his son, and he doesn't wrongly use Scripture as a manipulative tool for abstinence. In fact, he understands Scripture permits the moderate consumption of alcohol. But he also knows the kind of pressure his son might experience—a pressure for excess in violation of God's command. In love he makes a covenant right alongside his son. Excellent!

You see, we don't have to manipulate Scripture, invent two-wine theories, or engage in exegetical gymnastics at all. We just have to follow Scripture. Moderate consumption is permitted; drunkenness is condemned, and the obligation of love must infuse all of our behaviors. When we love someone we seek their very best. This father loves his son so much that he is willing to forego his own freedom. He exercises restraint, not because he has to, but because he wants to, and he does so in full honor of scriptural integrity. In all scenarios, whether alcohol related or not, we place our actions within the framework of loving others.

The point is that we have love obligations to one another. On occasion, we may abstain from certain freedoms, not because we must, but because we believe it to be the best course of action promoting love. This is where the Spirit of God can lead us while maintaining fidelity to Scripture. The preeminence of love becomes the hallmark of our interactions with one another. We can experience love obligations to one another in exemplary ways since the love of Christ has been poured into our hearts (Rom. 5:5).

Chapter 11 Summary:

Sin arises within the heart and does not intrinsically reside within material objects (even alcohol), and we honor God when we follow His written Word in both its freedoms and its prohibitions.

This truth is sometimes difficult to get our arms around, since we so easily associate abuse of a material item with the use of the item itself. As we have seen, however, this is incorrect thinking and would eventually cause us to disavow Christianity itself since it too is often abused. The path of least resistance often leads to easy, but incorrect, thinking—a sinkhole that is difficult to escape.

Commitment to scriptural truth is essential and must extend to *all* teaching of Scripture—everything. When we enjoy God's freedoms but disregard His prohibitions, we do not live according to His truth. When we enjoy His prohibitions but disregard His freedoms, we do the same thing. Either way, we merely play mental games to achieve what it is we desire. That isn't commitment, but spiritual arrogance seeking clever ways to skirt God's Word. Commitment entails following God's truth in its entirety, even the things we wish weren't there.

You don't like the fact that God permits alcohol consumption? Get over it. I've got news for you—you aren't God and you don't get to dictate the contents of Scripture. You *do* get to realign your thinking, words, and behaviors to its teaching. Are you willing to do that? Does your commitment extend to Scripture in its entirety or does it stop at the doorstep of what you want it to say? Scripture is wholly sufficient in its own right.

The Creator of the universe decrees that nothing is evil in itself, including alcohol, and moderate consumption is permitted while drunkenness is prohibited. Pretty simple, isn't it? To live by scriptural truth means that we live by all of its teaching, not just selected portions.

Now that the chapter summaries have been reviewed, a few more principles of application may be beneficial.

Practical Application:
There is no obligation, pressure, or command to drink. It is a matter of personal choice with freedom not to drink.

Sometimes well-intentioned Christians equate permission to moderately imbibe to mean that Christians should and must consume alcohol. Nothing could be further from the truth. If you don't want to partake, praise God, hallelujah. That is wonderful. Give God glory for the choice He permits you. But, don't force your choice on another, for that would violate the law of love. If you want to imbibe in moderation as an adult, praise God, hallelujah. Give God glory for the choice He permits you. Don't, however, force your choice on others when they have complete freedom in the matter, for that would violate the law of love.

Practical Application:
There may be times when abstinence is necessary or wise, not as a matter of scriptural law, but as a matter of wisdom and love.

This application principle is not acquiescing to prohibitionists or abstentionists, but is simply recognizing there may be times when abstinence is the way to go, not as a matter of scriptural law, but as a matter of wisdom and love. In fact, this is an offshoot of the love principle previously mentioned, but I want to draw special attention to it and say, don't be afraid to abstain when you feel a specific situation is best served by abstinence. This is not a plea for legalism, but the freedom you have—to show restraint and love when necessary.

My point is not to establish a list of when, where, and how we should abstain, for that is a legalistic approach. Before you know it, the list would grow to epic proportions and we would hold annual conferences to discuss additions to the list and maybe even start various denominations over the list's finer points. If you do abstain for a season or for a specific circumstance, that is absolutely fine. Just do so knowing that you are abstaining out of wisdom and love and not some twisted view of Scripture. I firmly believe the indwelling Holy Spirit can guide you in this regard.

Some churches make abstaining from alcohol a requirement of church membership or ordination. Are these requirements biblical? Does the Bible make abstinence a necessary requirement for becoming a member of God's family? Of course not. Does the Bible make abstinence a necessary requirement for leadership within the church? Of course not. So why do we add more rules and regulations to Scripture? It seems to me that of the two—moderately consuming alcohol or adding additional rules to the sufficiency of Scripture—the latter is the more grievous fault.

For many years, I have served in Christian colleges that typically make students, faculty, and staff sign some sort of life-together covenant. Some community covenants clearly articulate the sinfulness of alcohol and prohibit its use by faculty, staff, and students. Others note that while God doesn't prohibit alcohol, a pledge is signed not to imbibe as a matter of community living. Still others do not allow drinking on campus, but off campus the freedom to imbibe is permitted.

These institutions are trying to protect young, traditional college-age students from the cultural pressure of overindulgence. Whether these community covenants are effective and how extensive they should be is beyond the scope of this book. I mention the practice because it is something I have experienced within multiple Christian colleges and embodies the very issues covered in this book. Do schools require abstinence as a matter of scriptural prohibition or a matter of freedom tempered by wisdom?

Dealing with Abuse

How should the church deal with abuse of alcohol? Williamson believes alcohol abuse "should be dealt with in exactly the same way that any other form of abuse is dealt with."[3] Are we not becoming idiotized with the abuse of television and the amount of filth that fills our mind? Do we abuse the wonders of technology as it consumes our lives? Do we abuse a love of sports that enthralls our passions? The church doesn't ban televisions in the home, the owning of technological devices, or doing away with sports. The role of the church is to teach the freedoms and prohibitions of Scripture—the whole counsel of God—so believers can apply biblical principles to their lives.

Can the church caution its members against the dangers of abuse? Absolutely. The Bible warns us of the abuse of alcohol and why its excess is prohibited. The church can warn against the abuse of too much television watching, the excess of technology controlling our lives, and how a sports obsession can be problematic. But, the church doesn't *forbid* the use of television, technology, or sports. There is a difference. Williamson notes how man-made rules affect the church:

> When a church adopts a man-made rule (such as the rule of total abstinence from the use of wine) the tendency is as follows. Whenever a member uses any wine, even in moderation, he is immediately subjected to strict discipline. But when another member of the same church is gluttonous, or addicted to television, the church is excessively lenient. As long as those who are guilty of intemperance in these other things strictly abide by the man-made rule, the church tends to evade its duty. The result is that members of such churches tend to equate godliness with a lop-sided conformity to certain rules only, while other aspects of the law of God are virtually ignored. Or, to put the matter in a phrase, the church that forbids what God allows, will also tend to allow what God forbids.[4]

Did you catch that last phrase, "the church that forbids what God allows, will also tend to allow what God forbids"? Powerful and true. When we don't declare the whole truth of God's Word, we focus on selective issues (like alcohol abstinence) while ignoring others (like gluttony). Can we warn against the dangers of abusing alcohol? Absolutely. Can we prohibit the use of alcohol? Absolutely not. Why? Because the whole counsel of God only prohibits drunkenness while allowing moderate consumption of alcohol.

Principles of Application Summary

Here is a listing of the practical application principles (not an exhaustive list):

- Major on the majors and minor on the minors. Don't elevate non-pillar issues in a way that divides the body of Christ.
- Scripture speaks truth so seek to understand it and live by its principles.
- Do not get drunk under the influence of alcohol, but be under the influence of the Holy Spirit.
- Do not intentionally entice a weak brother to violate his conscience, for this is unloving.
- Living in community with others means that we have love obligations to one another and our actions should be guided by principles of love.

- There is no obligation, pressure, or command to drink. It is a matter of personal choice with freedom not to drink.
- There may be times when abstinence is necessary or wise, not as a matter of scriptural law, but as a matter of wisdom and love.

The Grand Finale

My quest to discover biblical teaching on alcohol is done. If I could boil the entire book down to a few sentences, here it is:

- The Bible permits the moderate consumption of alcohol.
- Drunkenness is not permitted and crosses a boundary established by God.
- We live in community with others where the preeminence of love must rule our interactions.

And now, it is time to bid you a fond farewell, turn out the lights, and lock the door. Farewell.

ENDNOTES & BIBLIOGRAPHY

Chapter 1: Another Book On Alcohol?
1. David Wilkerson, Sipping Saints (Old Tappan, NJ: Spire Book, Fleming H. Revell Company, 1978), 11.
2. Ibid., 61.

Chapter 2: Approaching Scripture With Integrity
1. Al Lunden and Alice Lunden, Jesus the Winemaker: Satan's Most Effective Lie (Bloomington, IN: WestBow Press, 2011).
2. Ibid., 51.
3. Ibid., 21.

Chapter 3: Drunkenology 101: The Abuse Of Alcohol
1. See Kenneth L. Gentry, God Gave Wine: What the Bible Says About Alcohol (Lincoln, CA: 2001), 17–32 for a clear presentation of the biblical teaching on drunkenness. Many of my thoughts are based upon Gentry's work.
2. G.I. Williamson, Wine in the Bible & the Church (Phillipsburg, NJ: Presbyterian and Reformed Publishing Company, 1976), 9.
3. Joel McDurmon, What Would Jesus Drink? (White Hall, WV: Tolle Lege Press, 2011), 57.
4. Brad Whittington, What Would Jesus Drink? (Wunderfool Press, 2011), 11.
5. Ibid., 13.
6. Ibid., 18.
7. Ibid.
8. Ibid.
9. Gentry, God Gave Wine: What the Bible Says About Alcohol, 32.

Chapter 4: History 101: Alcohol Through The Ages
1. James Norwood Pratt, The Wine Bibber's Bible (San Francisco, CA: 101 Productions, 1975), 93–94.
2. "Christian Views on Alcohol," Wikipedia, accessed on December 31, 2013, http://en.wikipedia.org/wiki/Christian_views_on_alcohol.
3. Ibid.
4. Edward R. Emerson, A Lay Thesis on Bible Wines (NY: Merrill & Baker, 1902), 20.
5. "Christian Views on Alcohol," quoting Raymond, 49 and also Wigoder, 799.

6. Howard H. Charles, *Alcohol and the Bible* (Scottdale, PA: Herald Press, 1966), 5, quoting from "The Story of Sinuhe," *The Ancient Near East: An anthology of Texts and Pictures*, ed. J. B. Pritchard, (Princeton, NJ: Princeton University Press, 1958), 5ff.
7. Much of the information from this section on the Church Fathers comes from "Christian Views on Alcohol," *Wikipedia*.
8. Everett Tilson, *Should Christians Drink?* (Nashville, TN: Abingdon Press, 1957), 41.
9. Ibid.
10. Ibid., 41–42.
11. "Christian Views on Alcohol."
12. Ibid.
13. Ibid.
14. Ibid.
15. Tilson, *Should Christians Drink?*, 42.
16. For an excellent look at the Reformers and drinking, see Jim West, *Drinking with Calvin and Luther* (Lincoln, CA: Oakdown Books, 2003), from which much of the Reformation material is taken.
17. West, *Drinking with Calvin and Luther*, 29.
18. Ibid.
19. Ibid., 30.
20. Ibid., 29.
21. Tilson, *Should Christians Drink?*, 48.
22. West, *Drinking with Calvin and Luther*, 54.
23. Ibid., 53.
24. Ibid.
25. Ibid.
26. Ibid., 61.
27. Ibid.
28. Ibid., 65.
29. Ibid., 70–71.
30. Ibid., 71–72.
31. Ibid., 68–69.
32. "Christian Views on Alcohol."
33. West, *Drinking with Calvin and Luther*, 80.
34. Ibid., 82–83.
35. Ibid., 84.
36. Ibid., 85.
37. Ibid., 96–97.
38. Ibid., 94.
39. "Christian Views on Alcohol."
40. West, *Drinking with Calvin and Luther*, 95.
41. Tilson, *Should Christians Drink?*, 51.
42. Ibid.
43. West, *Drinking with Calvin and Luther*, 102.
44. Ibid., 105.

45. Ibid., 106.
46. Ibid., 111.
47. Ibid., 112.
48. Tilson, *Should Christians Drink?*, 53.
49. "Christian Views on Alcohol."
50. Ibid.
51. Ibid.
52. Tilson, *Should Christians Drink?*, 55.
53. "Christian Views on Alcohol."
54. "Prohibition: A Film by Ken Burns & Lynn Novick," *PBS*, accessed on January 1, 2014, http://www.pbs.org/kenburns/prohibition/roots-of-prohibition/.
55. Tilson, *Should Christians Drink?*, 54.
56. Ibid., 56–57.
57. "Prohibition: A Film by Ken Burns & Lynn Novick."
58. Tilson, *Should Christians Drink?*, 58.
59. Williamson, *Wine in the Bible & the Church*, 2.
60. Ibid., 3.
61. Ibid., 4.
62. Ibid., 5.
63. "Alcohol and the Bible," David Hanson, accessed on January 18, 2014, http://www2.potsdam.edu/hansondj/controversies/1109209383.html#.UtqEVrTnYY0, quoting J.E. Royce, *Alcohol Problems and Alcoholism: A Comprehensive Survey*, (NY: Macmillan, 1981), 291.

Chapter 5: Biblical Teaching: An Overview

1. "Alcohol in the Bible," *Wikipedia*, accessed on January 18, 2014, http://en.wikipedia.org/wiki/Alcohol_in_the_Bible.
2. Charles, *Alcohol and the Bible*, 5.
3. The scriptures and outline for this section is adopted from "Fundamentally Reformed post 'Wine to Gladden the Heart of Man': Thoughts on God's Good Gift of Wine,'" accessed on January 18, 2014, http://www.fundamentallyreformed.com/2006/03/20/wine-gladden-heart/.
4. "Alcohol in the Bible."
5. Williamson, *Wine in the Bible & the Church*, 9–10.
6. Charles, *Alcohol and the Bible*, 8. The noncanonical examples in this section are also taken from Charles' work.
7. Ibid., 10.
8. Ibid., 11.
9. Ibid., 12.
10. Ibid., 14.
11. Ibid.
12. "Alcohol and the Bible," Daniel Whitfield, accessed on January 19, 2014, http://drbacchus.com/bible/alcohol.html. His search of Bible references for wine and alcohol is based on the New International and King James versions of the Bible.
13. Ibid.

Chapter 6: The Two-Wine Theory

1. Alvah Hovey, *Bible Wine* (reprinted from The Baptist Quarterly Review, 1888), 3.
2. Peter Lumpkins, *Alcohol Today: Abstinence in an Age of Indulgence* (Garland, TX: Hannibal Books, 2009), 120–121.
3. Tilson, *Should Christians Drink?*, 19, 21, 22.
4. Emerson, *A Lay Thesis on Bible Wines*, 8, 11.
5. Wilkerson, *Sipping Saints*, 30.
6. "Isaiah 16:10 and the Two-Wine Theory," post accessed on January 22, 2014, http://www.fundamentallyreformed.com/2008/08/07/two-wine-theory/, quoting from Gentry, *God Gave Wine: What the Bible Says About Alcohol*, 44, who quotes Dunlop Moore, "Wine," *A Religious Encyclopedia of Biblical, Historical, Doctrinal and Practical Theology* (Chicago, IL: Funk and Wagnalls, 1887), 3:2536–2537.
7. "Circular Reasoning," *Wikipedia*, accessed on January 22, 2014, http://en.wikipedia.org/wiki/Circular_reasoning.
8. Lumpkins, *Alcohol Today: Abstinence in an Age of Indulgence*, 123.
9. Ibid.
10. Ibid., 123–124, quoting Moses Stuart, *Scriptural View of the Wine-Question* (NY: Levitt, Trow and Company, 1848).
11. Charles Wesley Ewing, *The Bible and its Wine* (Denver, CO: The National Prohibition Foundation, 1985), XII.
12. Ibid., 10.
13. "Alcohol in the Bible." My list is a limited reflection of this article's expanded chart that contains the Hebrew or Greek word, its transliteration, Strong's number, meaning, Septuagint equivalent(s), and documentation regarding the source of the meaning.
14. Stephen M. Reynolds, *The Biblical Approach to Alcohol* (Princeton, NJ: Princeton University Press, and *Alcohol and the Bible* (Little Rock, AR: The Challenge Press, 1983).
15. Reynolds, *The Biblical Approach to Alcohol*, 33, as quoted in Gentry, *God Gave Wine: What the Bible Says About Alcohol*, 34–35.
16. Gentry, *God Gave Wine: What the Bible Says About Alcohol*, 35.
17. McDurmon, *What Would Jesus Drink: A Spirit-Filled Study*, 22.
18. Samuele Bacchiocchi, *Wine in the Bible: A Biblical Study on the Use of Alcoholic Beverages* (Berrien Springs, MI: Biblical Perspectives, 1989), 62.
19. "Wine, Alcohol, and the Bible," *Tekton Apologetics*, accessed on January 26, 2014, http://www.tektonics.org/lp/nowine.php.
20. Ibid.
21. Gentry, *God Gave Wine: What the Bible Says About Alcohol*, 35.
22. Ibid., 36.
23. Ibid., 37.
24. Ibid., 38.
25. Ibid., 39.
26. Ibid.
27. Ibid., 36, quoting Reynolds, *The Biblical Approach to Alcohol*, 60.
28. Ibid., quoting Reynolds, *The Biblical Approach to Alcohol*, 75, 78.
29. "Wine in the Ancient World," *Early Church History 101*, accessed on January 27, 2014, http://www.churchhistory101.com/feedback/wine-ancient-world.php.

30. Ibid.
31. R.A. Baker, "Wine in the Ancient World," downloadable PDF http://www.churchhistory101.com/docs/Wine-Ancient-World.pdf accessed on February 14, 2014, http://www.churchhistory101.com.
32. Gentry, *God Gave Wine: What the Bible Says About Alcohol*, 40.
33. Ibid., 41.
34. Ibid.
35. Ibid., 42, quoting Reynolds, *Alcohol and the Bible*, 20. Others who hold this view are Robert P. Teachout, "The Use of 'Wine' in the Old Testament" (doctoral dissertation, Dallas Theological Seminary, 1982), 282; William Patton, *Bible Wines: The Laws of Fermentation and the Wines of the Ancients* (Fort Worth, TX: Star Bible), 107; and Ewing, *The Bible and its Wine*, 14.
36. Ibid., quoting Reynolds, *The Biblical Approach to Alcohol*, 145.
37. Ibid.
38. Ibid., 42–43.
39. Reynolds, *Alcohol and the Bible*, 53.
40. Gentry, *God Gave Wine: What the Bible Says About Alcohol*, 47.
41. Ibid., 48.
42. Ibid., 50.
43. Alfred Edersheim, *The Temple: Its Ministry and Services* (Grand Rapids, MI: Eerdmans, 1958), 376, as quoted in Gentry, *God Gave Wine: What the Bible Says About Alcohol*, 50.
44. Gentry, *God Gave Wine: What the Bible Says About Alcohol*, 50.
45. Ibid., 57.
46. Ibid., 58.
47. Ibid.
48. "Wine, Alcohol, and the Bible."
49. Gentry, *God Gave Wine: What the Bible Says About Alcohol*, 60.
50. Ibid., 61.
51. Ibid., 62.
52. Ibid., 61.
53. Ibid., 63.
54. Ibid.
55. Ibid., 68–71.
56. Williamson, *Wine in the Bible & the Church*, 12.
57. Gentry, *God Gave Wine: What the Bible Says About Alcohol*, 68.
58. Ibid., 69.
59. Ibid., 70.
60. Ibid., 70–71. Gentry quotes W. Robertson Nicoll and J.H. Bernard, eds., *The Expositor's Greek New Testament*, (Grand Rapids, MI: Eerdmans, 1980), 3:363.
61. Williamson, *Wine in the Bible & the Church*, 14.

Chapter 7: Jesus And Alcohol

1. Williamson, *Wine in the Bible & the Church*, 12.
2. "Christian Views on Alcohol and Drug Addiction," post by Lance Gauthreaux on October 7, 2013, accessed on February 1, 2014, http://www.spiritualliving360.com/index/.php/christian-views-on-alcohol-and-drug-addiction-5-34039/.

3. Wilkerson, *Sipping Saints*, 19.
4. Lumpkins, *Alcohol Today: Abstinence in an Age of Indulgence*, 120–150.
5. Ibid., 143.
6. Gentry, *God Gave Wine: What the Bible Says About Alcohol*, 74-75.
7. Ibid., 75–79. The arguments presented here come from Gentry's fine defense of Reynolds' arguments.
8. Reynolds, *Alcohol and the Bible*, 37–38, quoted in Gentry, *God Gave Wine: What the Bible Says About Alcohol*, 75.
9. Gentry, *God Gave Wine: What the Bible Says About Alcohol*, 76.
10. Ibid.
11. Ibid.
12. Ibid., 78.
13. Ibid.
14. Ibid., 79.
15. Ibid.
16. Ibid.
17. Wilkerson, *Sipping Saints*, 33.
18. Moore, "Wine," *A Religious Encyclopedia of Biblical, Historical, Doctrinal and Practical Theology*, 3:2537–2538.
19. Tilson, *Should Christians Drink?*, 32.
20. Gentry, *God Gave Wine: What the Bible Says About Alcohol*, 81, quoting John D. Davis, "Wine," *Illustrated Davis Bible Dictionary* (Nashville, TN: Royal Publishers, 1973 [1924]), 868.
21. West, *Drinking with Calvin and Luther*, 129.
22. Gentry, *God Gave Wine: What the Bible Says About Alcohol*, 80, quoting Reynolds, *The Biblical Approach to Alcohol*, 108.
23. Tilson, *Should Christians Drink?*, 33–34, quoting Heinrich Graetz, *History of the Jews* (Philadelphia, PA., The Jewish Publication Society of America, 1891), I, 398.
24. McDurmon, *What Would Jesus Drink?*, 10–11.
25. West, *Drinking with Calvin and Luther*, 129.
26. "Wine-Drinking in New Testament Times," Robert H. Stein, accessed on February 14, 2014, http://www.swartzentrover.com/cotor/bible/Doctrines/Holiness/Drugs%20&%20Alcohol/Wine-Drinking%20in%20New%20Testament%20Times.htm.
27. West, *Drinking with Calvin and Luther*, 138.
28. Baker, "Wine in the Ancient World."
29. West, *Drinking with Calvin and Luther*, 138.
30. Ibid., 139.
31. Ferrar Fenton, *The Bible and Wine* (New York, NY: Loizeaux Brothers, reprinted in 1938), 8.
32. West, *Drinking with Calvin and Luther*, 127.
33. McDurmon, *What Would Jesus Drink: A Spirit-Filled Study*, 35.
34. Ibid., 36.
35. Reynolds, *The Biblical Approach to Alcohol*, 98.
36. Bacchiocchi, *Wine in the Bible: A Biblical Study on the Use of Alcoholic Beverages*, 146.
37. Hovey, *Bible Wine*, 12.
38. Emerson, *A Lay Thesis on Bible Wines*, 35.

39. Jimmy L. Albright, "Wine in the Biblical World: Its Economic, Social, and Religious Implications for New Testament Interpretation" (doctoral dissertation, Southern Baptist Theological Seminary, 1980), 129, 137.
40. R.C.H. Lenski, *The Interpretation of St. John's Gospel* (Columbus, OH: Lutheran Book Concern, 1942), 318.
41. McDurmon, *What Would Jesus Drink: A Spirit-Filled Study*, 106–107.

Chapter 8: Perceived Problem Passages

1. Much of this chapter is based on Gentry's fine work, *God Gave Wine: What the Bible Says About Alcohol*, Chapter 5: Alleged Negative Passages, 83–104.
2. Ibid., 86–87.
3. Ibid., 86.
4. Ibid., 84.
5. "Wine, Alcohol, and the Bible."
6. Gentry, *God Gave Wine: What the Bible Says About Alcohol*, 89–90.
7. Bacchiocchi, *Wine in the Bible: A Biblical Study on the Use of Alcoholic Beverages*, 91.
8. Reynolds, *Alcohol and the Bible*, 61.
9. ———. *The Biblical Approach to Alcohol*, 6.
10. Lumpkins, *Alcohol Today: Abstinence in an Age of Indulgence*, 134.
11. Reynolds, *Alcohol and the Bible*, 11.
12. McDurmon, *What Would Jesus Drink: A Spirit-Filled Study*, 69–70.
13. "Wine, Alcohol, and the Bible."
14. Gentry, *God Gave Wine: What the Bible Says About Alcohol*, 94.
15. Ibid., 96.
16. McDurmon, *What Would Jesus Drink?*, 65-69.
17. Ibid., 66.
18. Ibid., 67.
19. Ibid.
20. Ibid., 69.
21. Gentry, *God Gave Wine: What the Bible Says About Alcohol*, 98-99.
22. Ibid., 100.
22. Ibid., 100–101.
24. Ibid., 101–102.
25. Ibid., 102.

Chapter 9: Abstinence In The Bible

1. "Alcohol and the Bible." Whitfield's search of Bible references for wine and alcohol is based on the New International and King James versions of the Bible.
2. Charles, *Alcohol and the Bible*, 7.
3. Fenton, *The Bible and Wine*, 20.
4. Williamson, *Wine in the Bible & the Church*, 16.
5. "Nazarite," *Jewish Encyclopedia*, accessed on March 21, 2014, http://www.jewishencyclopedia.com/articles/11395-nazarite.
6. Charles, *Alcohol and the Bible*, 8.
7. Tilson, *Should Christians Drink?*, 27–28.

8. West, *Drinking with Calvin and Luther*, 149.
9. Williamson, *Wine in the Bible & the Church*, 17.
10. Gentry, *God Gave Wine: What the Bible Says About Alcohol*, 25.
11. Charles, *Alcohol and the Bible*, 8.
12. West, *Drinking with Calvin and Luther*, 144.
13. Lumpkins, *Alcohol Today: Abstinence in an Age of Indulgence*, 100–106.

Chapter 10: The Weaker Brother

1. R. Kent Hughes, *Romans* (Wheaton, IL:, Crossway Books, 1991), 264–265.
2. "Alcohol and the Bible."
3. Mark Reasoner, *The Strong and the Weak* (Cambridge, England: Cambridge University Press, 1999). This work began as part of his dissertation at the University of Chicago and focuses specifically on Romans 14-15:13.
4. Robert H. Mounce, *The New American Commentary: Romans* (Nashville, TN: Broadman & Holman, 1995), 255.
5. Whittington, *What Would Jesus Drink?*, 20.
6. Ibid.
7. Martin Luther, *Commentary on the Epistle to the Romans* (London, England: Oliphants, LTD, by Grand Rapids, MI: Zondervan Publishing House, 1954), 180.
8. Whittington, *What Would Jesus Drink?*, 21.
9. Ibid.
10. Mounce, *The New American Commentary: Romans*, 256.
11. Gentry, *God Gave Wine: What the Bible Says About Alcohol*, 110.
12. Mounce, *The New American Commentary: Romans*, 258.
13. John Stott, *Romans: God's Good News for the World* (Downers Grove, IL: InterVarsity Press, 1994), 365.
14. Williamson, *Wine in the Bible & the Church*, 21.
15. Ibid., 20.
16. John Murray, *The Epistle to the Romans* (Grand Rapids, MI: Wm. B. Eerdmans Publishers, 1959), 174.

Chapter 11: Tying Up Loose Ends

1. McDurmon, *What Would Jesus Drink?*, 78.
2. Ibid., 79.
3. Ibid., 80.
4. Ibid.
5. Williamson, *Wine in the Bible & the Church*, 37.
6. Gentry, *God Gave Wine: What the Bible Says About Alcohol*, 115–116, quoting John Murray, *The Epistle to the Romans*, 2:188–189.
7. Ibid. 127.
8. Williamson, *Wine in the Bible & the Church*, 27.
9. Ibid., 27–28.
10. Gentry, *God Gave Wine: What the Bible Says About Alcohol*, 131–132.
11. Ibid., 134.

12. Ibid., 141, quoting Gleason L. Archer, *Encyclopedia of Bible Difficulties*, (Grand Rapids, MI: Zondervan, 1982), 149.
13. "Sabbath Controversies," John Stevenson, accessed on April 20, 2014, http://www.angelfire.com/nt/theology/lk06-01.html.
14. Williamson, *Wine in the Bible & the Church*, 31.
15. Ibid., 33.

Chapter 12: What Now? A Practical Conclusion
1. West, *Drinking with Calvin and Luther*, 177.
2. Whittington, *What Would Jesus Drink?*, 41.
3. Williamson, *Wine in the Bible & the Church*, 49.
4. Ibid., 50.

www.ingramcontent.com/pod-product-compliance
Lightning Source LLC
Chambersburg PA
CBHW050635300426
44112CB00012B/1805